MAJOR
POINTS
—FROM THE—
MINOR
PROPHETS

MAJOR POINTS

FROM THE

MINOR PROPHETS

JOHN BLANCHARD

EP BOOKS (Evangelical Press):

Unit C, Tomlinson Road, Leyland, PR25 2DY

epbooks@10ofthose.com

www.epbooks.org

First published January 2012 Second impression June 2012 Third impression November 2012 Fourth impression June 2015 This edition 2017

British Library Cataloguing in Publication Data available

ISBN: 978-0-85234-782-9

Gratefully dedicated to Graham Hind, one-time pastor, long-time friend and constant encourager.

Contents

Foreword
The Right Rev. Kenneth Clarke,
Bishop of Kilmore, Elphin and Ardagh

The famous Irish playwright George Bernard Shaw is often quoted as having said, 'The Bible is as up to date as the morning newspaper.' As John Blanchard opens up the Minor Prophets section of the Bible you will discover the words of Shaw to be true. The message of these prophets is intriguingly contemporary. With courage and sacrifice, messages are declared to the people of God in the past which need to be heard and heeded by the people of God in the present. Here are powerful truths which can lead to the transformation of our generation. At a time of moral degeneration and immense social and cultural upheaval, God's call through these Minor Prophets is a word for our times. In this book the reader will find insights from John Blanchard which open up the life-changing prophetic messages found in some of the most neglected and least read parts of the Bible.

The author describes the historical context and culture, then provides useful background information on the lives and declarations of the prophets before highlighting some of the main thrusts of their messages. As in all good studies, there is observation, interpretation and application. This is clearly a book that has emerged from prayerful preparation, extensive reading and serious study.

As John Blanchard guides us through these books we discover Scripture reading us. We hear God speak. He probes and prods us through his Word. At times it is uncomfortable but the messages of prophets are not always comforting. Social injustice, rotten religion, poisonous hypocrisy, these and so much more come under the scrutiny of God's searing holiness. As the author of this book takes us to the Author of 'The Book' nothing can be hidden nor covered up. Spiritual heart surgery may very well be the outcome if we truly absorb the messages of these twelve books.

John Blanchard's work will prove a rich resource for many people.

Those who preach and teach will find a treasure trove of helpful quotations which are helpful and memorable illustrations. When expounding prophetic words about the dangers of pride, John quotes the Puritan preacher Thomas Adams, who wrote, 'He who is proud of his knowledge has gout in the wrong end.' In another place John comments, in words which can only be described as pithy and powerful, 'Delayed obedience is disobedience.'

The Bible student and Bible study leaders will benefit, not least from the extremely useful summaries of the main messages of each of these books.

Every Christian who is keen to explore God's heart and live a godly life will find help here. Here is food which will help us grow.

I suspect that, as a consequence of reading *Major Points from the Minor Prophets*, the cleanest pages in many Bibles may well get grubby as we turn to them again and again! Thank you, John Blanchard, for this excellent resource. It is full of information, explanation and inspiration. You have whetted my appetite to dig deeper in the Minor Prophets. I know others will find the same. Minor Prophets they may be called, but a major impact they have had—*and will have on all who prayerfully read this book!*

Preface

A friend of mine once began a sermon with the words, 'Please open your Bibles and turn with me to the clean pages.' When the congregation looked puzzled he added, 'In other words, turn to the Minor Prophets.' He had a good point! Although these twelve books constitute about twenty-five per cent of the Old Testament's prophetic teaching, one would be fairly safe in guessing that they are read much less often than the other five books, commonly known as the Major Prophets.

This is unfortunate to say the least, as the Minor Prophets go far beyond helping us to pin down historical events that took place some 3,000 years ago. Nor is it sufficient to agree with the twentieth-century American scholar Homer Hailey's conclusion that 'among the writings of these prophets are to be found some of the most beautiful, majestic and artistic expressions of all literature'. These twelve books contain much more than that. They give us a clear grasp of how God's chosen servants reacted to the massive political, social and religious changes that swept through Israel and Judea during their lifetimes. We see the devastating effects of corruption eating away the moral fibre of a nation and we are given breathtaking glimpses of God's sovereignty, his hatred of sin and his amazing love. Carefully read and wisely understood, they act as powerful stabilizers for God's people today as they face the twenty-first century's changes and challenges.

After he had completed a particularly taxing writing project at the famed Tenth Presbyterian Church, Philadelphia, a few years ago, the distinguished American preacher James Montgomery Boice wanted to preach a series of sermons based on biblical material that he supposed could be handled without an unusual amount of difficulty. He quickly settled on the Minor Prophets, but soon found he had bitten off more than he could easily chew. He promptly abandoned the short series he had in mind and his preaching on the Minor Prophets eventually spread over ten years. The two-volume printed version of these studies contains a wealth of valuable explanation and insight, but there is room for an even more detailed study of all twelve books, documenting in detail their historical background, explaining their linguistic nuances, giving a comprehensive interpretation of their prophecies and unpacking all the lessons they have for us today.

This is not it.

Instead, I want to give readers a general grasp of each prophet's place in history and a summary of his main theme and message, before concentrating in each case on one particular statement made by the prophet concerned. While not necessarily summarizing the particular prophet's ministry, each of the statements has something significant to say to us today. This is an unusual approach and will obviously not meet the needs of those looking for a full treatment of all twelve books. Yet as I pen these pages my constant prayer is that the life-changing truths these twelve men declared will equip Christians to get a firmer grasp of God's dealings with mankind in general and with his people in particular. In addition, I sincerely hope that what I have written will encourage its readers to turn with new enthusiasm to the Bible's 'clean pages'.

I am grateful to several friends who kindly read the manuscript of this book as it was emerging and helped to smooth out some of the wrinkles. I am especially indebted to the Rev. Graham

Hind and Mrs Marlene Williams for the many times when their excellent advice proved an invaluable help. Clare Baalham has been an excellent editor and I am very grateful for her important share in this particular project.

JOHN BLANCHARD
Banstead, Surrey
January 2012

Introduction

A simple way to introduce these studies in the Minor Prophets will be to ask and answer these questions about them: Who were they? Why are they known as 'Minor Prophets'? When and where did they live? What was their ministry? What message did they bring? Once we have answers to these questions we will be in a position to look at the prophets' main themes before focusing on one specific statement made by each one of them.

Identity parade

Who were the Minor Prophets? The answer to this first question is that they were the authors of the last twelve books in the Old Testament—Hosea, Joel, Amos, Obadiah, Jonah, Micah, Nahum, Habakkuk, Zephaniah, Haggai, Zechariah and Malachi. This is the order in which the books appear in our present Bible, although this has not always been the case. To give just one important example, in the Septuagint—the first Greek translation of the Old Testament—Hosea, Joel, Amos and Obadiah appear in order of their length, immediately followed by the last seven books in their current order, with Jonah tacked on at the end, as it was thought to be of a different character. The important thing to remember is that in this and all other arrangements they were always seen as a unit, not as twelve unconnected tracts or documents.

This is a striking example of a wider truth, which is that the Bible is not only amazing in its diversity but also in its unity. It is not so much a single book as a 'library' of sixty-six books written by some forty authors in three languages (Hebrew, Greek and Aramaic) on three continents (Africa, Asia and Europe) over a period of about 1,500 years. It contains history, laws, public records, biography, poetry, prophecy, sermons, hymns, personal correspondence, open letters and miscellaneous other documents. The writers were not professional authors, and included soldiers, priests, fishermen, shepherds, a Jewish rabbi and a Gentile doctor. If questioned about ordinary issues of everyday life they would have held a great variety of views coloured by their diverse backgrounds and cultures, yet in dealing with the most important issues that have ever occupied human minds, and without any collaboration or 'fixing', their individual contributions to the Bible combine to produce a unity and coherence unique in all literature. There is nothing more important to us when studying the Bible than to realize that while it uses many different 'accents' (reflecting the life and times of the authors concerned) *it speaks with one voice*. The critic who says that the God of the Old Testament is different from the God of the New Testament and that the two Testaments contradict each other has misread both.

The reason for the Bible's stunning unity is perfectly straight-forward. It is because every single word of it, as originally written, was 'breathed out by God' (2 Timothy 3:16). The human authors were not penning their personal opinions, nor were they merely expressing their deeply-held convictions. Instead, 'men spoke from God as they were carried along by the Holy Spirit' (2 Peter 1:21). This phrase was written when only the Old Testament was complete, but it is easy to show that it is also true of the New Testament. For example, the apostle Paul not only described the Old Testament as 'the oracles of God' (Romans 3:2) but without hesitation added that his own writings were 'the word of God' (1 Thessalonians 2:13). His fellow apostle John began the last book in the Bible by saying that he was about to write words 'which God gave him' (Revelation 1:1) and signed off by assuring his readers that the words he had written were 'trustworthy and true', having come to him from 'the Lord, the God of the spirits of the prophets' (Revelation 22:6).

In his superb book *Nothing but the Truth,* the modern British preacher Brian Edwards sums this issue up so well that I can do no better than quote him:

> The Holy Spirit moved men to write. He allowed them to use their own style, culture, gifts and character, to use the results of their own study and research, to write of their own experience and to express what was in their mind. At the same time, the Holy Spirit did not allow error to influence their writings; he overruled in the expression of thought and in the choice of words. Thus they recorded accurately all that God wanted them to say and exactly how he wanted them to say it, in their own character, style and language.

No wonder there is such a marvellous unity in Scripture! To borrow a brilliant illustration from the modern British theologian J. I. Packer, 'The Bible appears like a symphony orchestra, with the Holy Ghost as its Toscanini; each instrument has been brought willingly, spontaneously, creatively, to play his notes *just as the great conductor desired*, though none of them could ever hear the music as a whole' (emphasis added). With the entire Bible in our hands we are able to 'hear the music as a whole' and should not neglect any of it. To use a different analogy, the Old and New Testaments are like the two halves of a sentence: both are necessary before we can grasp its full meaning.

The trade name

Why are they called 'Minor Prophets'? This second question is also easily answered. In his famous book *City of God,* first published around AD 425, the great African theologian Aurelius Augustinius, better known as Augustine of Hippo, first gave them this name, but in doing so he was not suggesting that their contributions to Scripture were in any way inferior to the other fifty-four books. Nor could he have meant that they were the shortest books in the Old Testament, as four of the Minor Prophets' books are longer than the book of Ruth and two are longer than Ruth, Ezra and Esther. Instead, he was simply pointing out that the Minor Prophets are the shortest of the Old Testament's prophetical books (Ruth, Ezra and Esther are historical, not prophetical).

That deals with the question, but an important note needs to be added. The fact that in most cases these books are relatively short does not mean that their message is unimportant, because *nothing God says is unimportant.* Although he is concerned with even the tiniest details of our lives, he has no small talk.

As far as the Minor Prophets are concerned, we could have no greater incentive to treat their words seriously than to notice the way in which they are used in the New Testament. For instance, when Jesus said, 'I desire mercy, and not sacrifice' (Matthew 12:7) he was quoting Hosea; when he rode into Jerusalem on a donkey (see Matthew 21:1–5) he was fulfilling the words of Zechariah; when Paul wrote, 'The righteous shall live by faith' (Romans 1:17) he was quoting Habakkuk; and when on the Day of Pentecost Peter told the crowds that these were 'the last days' (Acts 2:17) he was quoting Joel. There are many other examples, but these alone should be sufficient to convince us that we must approach the Minor Prophets with a spirit of reverent submission, accepting their writings as integral parts of 'the living and abiding word of God' (1 Peter 1:23).

A slice of history

The third and fourth questions—*When and where did they live?*—can be answered together, though it means taking in a wide sweep of Old Testament history so as to get these men and their message in a right perspective. The simplest way to do this is to begin counting from 1,400–1,500 BC, when God's people, the Israelites, were miraculously delivered from their captivity in Egypt. This event is commonly called the Exodus, and after forty years of wandering in the desert the people arrived in the Promised Land of Canaan. For the next 300 years their national government was in the hands of locally-based judges, and then later passed to Eli (a priest and a judge) and eventually to

Samuel (a judge and a prophet), who both served as judicial and religious leaders.

When threatened by an invasion some time later, the people demanded a king who could unify the nation and set it on a firm footing. As a result of their lobbying, Saul was anointed as the first king of Israel, but he proved a failure and it fell to David, a young man from Bethlehem, to unite the kingdom around the new capital city, Jerusalem. David was in turn succeeded by his tenth son, Solomon, who strengthened the nation's unity by building an impressive temple in Jerusalem as a focal point of his people's worship.

Things were looking good, but they were soon to change. Around 930 BC Solomon died and his place was taken by his son, Rehoboam, whose economic policy and other follies caused ten of the nation's twelve tribes to revolt and form a breakaway northern kingdom which adopted the name of Israel (though also called Jacob or Ephraim), leaving the two tribes of Benjamin and Judah (together usually called Judah) in the south.

During the next 200 years the northern kingdom had no fewer than nineteen different kings, most of whom 'did what was evil in the sight of the LORD' (1 Kings 15:26), often in promoting blatant idolatry. The downward spiral continued until in 722 BC it was invaded by the Assyrians. Most of its population was deported and the northern kingdom was brought to an end. This was God's judgement on two centuries of rebellion against his ways: 'And this occurred because the people of Israel had sinned against the LORD their God, who had brought them up out of the land of Egypt from under the hand of Pharaoh king of Egypt' (2 Kings 17:7).

The southern kingdom of Judah fared somewhat better. It also had a succession of kings, but they were more of a mixed bag. Some, like Hezekiah, 'did what was right in the eyes of the LORD' (2 Kings 18:3) while others, like his son Manasseh, 'did what was evil in the sight of the LORD' (2 Kings 21:2). As the result of these radical changes of leadership Judah went on a spiritual roller-coaster ride of revival and recession until 586 BC, when Babylon, under its founder and ruler Nebuchadnezzar (more properly

Nebuchadrezzar), swept it aside, flattening Jerusalem, destroying the temple and deporting the cream of the population.

Yet unlike that of Israel, the exile of Judah lasted for only about seventy years. By then the Babylonians had been overthrown by Cyrus, King of Persia, who soon issued an edict allowing any exiles living in his newly acquired territory to return home and reinstate their national gods. Countless exiles from Judah took advantage of the programme and Zerubbabel was appointed to lead the first swathe of 50,000 deportees back to Jerusalem in 538 BC. Others followed in 458 BC and 444 BC and Zerubbabel supervised the rebuilding of the Jerusalem temple, a project that took twenty-two years and was completed in 515 BC. Seventy years later the walls of Jerusalem had been rebuilt and in the years that followed the religious and social structure of the nation was gradually reconstituted.

We can now zoom in a little closer to get a 'fix' on the Minor Prophets' place in history. To do this, we need to focus on the period from about 800 BC to 400 BC, that is to say from a point some time after the united kingdom had been split into Israel in the north and Judah in the south until after Judah's return to Jerusalem. Locating the individual prophets' positions within these four centuries is more difficult, but we can work to this general framework:

- Hosea and Amos prophesied to Israel at some time prior to the nation's exile in 722 BC.

- Micah, Habakkuk and Zephaniah prophesied to Judah prior to the Babylonians ransacking it in 586 BC. Nahum also seems to have prophesied during this time.

- Haggai, Zechariah and Malachi prophesied to Judah after its return from Babylon.

This leaves us with Joel, Obadiah and Jonah. Cases have been made out for dates ranging across almost the entire period from 800 to 400 BC, but exact dating is not critical for our present purposes.

Job description

The fifth question—*What was their ministry?*—is particularly important. One of the best ways to describe their function is to look at the two words used to describe these twelve authors in most English translations of the Old Testament—'seer' and 'prophet'.

In telling the story of Saul being anointed as Israel's first king there is the comment (put in brackets in some of our modern translations) that 'today's "prophet" was formerly called a seer' (1 Samuel 9:9). There is a significant point here that can easily be missed. The first thing to notice about a prophet is not what he says but what he *sees*; in other words he is a seer before he is a 'sayer'. Sometimes prophets saw such things as angels and visions, but above all else what they caught was a glimpse of *the mind of God*. In many ways they were quite ordinary people and were certainly not hand-picked by God because of their exceptional skills or ability. A New Testament writer says of Elijah, one of the Major Prophets, that he was a man 'with a nature like ours' (James 5:17). Simply put, he was no better than we are, prone to all our failures and weaknesses, exposed to the same temptations and trials and (as we can see by reading his story) liable to the same mood swings and inconsistencies. The all-important thing to grasp here is that for the furtherance of his own sovereign purposes God chose to open up his mind to the prophets, tell them how he saw certain things and what he intended to do as a result. The most beautiful expression of this comes in something the Bible says in relation to Moses, a great religious leader, law-giver and prophet. We are told that God 'used to speak to Moses face to face, as a man speaks to his friend' (Exodus 33:11). God took the prophets into his confidence and told them things they could not discover in any other way. Even Balaam, whose spiritual track record was decidedly mixed, openly declared that in his prophetic ministry he was a man 'whose eye is opened … who hears the words of God … who sees the vision of the Almighty' (Numbers 24:15–16).

There is a New Testament parallel, as Paul had no hesitation in pointing to the divine source of his words: 'We impart a secret and hidden wisdom of God, which God decreed before the ages for our glory. None of the rulers of this age understood this, for if they had, they would not have crucified the Lord of glory. But, as it is written: "What no eye has seen, nor ear heard, nor the heart of man imagined, what God has prepared for those who love him"—these things God has revealed to us through the Spirit' (1 Corinthians 2:7–9). Like the Old Testament prophets, the New Testament apostles were seers before they were 'sayers'.

Isaiah gives a brilliant illustration of this. He records some of God's people as saying to the prophets, 'Do not see ... do not prophesy to us what is right; speak to us smooth things, prophesy illusions' (Isaiah 30:10). These people rebelled against what the prophets were saying, and as the prophets were only saying what they were seeing, the people told them to stop seeing!

Yet God's special messenger was not only a 'seer' but a 'sayer' and the meaning of the word 'prophet' becomes clear as soon as we unpack the word. The *phet* part is based on a verb meaning 'to speak', while *pro* has two meanings—'before' and 'for'. Pulling these together, we can see that the prophet spoke *before* something happened and *for* (that is, on behalf of) someone else. The usual (and perfectly correct) way of expressing this is to say that the prophets both foretold and forthtold.

As far as *foretelling* is concerned, some people try to play this down and to suggest that the prophets' main ministry was one of forthtelling, of simply declaring what God was saying, but this is not the case. The prediction of future events is a major element in every prophetic book in the Old Testament. Some of these prophecies were fulfilled in the lifetime of the prophet concerned and some were fulfilled in New Testament times. Others—such as the Second Coming of Christ and the universal resurrection of the dead to final judgement—have yet to be fulfilled. Whatever the timing of the fulfilment, we dare not push the prophets' predictions into a corner and say that they were unimportant or irrelevant. They were a crucial part of their ministry. In fact, one of them goes so far as to say, 'For the Lord GOD does nothing without revealing his secret to his servants the prophets' (Amos 3:7). By reading Old Testament prophecies we can sketch in a broad scenario of world history from the time when they were given right up to the present day and even to the very end of time.

If brushing foretelling aside is one danger, another is that of trivializing it, reducing it to the level of showmanship or a claim to superior spirituality or power. Yet genuine biblical prophecy was never used in that way. No true prophet foretold the future to satisfy men's curiosity about what was about to happen, to project his own personality or ministry, or to prove he was in intimate touch with God. When a prophet spoke in the name of the Lord it was always to bring people to repentance, faith and obedience. The object of Old Testament prophecy was not to get people jumping to their feet but to get them falling to their knees in awe and in submission to the will of God. This is far removed from the kind of thing we sometimes see being projected as prophecy in certain areas of the Christian church today, especially in the antics of some preachers on religious television programmes. I recently heard one ludicrously declaring himself to be a Master Prophet, with the ability to 'decree' immediate blessing on all who met his terms (which inevitably had a price tag attached).

In *forthtelling*, the emphasis was on the fact that the prophet was God's spokesman and as such must be obedient to his divine commission. An incident in Exodus provides a perfect illustration of this. When God told Moses to go to Pharaoh, commanding him to release God's people from their captivity in Egypt, Moses protested that he was ill-equipped for the task: 'Oh, my Lord, I am not eloquent, either in the past or since you have spoken to your servant, but I am slow of speech and of tongue' (Exodus 4:10). God's reply could not have been clearer: 'Who has made man's mouth? Who makes him mute, or deaf, or seeing, or blind? Is it not I, the LORD? Now therefore go, and I will be with your mouth and teach you what you shall speak' (Exodus 4:11–12). Yet even this was not enough to motivate Moses, who feebly replied, 'Oh, my Lord, please send someone else' (Exodus 4:13).

This attempt to wriggle out of things angered God, yet he

graciously made a remarkable concession: 'Is there not Aaron, your brother, the Levite? I know that he can speak well. Behold, he is coming out to meet you, and when he sees you, he will be glad in his heart. You shall speak to him and put words in his mouth, and I will be with your mouth and with his mouth and will teach you both what to do. He shall speak for you to the people, *and he shall be your mouth, and you shall be as God to him*' (Exodus 4:14–16, emphasis added). I have drawn attention to the crucial words here. Aaron was to be the public spokesman, but both Aaron and Moses were to be *as the mouth of God*. God was to use them in such a way that the words they spoke would be the very words God would have spoken to the people had he chosen to do so directly.

This is a great illustration of the biblical truth that when the Old Testament prophets spoke in God's name they used the very words God wanted them to use, making the source of their message the guarantee of its authority and inerrancy. This is stated throughout the prophetic books, not least in those written by the Minor Prophets. Hosea begins, 'The word of the LORD that came to Hosea' (Hosea 1:1) and Joel, Micah, Zephaniah, Zechariah and Malachi introduce all they have to say in much the same way. Earlier in the Old Testament there is another beautiful illustration of the same truth when among his last words David claimed, 'The Spirit of the LORD speaks by me; his word is on my tongue' (2 Samuel 23:2). This is exactly the kind of thing the apostle Peter meant when centuries later he wrote, 'For no prophecy was ever produced by the will of man, but men spoke from God as they were carried along by the Holy Spirit' (2 Peter 1:21). It is precisely what Paul had in mind when he insisted, 'All Scripture is breathed out by God' (2 Timothy 3:16). He underlined this when commending the Christians at Thessalonica for accepting his ministry 'not as the word of men but as what it really is, the word of God' (1 Thessalonians 2:13). This is the only consistent biblical way of interpreting Scripture: *what the Bible says, God says*. As the Puritan divine Thomas Watson put it, 'The two Testaments are the two lips by which God has spoken to us.'

There are those in certain church circles today who dare to make claims on a par with those made by the Old Testament prophets. They can be heard on religious television and radio programmes and in pulpits all around the world, making strident claims to be prophets for today, or apostles for today's church, entrusted with a special word from God for today's generation. Is there no difference between these men (and women) and the Bible's prophets? The simplest way to answer the question is to notice that an Old Testament prophecy was a means by which an infallible God used fallible men to bring an infallible word to fallible people. This meant that when exercising their ministries *Old Testament prophets never made a false statement*, because God guaranteed the integrity of every word he gave them to speak.

These prophets were subject to a very stringent test, which God explained like this: 'And if you say in your heart, "How may we know the word that the LORD has not spoken"—when a prophet speaks in the name of the LORD, if the word does not come to pass or come true, that is a word that the LORD has not spoken; the prophet has spoken it presumptuously. You need not be afraid of him' (Deuteronomy 18:21–22). Notice carefully what is being said here. God does *not* say that if someone claims to make a God-given prophecy and the prophecy comes to pass, this proves it to have been a genuine message from God. What he *does* say is that if the prophecy is not fulfilled the so-called prophet is not genuine. Notice how strict this test is! If someone claims to make a prophecy in God's name—even a small, 'localized', seemingly insignificant prophecy—and the event prophesied does not come to pass, the person concerned is disqualified; he is not what he claims to be. It would not do for someone to shrug off a failed prophecy by saying, 'But I am only human and I am bound to get a prophecy wrong from time to time.' When claiming to speak in God's name, his own integrity was on the line, as a true prophet never got it wrong.

This has serious implications at the present time. It is not enough to say that some predictions come to pass; they all have to be infallibly accurate. We must also note that the slightest error in a prophecy does not merely dismantle the prophecy, *it disqualifies the person claiming to be a prophet.* There is a great deal of ducking and weaving on this issue. There are those who speak of prophecy as a mixed phenomenon; sometimes it is true, but there are other times when it does not quite work out, because the human instrument is fallible. Some say that prophecy 'is nearly always a mixture of God's Spirit and our thinking', while others speak of 'non-infallible prophecy'. But 'non-infallible prophecy' is a contradiction in terms! As the modern Welsh preacher Geoff Thomas puts it, 'The question of how it is possible for men to receive a word from the throne of the universe and then give it out mixed with error cannot be answered satisfactorily.'

Thomas is right. How can there possibly be a God-inspired word that is 'non-infallible'? How can anyone hear a word from God, deliver a garbled or compromised version of it, and then claim that it remains divinely inspired? A crucial New Testament statement draws a line under the whole issue: 'Long ago, at many times and in many ways, God spoke to our fathers by the prophets, but in these last days he has spoken to us by his Son' (Hebrews 1:1–2). *We do not have biblically-endorsed prophets today as we no longer have any need of them; we have the complete Word of God.* Instead, we need exegetes, expositors, preachers and teachers of the faith that was 'once for all delivered to the saints' (Jude 3). J. I. Packer puts it well: 'The preacher will take care that what he offers is not his own ideas but God's message from God's book, and will see it as his task not to talk for his text, but to let the text talk through him.'

Another important point needs to be made here. Not only should we rely wholeheartedly on the faithful exposition of the Bible as the written Word of God, we should not insist on signs and wonders as an authentication of a preacher's ministry. This is made crystal clear in a story Jesus told about a rich man and Lazarus. When the rich man had died and was in Hades, he pleaded with Abraham to send Lazarus (who had also died but was by then in 'Abraham's bosom', a synonym for Paradise) back to earth to warn the rich man's five brothers of the appalling fate awaiting them if they did not repent. Abraham's reply was terse and telling: 'If they do not hear Moses and the Prophets, neither will they be convinced if someone rises from the dead' (Luke 16:31). The message is clear: if people will not listen to the Word of God and turn to him in repentance and faith as a result, no 'signs and wonders' will move them to do so, not even a long-buried friend coming back to life.

The Bible is the only infallible word we have or need, revealing to us that in the Lord Jesus Christ we have the Prophet to end all prophets, the Priest to end all priests and the King to end all kings. Our great need today is not for prophets but for preachers, men who will give themselves sacrificially to the study of the Word of God and to its systematic exegesis and exposition, 'rightly handling the word of truth' (2 Timothy 2:15) and applying its truth to their hearers.

The big five

The final question to be answered is crucial: *What message did they bring?* These sixty-six chapters touch on a vast variety of subjects—theological, spiritual, moral and political, as well as prophetical. Yet there are five themes that dominate their authors' writings.

The first is *the utter and undeniable sovereignty of God*. When Haggai records God as saying, 'I will shake the heavens and the earth and the sea and the dry land' (Haggai 2:6) he is declaring a bedrock truth that underlies all of Scripture from Genesis to Revelation. Not a single atom exists, nor does a single event occur, other than under the settled sovereignty of God. As David says, 'Whatever the LORD pleases, he does, in heaven and on earth, in the seas and all deeps' (Psalm 135:6). The twentieth-century British hymn-writer George Wallace Briggs expressed it well:

> God has spoken by his prophets,
> Spoken his unchanging word;
> Each from age to age proclaiming
> God, the one, the righteous Lord;
> In the world's despair and turmoil
> One firm anchor still holds fast;

God is king, his throne eternal,
God the first and God the last.

The second is *God's inevitable judgement against sin*. The Minor Prophets have a great deal to say about God's hatred of sin and his righteous punishment of it, not only at the time they were writing but as a general principle and finally at the end of time, when all nations will stand before God on 'the great and awesome day of the LORD' (Malachi 4:5). This will be the moment when 'each of us will give an account of himself to God' (Romans 14:12). When God tells Joel, 'I will sit to judge all the surrounding nations' (Joel 3:12) he is crystallizing awesome truth repeated throughout the Minor Prophets. There are times when these prophets couch their denunciation of sin in devastating language, leading the modern American scholar Gene Edward Veith to admit, 'Reading the prophets can be an unsettling experience. Here we see God's utter, absolute fury against sin. The graphic accounts of what God is going to do to his own faithless, immoral, complacent people constitute some of the scariest words in all of literature.'

The third is *God's amazing love*. The love of God runs like a river through all of their writings, reflecting Joel's declaration that God is 'gracious and merciful, slow to anger, and abounding in steadfast love' (Joel 2:13). Many people wrongly think that whereas the wrath of God is emphasized in the Old Testament, the emphasis in the New Testament is on the love of God, but this gives a distorted picture. The truth is that there are more references to the love of God in the Old Testament than in the New and the most complete statements about the final wrath of God against sin are in the New Testament rather than in the Old. The modern Canadian theologian D. A. Carson makes this clear point when he writes, 'The move from the Old Testament to the New Testament is not a move from a wrathful God to a loving God. Rather, the New Testament ratchets up both themes.' For their part, the Minor Prophets reflect both 'the kindness and the severity of God' (Romans 11:22) and only when we give full weight to all the Bible says about both do we have a true picture.

If we ignore either the kindness or the severity of God we are left with a lopsided caricature.

The fourth is *a passionate call to get right with God*. Superficial readers of their writings tend to picture the prophets as dealing out unrelenting condemnation, but this is a distortion and not a true reflection of their message. They certainly paint sin and its consequences in stark and dreadful colours, but they have a passion for people to repent of their sin, to abandon their backsliding, to stop compromising, to seek after holiness and to enter into the blessing God longs to bring them. They repeatedly draw attention to this in statements such as, 'Return to me ... and I will return to you' (Zechariah 1:3).

The fifth is *the coming of Messiah*. All of the prophets, Major and Minor, are like so many signposts dotted throughout Old Testament history, all pointing to Christ, to great David's greater Son, the Suffering Servant, the anointed Conqueror of his people's enemies and 'King of kings and Lord of lords' (1 Timothy 6:15) to whom all should submit in repentance, faith and obedience. As the great sixteenth-century German Reformer Martin Luther said, 'As we go to the cradle only to find the baby, so we go to the Scriptures only to find Christ.' He was right—and the writings of the Minor Prophets lead us to him again and again. Only in the light of the Old Testament can we properly understand the coming of Christ and only through Christ can we properly understand the Old Testament.

The Minor Prophets provide a veritable feast of good things to nourish God's people and in this introduction I have merely been laying the table. It is time to eat.

Bon appétit!

HOSEA

'**G**od told me to marry a prostitute!

Any writer trying to seize his readers' attention with an explosive opening to his story could hardly imagine anything more riveting than this. A God of infinite holiness and purity, who 'cannot look at wrong' (Habakkuk 1:13), who commands us to avoid 'sexual immorality and all impurity' (Ephesians 5:3) and who warns us that he will 'judge the sexually immoral and adulterous' (Hebrews 13:4), tells one of his prophets to marry a woman who was steeped in the permissive culture of her day and rode roughshod over all God-given standards about sexual morality.

Hosea's opening words are so shocking that many people think this book is not a historical account but an allegory, a vision or parable. We will look at this issue later, but begin by finding out something about Hosea and his prophecy.

The survivor

Some of the Old Testament prophets appear on the scene for a very short time; for example, all of Haggai's recorded prophecy was spoken in the course of a few months. By contrast, Hosea had a very long ministry. His book is 'The word of the LORD that came to Hosea, the son of Beeri, in the days of Uzziah, Jotham, Ahaz, and Hezekiah, kings of Judah, and in the days of Jeroboam the son of Joash, king of Israel' (1:1). The reigns of the four kings of Judah ran from 790 to 686 BC and the 'Jeroboam' mentioned was Jeroboam II, Israel's fourteenth king, who reigned from 793 to 753 BC. The five reigns therefore covered a period of about 100 years. Hosea's ministry may have lasted for at least half of that time and it extended long after Jeroboam died. This would date Hosea's prophecy somewhere around the middle of the eighth century BC and make him one of the earliest of the prophets. He was a contemporary of Isaiah, who also prophesied 'in the days of Uzziah, Jotham, Ahaz, and Hezekiah, kings of Judah' (Isaiah 1:1), but while Isaiah's message was directed to the southern kingdom of Judah, Hosea prophesied almost exclusively to the northern kingdom of Israel.

We know very little about Hosea's background—except that he was 'the son of Beeri' (1:1)—yet there is a sense in which we know him at a deeper level than any of the other Minor Prophets. He has been called 'The Prophet of the Sorrowing Heart' and the title fits him well. Two things combined to produce the wrenching grief that gripped Hosea's heart, a national tragedy and a personal tragedy. Our 'major point' comes in the context of the second, but we begin by unpacking the first.

National tragedy

Jeroboam's predecessor, King Jehoash, was a successful military commander, and when he died Jeroboam built on his success. He 'restored the border of Israel from Lebo-hamath as far as the Sea of Arabah, according to the word of the LORD, the God of Israel, which he spoke by his servant Jonah' (2 Kings 14:25). This meant that Israel then occupied virtually all of the land God had promised to their forefathers.

So far, so good—but the outward signs of peace, power and prosperity were not the whole story. Jeroboam 'did what was evil in the sight of the LORD' and 'did not depart from all the sins of Jeroboam the son of Nebat' (2 Kings 14:24), Israel's first king. As a result, the moral and spiritual climate of the nation began to crumble, and soon after Jeroboam II died it fell apart.

An old proverb says, 'A fish rots from the head down' and in Israel's case it proved to be true as the nation's moral and spiritual decline began with royalty. Although the slide had started before Jeroboam's death it accelerated afterwards. His son and successor Zechariah was murdered within six months and replaced by Shallum. He reigned for just a month before being assassinated by the brutal Menahem, who clung on to power for ten years but was then killed and succeeded by Pekahiah. Two years later Pekahiah's military commander Pekah killed the king and took the throne in a military coup. Two years later he was murdered by Hoshea, whose godless behaviour dragged the nation the rest of the way down the slippery slope that led to it being swept into captivity by the Assyrians in 722 BC. From that time on the kingdom of Israel ceased to exist.

Hosea mentions only Jeroboam as a king of Israel and makes no mention of the other six rulers who reigned in just over twenty years during Hosea's lifetime. This may be because none made a significant difference to the direction in which things were going. Be that as it may, corruption among the leadership was matched by moral and spiritual degradation throughout the land. Society was stained by injustice, corruption, immorality and idolatry, as we can see from these statements in Hosea's message to the nation:

> There is no faithfulness or steadfast love, and no knowledge of God in the land; there is swearing, lying, murder, stealing, and committing adultery; they break all bounds, and bloodshed follows bloodshed (4:1–2).

> … they have deserted the LORD to give themselves to prostitution, to old wine and new, which take away the understanding of my people (4:10–12, NIV).

> My people enquire of a piece of wood, and their walking staff gives them oracles. (4:12)

> They utter mere words; with empty oaths they make covenants; so judgement springs up like poisonous weeds in the furrows of the field. (10:4)

Many other statements show how Israel went from bad to worse in a rapid downward spiral that eventually led to it being wiped out of history altogether, but everything was rooted in this: *'Israel has forgotten his Maker'* (8:14). What added to the tragedy was that when the nation had been on its forty-year trek through the desert to the Promised Land God had warned it again and again about the danger of doing this. Three examples will serve to represent the others:

> And when the LORD your God brings you into the land that he swore to your fathers, to Abraham, to Isaac, and to Jacob, to give you—with great and good cities that you did not build, and houses full of all good things that you did not fill, and cisterns that you did not dig, and vineyards and olive trees that you did not plant—and when you eat and are full, *then take care lest you forget the LORD, who brought you out of the land of Egypt, out of the house of slavery.*
>
> (Deuteronomy 6:10–12, emphasis added)

> *Take care lest you forget the LORD your God* by not keeping his commandments and his rules and his statutes, which I command you today, [lest] … your heart be lifted up, and you forget the LORD your God, who brought you out of the land of Egypt, out of the house of slavery.
>
> (Deuteronomy 8:11–12, 14, emphasis added)

> *And if you forget the LORD your God* and go after other gods and serve them and worship them, I solemnly warn you today that you shall surely perish.
>
> (Deuteronomy 8:19, emphasis added)

God could not have made things any clearer, yet although he delivered them from centuries of slavery, established a covenant with them, guided and protected them throughout four decades in the desert, met all their needs, enabled them to defeat all their enemies, brought them safely into Canaan, constituted them as a nation and settled them in a land so fertile that it could be described as 'flowing with milk and honey' (Exodus 3:17), *they forgot him!* They became so engrossed in their prosperity and progress that they often acted as if God did not exist. Their material prosperity spawned their spiritual poverty, and Hosea makes the point perfectly when he records God saying, 'when they had grazed, they became full, they were filled, and their heart was lifted up; *therefore they forgot me*' (13:6, emphasis added).

In 1863, halfway through the American Civil War, President Abraham Lincoln made a statement that reflected the same pattern—prosperity, pride, internal strife, the deceitfulness of the human heart and moral decline:

> It is the duty of nations, as well as of men, to own their dependence upon the overruling power of God, to confess their sins and transgressions in humble sorrow, yet with the assured hope that genuine repentance will lead to mercy and pardon, and to recognize the sublime truth announced in the Holy Scriptures, and proven by all history, that those nations are blessed whose God is the Lord. We know that by his divine law nations, like individuals, are subjected to punishments and chastisements in this world. May we not justly fear that the awful calamity of civil war which now desolates the land may be a punishment inflicted upon us for our presumptuous sins, to the needful end of a national reformation as a whole people? We have been the recipients of the choicest bounties of heaven. We have been preserved these many years in peace and prosperity. We have grown in numbers, wealth and power as no other nation has ever grown, *but we have forgotten God*. We have forgotten the gracious hand that preserved us in peace and multiplied, enriched and strengthened us, and we have vainly imagined in the deceitfulness of our hearts that all these blessings were produced by some superior wisdom and virtue of our own. Intoxicated by our own unbroken success, we have become too self-sufficient to feel the necessity of redeeming and preserving grace, too proud to pray to the God who made us.

With the exception of the reference to the civil war, every word of Lincoln's lament would apply to many nations today.

Almost never do we hear biblical truth being declared with conviction and authority in the corridors of power. Even many church leaders speak and act as if it is more important to be politically correct than to be biblically truthful. Alongside the Queen's name, British coins have the abbreviations D.G. REG. F.D. stamped on them. They represent the Latin terms, 'By the grace of God', 'Queen', 'Defender of the Faith', yet they mean very little to most people living in the land. In the same way, having statements of faith on the circumference of our lives is worthless if those lives are not being transformed by the Spirit of God.

The Spanish-born American author George Santayana, who died in 1952, famously said, 'Those who cannot remember the past are condemned to repeat it' and we need to learn, relearn and never stop learning the lessons of God's dealings with his people as recorded in the Bible. The apostle Paul told New Testament Christians, 'For whatever was written in former days was written for our instruction, that through endurance and through the encouragement of the Scriptures we might have hope' (Romans 15:4). We ignore this powerful and vital resource at our peril. Every national issue, every social issue, every moral issue, every church issue and every personal issue should be illuminated and evaluated by the light of Scripture, or we will not have it properly in focus.

Hosea lived at a time when material prosperity went hand in hand with spiritual poverty—and the danger has not gone away. I think of a friend I knew forty years ago whose dedication and sacrificial commitment to God's service not only challenged my own feebler efforts, but rebuked them. His outstanding talents also enabled him to make rapid progress in his chosen profession, but as his business successes gathered pace, his involvement in Christian service slowed down. He gradually withdrew from positions of leadership, then got less involved in evangelistic programmes, then decided that one Sunday service was sufficient, and eventually stopped attending church altogether. The last I heard he and his wife showed no obvious signs of spiritual life. Reader, beware! Backsliding never begins with a bang. It begins quietly, slowly, subtly. As the twentieth-century American preacher Donald Grey Barnhouse put it,

'Withering is a slow process, barely perceptible at first, either to the one who is being withered or to those who look on.'

This all ties in with Hosea's prophecy. He watched with growing grief as he saw the nation's prosperity eating away at its moral and spiritual integrity. The lesson is crystal clear. Outward success always carries the risk of inward failure and material plenty can mask spiritual poverty. Big is not necessarily beautiful; it may be fatal, as it was in Israel's case. Hosea's beloved nation had sidelined God while pretending to serve him, and this terrible truth broke the prophet's heart.

Personal tragedy

The second tragedy to strike Hosea was not national but intensely personal and the two disasters are linked at the very beginning of his book: 'When the LORD began to speak through Hosea, the LORD said to him, "Go, take to yourself an adulterous wife and children of unfaithfulness, because the land is guilty of the vilest adultery in departing from the LORD"' (1:2, NIV).

For some, this raises not only eyebrows but objections. Would God really say such a thing? There were strict rules laid down regarding women suitable for priests to marry; surely the same high standard would apply to the prospective wives of prophets? What is more, Hosea marrying a woman of loose morals would violate a well-known biblical principle that had been laid down in the Law of Moses and was crystallized centuries later in the rhetorical question, 'For what partnership has righteousness with lawlessness? Or what fellowship has light with darkness?' (2 Corinthians 6:14).

These two objections lead some highly respected Bible students and expositors to say that Hosea was not recording history but reciting an allegory. Yet this solves nothing because even if this were the case both objections would remain. In any event, God is sovereign and can deal with his creatures in any way he chooses, even if our immediate reaction is to question his wisdom and even his integrity. Though he cannot lie, sin or deny himself, God has no 'no go' areas and may bring his choicest servants into the most puzzling or traumatic circumstances for his own eternal purposes and glory. Recognizing this debunks the superficial and fallacious idea that as long as we are committed, faithful and obedient our situations and circumstances will be free from stress and trauma and unaffected by the trials and perplexities that others face. Nothing could be further from the truth. Job was 'blameless and upright, one who feared God and turned away from evil' (Job 1:1) yet God called him to go through an almost unbelievable sequence of material, physical and spiritual traumas. Even Job's experience pales into insignificance compared to that of the Lord Jesus Christ, who was utterly perfect, yet was 'despised and rejected by men; a man of sorrows, and acquainted with grief' (Isaiah 53:3).

Any Christian who measures his or her spirituality in terms of outward comfort or success is making a dangerous mistake, and anyone who believes that tough times are an infallible index of God's displeasure is doing the same. Paul's testimony makes that clear:

> We are afflicted in every way, but not crushed; perplexed, but not driven to despair; persecuted, but not forsaken; struck down, but not destroyed... So we do not lose heart. Though our outer self is wasting away, our inner self is being renewed day by day. For this light momentary affliction is preparing for us an eternal weight of glory beyond all comparison, as we look not to the things that are seen but to the things that are unseen. For the things that are seen are transient, but the things that are unseen are eternal. (2 Corinthians 4:8–9, 16–18)

Enter Gomer

The link between the national and personal tragedies that tore at Hosea's heart surfaces in God's instruction to the prophet to marry 'a wife of whoredom'. The woman concerned was called Gomer. We know nothing about her family except that she was 'the daughter of Diblaim' (1:3), but to be called 'a wife of whoredom' points to her being a woman of her times, which were steeped in corruption and immorality. They were like the

Swinging Sixties (1960–1969) when there was dynamic reaction against social and moral conservatism. The decade was marked by sexual permissiveness that was part of the so-called New Morality, a strange name as it was neither new nor moral. I was reminded at the time of an American breakfast cereal called Grape Nuts, which contains neither grapes nor nuts. The phrase 'New Morality' trivializes the truth as it does nothing more than give the old immorality a more socially acceptable name.

Bible scholars differ as to whether Gomer was living an immoral life when Hosea met her, but John Calvin had no doubt. He said she was 'a common harlot' who 'prostituted herself, not once, nor twice, nor to few men, but to all'. Hosea must have agonized over the issue but the important thing to notice is his unqualified obedience—he 'went and took Gomer' (1:3). The story then moves rapidly on: 'and she conceived and bore him a son' (1:3). I remember the long discussions my wife and I had over what names to give our five sons when they were born. Things were different for Hosea and Gomer, because God told him, 'Call his name Jezreel' (1:4). Only one other person in the Bible has that name (see 1 Chronicles 4:3) but it also occurs nearly forty other times as the place name of two towns and the largest and richest valley in Israel.

This is the point at which massive clouds began to gather, because God's explanation of the choice of the name Jezreel was the first part of what was to become a devastating message to the nation of Israel. Hosea was told, 'Call his name Jezreel, for in just a little while I will punish the house of Jehu for the blood of Jezreel, and I will put an end to the kingdom of the house of Israel. And on that day I will break the bow of Israel in the Valley of Jezreel' (1:4–5).

The key to Hosea's prophecy lies in the name given to this child—and, as we will see—to the others that were to follow. Years earlier, a military commander called Jehu was God's instrument in securing a significant victory in the valley of Jezreel, but Jehu went far beyond his mandate and in a series of ruthless strikes slaughtered countless people, including Jezebel and Jehoram, the king of Judah. His murderous excesses were motivated by naked ambition, and he seized the nation's throne, but 'was not careful to walk in the law of the LORD, the God of Israel, with all his heart' (2 Kings 10:31). In response to Jehu's brutality and the nation's rampant sin, God vowed to bring retribution four generations later. This period of time had now elapsed and Hosea was told that naming his firstborn son Jezreel was a warning that judgement was to fall upon Israel 'in just a little while'. Hosea's chronic grief over Israel's godlessness must surely have deepened as he realized that national disaster was now looming. Soon afterwards a fierce battle in the valley of Jezreel began the collapse that led to the nation being swept off into captivity by the Assyrians in 722 BC.

The symbolic truth of Hosea's story becomes clearer as the narrative moves on: Gomer 'conceived again and bore a daughter' (1:6). In the case of Gomer's firstborn we are told that 'she bore [Hosea] a son', but in this case Hosea is not mentioned. The absence seems significant and suggests that Gomer was reverting to type and already being unfaithful. This would have been a sickening body blow to Hosea, but with remarkable restraint he chose not to exercise his right to divorce her. God then directed that the baby girl be named 'Lo-Ruhamah' (1:6, NIV). The name means 'No Mercy' and God explained exactly why it had been chosen: 'for I will no more have mercy on the house of Israel, to forgive them at all' (1:6). Yet again, Hosea must have reeled under the added pain. God's dealings with Israel had for centuries been tempered by mercy, love, compassion and patience, but now the axe was to fall.

God then added a significant rider to his devastating prophecy: 'But I will have mercy on the house of Judah, and I will save them by the LORD their God. I will not save them by bow or by sword or by war or by horses' (1:7). This astonishing promise was fulfilled in two ways. When the Assyrians had devastated Israel they turned their attention to Judah, but their plans were wrecked, not in a military battle, but when 'the LORD sent an angel, who annihilated all the fighting men and the leaders and officers in the camp of the Assyrian king' (2 Chronicles

32:21, NIV). Much later, after Judah had spent seventy years in captivity in Babylon, it was delivered not by military force but by God moving the pagan king Cyrus (who had by then captured Babylon) to allow captured expatriates to return to their own nation. Even a writer of fiction would have been hard pressed to invent such a turn of events, but they fulfilled to the letter God's infallible promise.

Hosea's story moves on. Once more Gomer conceived and 'bore a son' (1:8). Again the father is not mentioned and God's instruction to call the baby boy 'Lo-Ammi' (1:9) added another terrible blow. 'Lo-Ammi' means 'not my people' and carried to Israel the appalling message, 'you are not my people, and I am not your God' (1:9).

With the birth of each of the three children God's warnings to Israel became increasingly serious. Firstly, 'I will scatter you'; then, 'I will have no mercy on you'; finally, 'You will no longer be my people'. For God to remove his protection was alarming; to remove his pardon was even worse; but to remove his presence was worst of all. Yet despite the impending disaster, the way the story plays out suggests God's reluctance to withdraw anything from his people. We can assume that there was at least a year—it may have been much longer—between the births, giving Gomer time to change her ways. There was also time for Israel to repent of its violence, immorality and godlessness and to turn back to God, who had shown himself to be 'merciful and gracious' and 'slow to anger' (Exodus 34:6), but it was hell-bent on its own course. Hosea's marriage was now in ruins; Gomer's life was in ruins; Israel's moral and spiritual status was in ruins. No wonder Hosea is called 'The Prophet of the Sorrowful Heart'.

The 'impossible' command

The next part of what amounts to Hosea's autobiography is in Chapter 3 of his book. Except for Psalm 117 it is the shortest chapter in the Old Testament, yet its message is stunning. Hosea's marriage to Gomer was over. As the innocent party, he had gone through the searing agony of seeing his marriage come apart at the seams. Now there was an empty place at the table, an empty chair in the room and an empty space in the bed. Some time later, with Gomer presumably offering her body to anyone who wanted it, she had also become a slave. Disgraced, destitute and derelict, there was not a good thing to be seen in her and not a good thing to be said about her. Who knows how many men she had slept with, or what degradation she had plunged into? Then comes our utterly shocking 'major point':

> And the LORD said to me, 'Go again, love a woman who is
> loved by another man and is an adulteress'.   (3:1)

For many men this would have been too much to ask. After Gomer's serial unfaithfulness they would have sued for divorce, been glad to get rid of her, and never given her another charitable thought. Instead, and in spite of the conflicting emotions that must have torn at his heart, Hosea obeyed God's instruction and made his way to the slave market. Slaves were sold naked and we can imagine Hosea making his way among them, looking for Gomer and scarcely able to recognize this wretched woman with her sunken eyes and ravaged body. The going rate for a slave, laid down in Exodus 21, was thirty shekels of silver, but it seems that Gomer was being sold at a discount. She was not just shop-soiled or second-hand, she was a disgusting leftover. Nobody wanted her, whatever the asking price, but Hosea bought her for 'fifteen shekels of silver and a homer and a lethech [one and a half bushels] of barley' (3:2).

Hosea now owned her and could do whatever he chose with her. He could even kill her if he wanted to (and some men might have thought that fifteen shekels of silver and some barley was a good price to pay for giving them that opportunity). Instead, Hosea told her, 'You must dwell as mine for many days. You shall not play the whore, or belong to another man; so will I also be with you' (3:3). The choice of words here is very important. 'You must dwell as mine *for many days*' points to the need for a 'probation' period, giving Gomer a chance to show that she was willing to change her ways and from now on to remain faithful to Hosea. He would provide for her, protect her, care for her and seek her good, yet there would be a certain distance between them for a while. Only when she had proved herself to be faithful to Hosea would they resume a full relationship as man and wife.

The message

Hosea's is a stunning story, unique in Scripture, but we will only understand its full meaning if we see it as reflecting a message from God to the backslidden nation of Israel, a message filled out in the rest of Hosea's prophecy. In his excellent work *The Old Testament Explained and Applied* the modern British preacher Gareth Crossley suggests of Hosea, 'It is pre-eminently a book for the backslider.' What is beyond question is that Hosea wrote with passion. The seventeenth-century British preacher and writer John Bunyan, the author of *The Pilgrim's Progress*, said, 'I preached what I did feel, what I smartingly did feel,' and Hosea did the same. Our right response to what Hosea 'smartingly' felt should begin by taking careful note of three things in his deeply moving story.

The first is Israel's terrible unfaithfulness, of which Gomer is a picture. At the outset, God told Hosea that Israel 'commits great whoredom by forsaking the LORD' (1:2). Later, God told the nation, 'You have played the whore, departing from your God. You have loved a prostitute's wages on all threshing floors' (9:1). One of the most beautiful biblical pictures of the relationship between God and his people is that of husband and wife. In the Old Testament God tells them, 'For your Maker is your husband, the LORD of hosts is his name' (Isaiah 54:5) and in the New Testament the people of God are pictured as 'a bride adorned for her husband' (Revelation 21:2) Using the same metaphor, one of the Bible's most searing descriptions of a believer's sin is to call it adultery: 'You adulterous people! Do you not know that friendship with the world is enmity with God?' (James 4:4). Worldliness shows itself in a lifestyle conformed to the spirit and standard of the age. John Henry Jowett, Minister of Westminster Chapel, London, from 1918 to 1922, wrote, 'Worldliness is a spirit, a temperament, an attitude of soul. It is life without high callings, life devoid of lofty ideals. It is a gaze horizontal, never vertical. Its motto is "Forward", never "Upward."' Bluntly put, worldliness is breaking a solemn vow of commitment to Christ and flirting with other gods.

Addressing the graduates of Harvard University in 1978, the Russian dissident Aleksandr Solzhenitsyn pointed out the danger and disaster of doing so: 'The human soul longs for things higher, warmer and purer than those offered by today's mass living habits, introduced by the revolting invasion of publicity, by TV stupor, and by intolerable music... We have turned our backs upon the Spirit and embraced all that is material with excessive and unwarranted zeal.'

We need to ask ourselves a serious question here. Are we ever guilty in any way or to any degree of the same sin? The nineteenth-century Scottish divine Thomas Guthrie wrote these searching words: 'If you find yourself loving any pleasure better than your prayers, any book better than the Bible, any house better than the house of God, any table better than the Lord's table, any person better than Christ and any indulgence better than the hope of heaven, take alarm.' No Christian should read these deeply challenging words without careful self-examination.

The second is God's amazing love, of which Hosea's love is a picture. Greatly as he loved Gomer, even his amazing example is as nothing when compared with God's love for his people. We have already noted God's reluctance to punish them and his eagerness to bless them. The message to Hosea has another pointer to this, as he was told to love Gomer 'even as the LORD loves the children of Israel, though they turn to other gods and love cakes of raisins' (3:1). The raisin cakes offered to pagan gods were not like 'ready meals' bought at a supermarket and pushed into a microwave for a few minutes. The whole process of sacrificing these cakes to false gods took time. The ingredients had to be gathered together, then carefully mixed before a slow baking process took place. In the same way, Israel did not suddenly rush into sin. They spent years disobeying God's commands, yet his message to them was 'I love you!' Even when Israel had systematically broken its part of the divine covenant, God had kept his part, and his commitment to them remained unchanged.

Hosea loved Gomer even during and after her disgusting moral collapse, yet his love had a beginning and death eventually brought it to an end. God's love for his people knows no such limits. He tells them, 'I have loved you with an everlasting love' (Jeremiah 31:3). Paul goes to great lengths to emphasize this: 'For I am sure that neither death nor life, nor angels nor rulers, nor things present nor things to come, nor powers, nor height nor depth, nor anything else in all creation, will be able to separate us from the love of God in Christ Jesus our Lord' (Romans 8:38–39).

What is more, God's amazing love for his people is beyond time, as they were chosen in Christ 'before the foundation of the world' (Ephesians 1:4). This great truth led the nineteenth-century British preacher C. H. Spurgeon to say, 'I believe the doctrine of election, because I am quite certain that, if God had not chosen me, I should never have chosen him; and I am sure he chose me before I was born, or else he never would have chosen me afterwards; and he must have elected me for reasons unknown to me, for I never could find any reason in myself why he should have looked upon me with special love.'

God's never-ending love for his people is rooted in his own character, a truth beautifully expressed by the eighteenth-century British preacher and hymn-writer Joseph Hart:

How good is the God we adore,
Our faithful, unchangeable Friend!
His love is as great as his power,
And knows neither measure nor end!

True or false?

Thirdly, there is God's call to genuine repentance, of which Gomer's requirement to prove herself is a picture. As Hosea's prophecy comes to an end, we find God calling for a radical change: 'Return, O Israel, to the LORD your God. Your sins have been your downfall! Take words with you and return to the LORD. Say to him: "Forgive all our sins and receive us graciously, that we may offer the fruit of our lips"' (14:1–2, NIV). There is nothing superficial here. Firstly, they needed to recognize the reality and nature of sin. Previously, they realized that they had been 'torn' and 'struck down' (and even saw God's hand in this) but there was no mention of their own guilt. They are now told to realize that there was more to repentance than feeling sorry for themselves. They had to own up to the fact that their sins were responsible for their downfall. Secondly, they were to be specific in naming their sins. One of their greatest sins was idolatry; they were guilty of calling out 'Our god' (14:3) to idols they had made with their own hands. But there were many other sins to be named and repented of: 'swearing, lying, murder, stealing, and committing adultery' (4:2), 'evil' and 'treachery' (7:3), drunkenness (see 7:5), 'intrigue' (7:6), assassinations (see 7:7), failure to seek God's face (see 7:7) and even slander against him (see 7:13).

The nation was steeped in sin, but the people seemed to think that if they went through formal religious rituals God would sweep all their sin under the carpet and pour out his blessing on them. One of the most precious statements in the Word of God promises, 'If we confess our sins, he is faithful and just to forgive us our sins and to cleanse us from all unrighteousness' (1 John 1:9)—and the key word is 'confess', which literally means 'to say together with'. Confession of sins means agreeing with God's verdict on them and admitting them to him in specific detail. The people were to 'take words' to God, not merely vague concepts. They were to name their sins, not smother them under religious phrases.

Their response fell far short of this. Hosea records the people of both Israel and Judah as saying, 'Come, let us return to the LORD; for he has torn us, that he may heal us; he has struck us down, and he will bind us up. After two days he will revive us; on the third day he will raise us up, that we may live before him. Let us know; let us press on to know the LORD; his going out is sure as the dawn; he will come to us as the showers, as the spring rains that water the earth' (6:1–3).

At first glance this seems fine and to speak of a genuine turning to God. Yet vital elements are missing. There is no sense of guilt and no confession of sin, but merely an acknowledgement of the mess and pain that sin has caused. To make matters worse, there is the presumption that in response God will come running and take care of all their problems. The phrases 'after two days' and 'on the third day' are not to be taken literally. They mean that the people were sure that as long as they went through the motions of worship God would respond very quickly. They were equally sure that God's forgiveness was as certain as the rising of the sun and the coming of spring rains.

God's response was far from what they expected and he began by exposing their superficial approach: 'What shall I do with you…? … Your love is like a morning cloud, like the dew that goes early away' (6:4). Although they were using some of the right words God saw that these lacked any real depth and that the elements of true contrition were missing. James Montgomery Boice warns, 'We are never in greater danger than when we assume that [God] will always forgive us as long as we go through the outward forms of repentance.'

The danger is as true on the corporate church level as it is on the personal level. In advising on the compilation of a modern hymn book I decided to see how many hymns and songs written in the last twenty years referred to the holiness of God, his intolerance of sin or the need for genuine repentance— and found that just three per cent did so. Many churches fail to notice this. Some (though certainly not all) of these recent hymns and songs call for lively and upbeat singing, with worshippers sometimes encouraged to sway in time to the music, clap their hands, raise their arms or express themselves in other physical ways—but is this exuberance matched by sorrow for sin, the seeking of forgiveness and the cry for God's mercy? God requires more than an outward show of excitement. Donald Grey Barnhouse once went so far as to say, 'God hates the sanctimonious hallelujah more than he hates the godless curse.' That may sound harsh, but God says of enthusiastic but superficial worship, 'I hate, I despise your feasts' (Amos 5:21), whereas David rejoices that 'a broken and contrite heart, O God, you will not despise' (Psalm 51:17).

Halfway through a preaching series at a church in Texas the pastor asked me over coffee whether I had any comments on the services. When I began by telling him that while we can never praise God too highly we can praise him for too long, he nearly choked over his cappuccino! I explained that throughout that week every item chosen by the worship group had been a modern song of praise. I told him that while uninterrupted praise was fine for angels who had never sinned, our singing needed to include the confession of sin, a spirit of repentance, a cry for forgiveness and a longing for God's gracious help as we strove for holiness. This had never occurred to him; nor had my other observation that the congregation was being systematically robbed of the riches contained in the hymns of writers such as Isaac Watts, Augustus Montague Toplady, John and Charles Wesley, Joseph Hart, Philip Doddridge, William Gadsby and James Montgomery, to name but a few.

Not even all the Psalms—'the Bible's hymn book'—are comprised only of praise. They also sound deep notes of contrition, confession and repentance, as well as longings for holiness and guidance. Those responsible for the planning and conduct of public worship should first and foremost seek to reflect what God requires, not what the worshippers might prefer. They should ask important questions when choosing hymns and songs, whether they were written recently or long ago. Does this magnify God's name and reflect something of his character? Does it communicate clear biblical truth? Does it encourage worship that truly reflects biblical truth? Does it help people to express their sorrow for sin and to cry out for God's mercy, grace and forgiveness? Does it put into words a longing for holiness? Just as importantly, when joining in congregational singing, we all need to ask whether we are genuinely opening our hearts as well as our mouths and truly seeking to worship God 'in spirit and truth' (John 4:24).

We need to dig a little deeper. Are our personal and private times of prayer truly serious and earnest, or are there times when they are as mechanical as Tibetan prayer wheels placed so as to be spun by wind or water without engaging the hearts of those who placed them there? If our prayer times are no more than a lifeless repetition of a largely self-centred shopping list we are almost certainly speaking to ourselves. The Puritan preacher Thomas Brooks warned, 'God hears no more than the heart speaks, and if the heart be dumb God will certainly be deaf.'

'The greatest chapter'

James Montgomery Boice called Hosea 3, with its story of Hosea and Gomer, 'the greatest chapter in the Bible because it portrays the greatest story in the Bible—the death of the Lord Jesus Christ for his people—in the most concise and poignant form to be found anywhere.' Hosea is recording historical events, yet they form a kind of pageant, a dramatic illustration of even greater events, when Jesus came into the world to save sinners. In telling this greatest of all stories, the New Testament uses two words that link it unmistakeably with Hosea. Christians are told, 'You are not your own, for you were bought with a price' (1 Corinthians 6:19–20)—and the word 'bought' translates the original Greek word *agorazo*, which was used of buying something *in* the marketplace. We are also told, 'Christ redeemed us from the curse of the law' (Galatians 3:13)—and the word 'redeemed' translates the original Greek word *exagorazo*, which was used of buying something *out of* the marketplace. The picture is perfect! Hosea left his home, went into the squalid surroundings of the marketplace, chose Gomer in spite of her disgusting sin and its consequences, rescued her, forgave her, took her home and supplied all her needs. In infinite love and amazing grace God's beloved Son left the glories of heaven, came to live in all of earth's squalor, chose us in spite of the fact that we were steeped in sin, claimed us, cleansed us and (going further than Hosea) covenanted never to leave us or forsake us, all at the cost not of 'perishable things such as silver or gold, but with the precious blood of Christ' (1 Peter 1:18–19).

On one occasion while I was leading a tour to the Holy Land, I left Jerusalem by the Damascus Gate, then turned right towards the bus station. Looking at the buses for the destination sign I needed, my eyes caught sight of a little hill just behind the bus station. The front of the hill looked as if it had been ripped off, leaving a rough cliff face. It had two distinct indentations, looking for all the world like eye sockets in a human skull, and in between them the cliff face jutted out like the bridge bone of a nose. Ever since the British General Charles Gordon suggested in the eighteen-eighties that this was where Jesus was crucified this hill has become known as 'Gordon's Calvary'. The Church of the Holy Sepulchre, inside the present city walls, is thought by many others to mark the place of the crucifixion, but as I stood at the bus station I could not help thinking that I might actually be looking at the 'Place of a Skull' (Matthew 27:33), the very spot where two thousand years ago the man described by the eighteenth-century British hymn-writer Isaac Watts as 'the young Prince of Glory' surrendered himself into the hands of 'lawless men' (Acts 2:23) and bore in agonizing fullness the penalty for every sin that was to stain and scar my life. I am not ashamed to say that while hundreds of others scrambled for buses at the height of the afternoon rush hour I stood with tears of gratitude running down my face.

In the substitutionary death of Jesus the sin of God's people was judged and its penalty paid. No Christian who grasps this can do other than marvel at the staggering truth reflected in these words by the modern British composer Stuart Townend:

> Behold the Man upon a cross,
> My sin upon his shoulders;
> Ashamed, I hear my mocking voice
> Call out among the scoffers.
> It was my sin that held him there
> Until it was accomplished.
> His dying breath has brought me life;
> I know that it is finished.

JOEL

At 7.38 a.m. local time on 26 December 2004, tectonic plates several miles under the sea off the north-western tip of Indonesia sprang apart with the force of 1,000 atomic bombs, triggering thirty-six earthquakes. Trillions of tons of water were displaced and a 600-mile section of the Indian Ocean's seabed was re-aligned. The massive upheaval generated a series of tsunamis—long, high sea waves that raced across the ocean at 500 miles an hour and tore into the coastlines of eleven countries. Whole towns were devastated and entire islands disappeared under water. In Sri Lanka, hundreds of miles away from the initial event, a train crowded with 1,000 passengers was tossed into the trees like an unwanted toy.

A United Nations spokesman said that in terms of the area affected this was the greatest natural catastrophe in the world's history. In what the *Independent* called 'The wave that shook the world' the death toll was put at 288,000. One survivor of the tsunamis said, 'It is as if someone had pulled out the plug to the earth.' An article in the *Daily Telegraph* claimed, 'Our brains are not designed to compute suffering on such a scale ... the swallowing up of whole communities is literally unimaginable.' One reader argued, 'On the abundant available evidence does it not seem that, if there is or was a God, it is now malevolent, mad or dead?'

Over 2,500 years earlier the prophet Joel lived in a country that was devastated by another terrifying disaster, to which his response was very different.

The deadly invasion

We have no information about Joel except that he was 'the son of Pethuel' (1:1), whose name appears nowhere else in the Bible. There are twelve other men named Joel in the Old Testament and each one held a prominent position in society. As the prophet's name meant 'Jehovah is God' his parents may well have chosen it as a declaration of their personal faith. It has proved impossible to date his prophecy, with scholars suggesting various times between the ninth century BC and the fourth century BC, a range of some 500 years. Joel mentions none of the kings of Israel or Judah (something that in some other Minor Prophets is helpful in dating their prophecies) nor does he name any priest, prophet or other leader whose time frame would help.

A good case can be made for it having been written in the early years of Judah's King Joash (sometimes called Jehoash), who reigned from 835 BC to 796 BC. One good reason for suggesting this early date is that in the oldest Hebrew Scriptures Joel was always placed second (immediately behind Hosea) in the collected writings of the Minor Prophets. There are other clues. Joel makes no mention of Assyria, Babylon or Persia, arch-enemies of Israel and Judah in the eighth century BC, but he does mention 'Tyre and Sidon' (3:4) and 'Egypt ... and Edom' (3:19), who were Judah's enemies during the reign of King Joash. In addition, the prophet Amos seems to quote Joel 3:16 at Amos 1:2 and we know that Amos prophesied during the reigns of Israel's King Jeroboam II and Judah's King Uzziah (sometimes called Azariah), whose reigns covered the period from 793 BC to 753 BC. This would place Joel in or very close to the eighth century BC. That said, these are slim pickings and some scholars suggest that Joel quoted Amos rather than the reverse. After over 2,500 years the jury is still out on the issue and for our present purposes we can settle for the sixteenth-century French Reformer John Calvin's comment: 'As there is no certainty, it is better to leave the time in which he taught undecided; and, as we shall see, this is of no great significance.'

What is of significance is that Joel's prophecy was triggered off by a catastrophic plague of locusts. Some may think that the havoc wreaked by insects no more than two inches long could never be compared to that caused by the 2004 tsunami—but they would be wrong. Ever since written records were kept there is evidence of plagues of locusts devastating crops over vast areas. Swarming in their billions, they can blot out the sun, cover distances of several hundred miles in twenty-four hours, and jump from one continent to another. Nothing can stop a swarm of locusts that can be several miles wide, interfere with land and air travel and devour an entire country's food supply in a matter of hours. A massive plague of locusts can affect twenty per cent of the earth's surface. The United Nations' Desert Locust Information Service reports that during such plagues locusts may endanger one in every ten people on earth. In *City of God*, Augustine of Hippo (AD 354–430) wrote about a plague of locusts that hit Africa when it was a Roman province. After destroying countless square miles of vegetation a massive swarm drowned in the sea and Augustine records that when they were washed up on the shore, 'The putrefaction of these insects so infected the air as to cause a pestilence so horrible that in the Kingdom of Masinissa alone 800,000 and more are said to have perished'.

The invasion cited by Joel was 'powerful and beyond number' (1:6) and so destructive he suggested to his fellow countrymen that it was unique in the nation's history, asking, 'Has such a thing happened in your days, or in the days of your fathers?' (1:2). It had stripped the land bare and Joel summarized the destruction in one of the most graphic verses in the entire Bible: 'What the cutting locust left, the swarming locust has eaten. What the swarming locust left, the hopping locust has eaten, and what the hopping locust left, the destroying locust has eaten' (1:4). Scholars have had a rare time debating whether these locusts were real or whether they were Joel's vivid metaphor for a vast army of soldiers, but it seems best to take the words at face value. The four terms Joel uses about them may refer to different species of locust or four different stages in the growth of a single species but the modern American scholar O. Palmer Robertson covers all the bases: 'The picture is clear: locusts, locusts and more locusts.'

To make matters worse, a terrible fire had 'devoured the pastures of the wilderness ... burned all the trees of the field' and left the precious water brooks 'dried up' (1:19–20). Nobody could escape the outcome of these twin tragedies and Joel pinpoints several groups that would have been severely affected. 'Tillers of the soil' and 'vine dressers' were obviously hit hard 'because the harvest of the field has perished' (1:11). He also singles out priests, no longer able to carry out the sacrificial duties that lay at the heart of the nation's covenant relationship with God because 'the grain offering and the drink offering are cut off from the house of the LORD' (1:9). Eventually, the entire population was affected and normal life was reduced to mere existence: in Joel's poetic words, 'gladness dries up from the children of man' (1:12). Even drunkards would have felt the plague's impact because, 'The sweet wine ... is cut off from your mouth' (1:5).

The people hardly needed Joel to point out these things, but his message went far beyond stating the obvious and can be summarized in one phrase: 'For the day of the LORD is near, and as destruction from the Almighty it comes' (1:15). The phrase 'the day of the LORD' occurs many times in the Old Testament, always referring to momentous times or events. Sometimes these events are imminent and sometimes they are to occur years later, all of them leading up to the final 'day of the LORD' at the end of time. Joel now uses it to explain the source and significance of the plague of locusts and he does so by drawing the people of Judah's attention to two massively important truths.

God is God

The first of these is that *God is sovereign*. For many people the plague would have been seen as a natural disaster that raised painful questions. How could God allow such a thing to happen to his covenant people? Why should they have been exposed to a terror over which they had no control? Some may even have found themselves as stripped of faith as their land had been of vegetation, leaving them at least tempted to decide, like the *Daily Telegraph* correspondent about the 2004 tsunami, that God was 'malevolent, mad or dead'. Joel's response to the deadly invasion of locusts was to see it through a very different lens.

Although the word 'sovereignty' (like the word 'trinity') does not occur anywhere on its pages, the Bible is saturated with the subject, beginning with the very first verse: 'In the beginning, God created the heavens and the earth' (Genesis 1:1). The Hebrews had no single word to describe what we would now call the universe and the phrase 'the heavens and the earth' simply means all reality outside of God himself. As the modern American scholar Douglas Kelly puts it, Genesis 1:1 records 'the absolute creation of all things out of nothing'. *All things*, from angels to amino-acids, from light to life, from galaxies to gravitons, from stars to stem cells, from time to termites, from space to spiders, from elephants to electrons, from lizards to the laws of physics, all were created by God. There is not a single atom, proton, neutron, photon, quasar or quark that God did not bring into existence. In his revelation of things to come the apostle John recorded heavenly beings worshipping God by crying out, 'Worthy are you, our Lord and God, to receive glory and honour and power, for you created all things, and by your will they existed and were created' (Revelation 4:11).

Yet the sovereignty of God goes far beyond creation. It also means that God is in constant and active control of all that he created. He told Isaiah, 'My counsel shall stand, and I will accomplish all my purpose' (Isaiah 46:10). One of the psalmists declares, 'Our God is in the heavens; he does all that he pleases' (Psalm 115:3). God is not an absentee landlord who created the universe and then left it to fend for itself. Instead, he controls every part of it and everything that lives in it. John Calvin is exactly right: 'God is deemed omnipotent not because he can indeed act, yet sometimes ceases and sits in idleness, or continues by a general impulse that order of nature which he previously appointed; but because, governing heaven and earth by his providence, he so regulates all things that nothing takes place without his deliberation' (emphasis added). The modern American theologian R. C. Sproul fine-tunes the point: 'If there is one molecule in this universe running around loose outside the scope or the sphere of God's divine control and authority and power ... it would mean that God is not sovereign. If there is any element of the universe that is outside of his authority, then he is no longer God over all... *God owns what he makes and he rules what he owns*' (emphasis added). This has to be the case. If he is not sovereign, he is not God. If he is not God, he is not sovereign.

Lord of the locusts

We must now take this further. If God 'works *all things* according to the counsel of his will' (Ephesians 1:11, emphasis added) it must mean that we dare not 'edit' his authority and limit it to events that we find pleasant or that obviously benefit us in some way. 'All things' must include events that leave us puzzled or in pain, and God himself tells us that this is the case: 'I form light and create darkness, I make well-being and create calamity' (Isaiah 45:7). Elsewhere, the Bible states, 'Whatever the LORD pleases he does, in heaven and on earth, in the seas and all deeps. He it is who makes the clouds rise at the end of the earth, who makes lightnings for the rain and brings forth the wind from his storehouses' (Psalm 135:6–7). As the modern Irish scholar J. A. Motyer writes, 'The Lord is executively behind all the diversities of experience which life contains; he also ordains the order in which things happen, the course of experience.'

This comes across powerfully in the story of Job, a man who was 'blameless and upright, one who feared God and turned away from evil' (Job 1:1), yet in a single day was told that all his livestock had been stolen or destroyed and all ten of his children wiped out. Far from believing that this personal tsunami was beyond God's control, at the end of the day he fell to the ground in worship and cried out, 'The LORD gave, and the LORD has taken away; blessed be the name of the LORD' (Job 1:21). When in addition to his catastrophic losses Job's health broke down, his wife could take no more and asked him, 'Do you still hold fast your integrity? Curse God and die.' But Job rejected her suggestion as foolish and replied, 'Shall we receive good from God, and shall we not receive evil?' (Job 2:9–10). The prophet Jeremiah asked a similarly rhetorical question: 'Is it not from the mouth of the Most High that good and bad come?' (Lamentations 3:38). The worst calamities, the greatest pains and the sorest trials that touch our lives originate with God, not with anyone or anything else. The renowned British author C. S. Lewis advised, 'The great thing, if one can, is to stop regarding all the unpleasant things as interruptions of one's own or real life. The truth is of course that what one calls the interruptions are precisely one's real life—the life God is sending one day by day.'

When things go wrong we have a tendency to concentrate our thinking on secondary causes instead of looking beyond them to their ultimate source. Nowhere is this more clearly stated in the Bible than when we consider the worst sin that has ever been committed and which caused the greatest pain that any human being has ever suffered—the crucifixion of Jesus. When he was arrested in the Garden of Gethsemane and one of his disciples attacked a high priest's servant, Jesus told him, 'Put your sword into its sheath; shall I not drink *the cup that the Father has given me*?' (John 18:11, emphasis added). On the day of Pentecost, the apostle Peter told the crowds that although Jesus had been 'crucified and killed by the hands of lawless men' he had been 'delivered up according to the definite plan and foreknowledge of God' (Acts 2:23). Centuries earlier the prophet Isaiah foresaw this and wrote of Messiah being 'smitten by God, and afflicted' (Isaiah 53:4).

From what he is about to say it is obvious that Joel's prophecy drives home the same truth and sees the hand of God behind the invasion. Far from being outside of his control God called it 'my great army, which I sent among you' (2:25). The locusts swept across the land in their billions, but not a single one of them could have moved a wing unless God had decreed that it would do so.

The message

In *The Problem of Pain* C. S. Lewis wrote, 'God whispers to us in our pleasures, speaks in our conscience, but shouts in our pains: it is his megaphone to rouse a deaf world.' Joel anticipated Lewis by nearly 3,000 years and the second massively important truth he wanted to convey to his fellow countrymen was that in sending the plague *God was shouting to them*. The seventeenth-century Scottish theologian Samuel Rutherford declared, 'I would wish each cross were looked in the face seven times, and were read over and over again. It is the messenger of the Lord *and speaks something*' (emphasis added).

Some people no doubt saw the locust plague as a natural disaster with no explanation. Joel wanted them not merely to see it but to hear it telling them that it was God's judgement on them because of their sin. Centuries before, God had warned their predecessors that if they turned away from him, 'You shall carry much seed into the field and shall gather in little, for the locust shall consume it' (Deuteronomy 28:38); now, he was putting his promise into practice. Yet God's aim was not the people's destruction but their restoration, and no sooner has Joel laid out the devastating effects of the plague than he issues a call to repentance, urging them to consider their ways and to turn back to God.

The nation's spiritual leaders were to set an example in doing this: 'Put on sackcloth and lament, O priests; wail, O ministers of the altar. Go in, pass the night in sackcloth, O ministers of my God!' (1:13). This was not to be some pleasant religious ritual. Sackcloth was rough, unfinished material and would have been very uncomfortable to wear, and its real significance was as a mark of grief, sorrow and penitence. In the Old Testament we find it being worn in times of national and personal crisis, danger and distress. In Jonah's day, the king of Nineveh not only 'covered himself with sackcloth' (Jonah 3:6) but ordered that every 'man and beast' (Jonah 3:8) be covered.

Joel emphasizes the importance of the call to repentance by adding further instructions: 'Consecrate a fast; call a solemn assembly. Gather the elders and all the inhabitants of the land to the house of the LORD your God, and cry out to the LORD' (1:14). Fasting is often mentioned in the Old Testament and specifically linked with confessing sin and seeking God's favour. When disaster threatened Israel, Samuel, the last of the nation's judges and its first prophet, gathered the people at Mizpah 'and fasted on that day and said there, "We have sinned against the LORD"... And Samuel cried out to the LORD for Israel' (1 Samuel 7:6, 9).

Just as 'all inhabitants of the land' (1:2) were to hear Joel's announcement about the plague, so they were all to understand its meaning and engage in wholehearted repentance. Later in his prophecy, Joel drives this home by giving no fewer than seven directives to ensure that it was done: 'Blow the trumpet in Zion; consecrate a fast; call a solemn assembly; gather the people. Consecrate the congregation; assemble the elders; gather the children, even nursing infants. Let the bridegroom leave his room, and the bride her chamber' (2:15–16). Nobody was overlooked. Pleading old age would not work. Having babies and children to look after would be no excuse. Newly-weds were expected to interrupt their honeymoon.

Why was this nationwide call to repentance so rigorous and urgent? It was because as well as wreaking terrible havoc, the plague of locusts was also a warning that if the people failed to repent an even more devastating invasion was to follow very shortly. Joel writes about this in 2:1–11 and says the people should tremble, 'for the day of the LORD is coming; it is near' (2:1). In this case it may have meant a foreign military invasion, but whatever it was it would be under God's immediate and total control: 'The LORD utters *his* voice before *his* army, for *his* camp is exceedingly great; he who executes *his* word is powerful' (2:11, emphasis added).

The warning and the promise

Although Joel has no direct prophecy about the coming Messiah and nowhere identifies him, he does link future judgement on the nation of Israel with events that lie beyond the coming, death and resurrection of Jesus and he does say that at some time in the future terrible events would take place. There would be 'blood and fire and columns of smoke ... the sun shall be turned to darkness, and the moon to blood' (2:31). There have been cartloads of comments as to what these phenomena mean, and there is no room to discuss them here. What we can be clear on is that they will precede 'the great and awesome day of the LORD' (2:31). This will herald the final day of judgement, when 'the heavens will be set on fire and dissolved, and the heavenly bodies will melt as they burn!' leading to 'new heavens and a new earth' (2 Peter 3:12–13).

The whole of Chapter 3 is taken up with Joel recording God's direct words on the subject. 'All the nations' would be brought to 'the Valley of Jehoshaphat' (3:2). There was such a place, but 'Jehoshaphat' means 'Jehovah has judged' and the prophecy is about 'the day of judgement and destruction of the ungodly' (2 Peter 3:7). 'Tyre and Sidon, and all the regions of Philistia' (3:4) are singled out for punishment because of the way they had treated God's people, especially in capturing and trading or selling them, while 'Egypt shall become a desolation and Edom a desolate wilderness, for the violence done to the people of Judah' (3:19). Yet nobody opposed to God will escape from facing him in 'the valley of decision' (3:14), when 'The LORD roars from Zion, and utters his voice from Jerusalem, and the heavens and the earth quake' (3:16).

Joel's message lists a fearful catalogue of dreadful events—past, present and future—yet his prophecy also rings with hope rooted in the promises of a sovereign God who is 'a refuge to his people' (3:16). This brings us to our 'major point', a glorious promise that resonates throughout the Bible, both historically and prophetically:

> **And it shall come to pass that everyone who calls on the name of the LORD shall be saved.** (2:32)

The first thing to notice is the universality of this promise. In what theologians call the *protoevangelium* (the first gospel) God told the serpent in the Garden of Eden, 'I will put enmity between you and the woman, and between your offspring and her offspring; he shall bruise your head, and you shall bruise his heel' (Genesis 3:15). The bruising of the serpent's head speaks of the fatal blow dealt to Satan in the death and resurrection of Jesus Christ and this statement in Genesis was the first announcement of God's amazing plan of salvation which was to open the kingdom of heaven to all believers.

When establishing a covenant with Abram, God 'brought him outside and said, "Look towards heaven, and number the stars, if you are able to number them." Then he said to him, "So shall your offspring be." And he believed the LORD, and he counted it to him as righteousness' (Genesis 15:5–6). Changing the patriarch's name to Abraham, God later told him, '… you shall be the father of a multitude of nations' (Genesis 17:4). Centuries later, the apostle Paul made it clear that the patriarch's offspring consisted not necessarily of physical descendants but of everyone who 'shares the faith of Abraham, who is the father of us all' (Romans 4:16).

Just before ascending to heaven after his resurrection from the dead, Jesus underlined the universality of the gospel by telling his disciples, 'But you will receive power when the Holy Spirit has come upon you, and you will be my witnesses in Jerusalem and in all Judea and Samaria, and to the ends of the earth' (Acts 1:8). In the providence of God their worldwide mission got off to an explosive start even before they left Jerusalem, as on the Day of Pentecost people from about fifteen nations heard the gospel in their own language and 'about three thousand souls' (Acts 2:41) were converted.

Even if we confine ourselves to reading the early chapters of Acts we cannot miss the powerful evidence that the gospel breaks through national, social, religious, cultural, physical and other barriers. A man 'lame from birth … laid daily at the gate of the temple' came to faith (Acts 3:2). A little later the church had grown so rapidly that 'the number of the men came to about five thousand' (Acts 4:4), while soon after that 'more than ever believers were added to the Lord, multitudes of both men and women' (Acts 5:14). One remarkable conversion was 'an Ethiopian … a court official of Candace, queen of the Ethiopians' (Act 8:27). Even more astonishing was the conversion of Saul of Tarsus, who was brought to faith while on a search-and-destroy mission against the Christian church, 'breathing threats and murder against the disciples of the Lord' (Acts 9:1). Later, a Roman non-commissioned officer named Cornelius, 'a centurion of what was known as the Italian Cohort' (Acts 10:1) trusted Christ. When the gospel was preached in Antioch 'a great number who believed turned to the Lord' (Acts 11:21), while back in Jerusalem 'the word of God increased and multiplied' (Acts 12:24).

These and all the other biblical examples we could give will find their consummation in eternity. In his preview of heaven the apostle John wrote, 'After this I looked, and behold, a great multitude that no one could number, from all tribes and peoples and languages standing before the throne and before the Lamb, clothed in white robes, with palm branches, and crying out with a loud voice, "Salvation to our God who sits on the throne, and to the Lamb!"' (Revelation 7:9–10). This vision of heaven points to the fact that while the door into heaven is narrow it is wide open. *Any theological system that restricts the free offer of the gospel has no biblical basis.* When the eighteenth-century British preacher Rowland Hill was told that as he believed in election he should preach only to the elect, he told his critic to chalk a mark on the elect and he would then gladly do so! Preaching in the hope that sinners might somehow stir themselves to respond is asking for the impossible, because if election is false, evangelism is futile. We can preach the gospel without constraint, in complete confidence that God will cause it to take root in the hearts of all those he has graciously chosen to draw to himself in saving faith.

Repentance—true and false

Joel's message was to different parts of society, but it was the same to all of them—they were to 'cry out to the LORD' (1:14). We have already seen that this was not to be a purely formal religious ceremony or ritual. There was to be a 'solemn assembly' (1:14) and Joel announced, 'Let all the inhabitants of the land tremble' (2:1). It was a call to genuine repentance, and God himself issued it: "'Yet even now," declares the LORD, "return to me with all your heart, with fasting, with weeping, and with mourning; and rend your hearts and not your garments'" (2:12–13).

Other than the reference to drunkards in Chapter 1, no specific sin is mentioned, but Joel's passionate plea and God's searching command are clear indications that things were seriously wrong. The call to 'rend your hearts and not your garments' shows that God was looking for more than an outward symbol. In biblical times tearing one's clothing was often a symbol of sorrow, grief or distress. When Israel's idolatrous King Ahab was condemned for his vicious wickedness, 'he tore his clothes and put sackcloth on his flesh and fasted and lay in sackcloth and went about dejectedly' (1 Kings 21:27). Yet we know that in spite of these outward actions there was no genuine repentance, as shortly afterwards we find him saying of the prophet Micaiah, 'I hate him, for he never prophesies good concerning me, but evil' (1 Kings 22:8). When people at Lystra 'tore their garments and rushed out into the crowd' (Acts 14:14), trying to worship the apostle Paul and his companion Barnabas, they were passionately condemned for their idolatry.

There would have been nothing wrong in Joel's hearers tearing their clothes as a sign of sorrow, but this alone would not have been sufficient; 'man looks on the outward appearance, but the LORD looks on the heart' (1 Samuel 16:7). Outward, empty symbols of repentance would only add to the sins for which inward repentance was required. God's command was, '... rend your hearts'. This exact phrase is not used anywhere else in the Bible, but its meaning is clear. The heart of the people's problems was the problem of their hearts, which were 'deceitful above all things and desperately sick' (Jeremiah 17:9). This was where the change was needed.

There is more to true repentance than apologizing to God. Israel's King David, guilty of adultery and serial dishonesty and of being an accessory to murder, provides a clear illustration of what true repentance is and why nothing less is acceptable to God: 'Behold, you delight in truth in the inward being... Create in me a clean heart, O God, and renew a right spirit within me... The sacrifices of God are a broken spirit; a broken and contrite heart, O God, you will not despise' (Psalm 51:6, 10, 17).

True repentance involves a change of mind. The person who truly repents has a totally different view of sin from the one they previously held. They no longer see sin as trivial or as merely a personal matter and entirely their own business. Instead, they realize that all sin is an offence against God. The modern American preacher Jerry Bridges says, 'Sin is a serious business to God, and it becomes a serious business to us when we reflect upon the fact that every sin, regardless of how seemingly insignificant it appears to us, is an expression of contempt towards the sovereign authority of God.'

True repentance involves a change of heart. It means being heartbroken as we realize that sin is not only the cause of everything degrading and shameful in human experience but that it was sin that nailed Jesus to the cross and brought his earthly life to such a horrific end. The nineteenth-century American scholar Thomas Moore was not exaggerating when he says, 'All true repentance arises from a sight of a dying Saviour, one who has died for us.'

True repentance involves a change of life. God does not merely call us to repent *of* sin but also *from* sin. God has nowhere undertaken to forgive a sin that a man is not prepared to forsake. Repentance involves not only an inner change of heart and mind but an outer change of life. When John the Baptist was baptizing those who confessed their sins, hypocritical Pharisees and Sadducees wanted to get in on the act, but John turned them away, bluntly telling them, 'Bear fruit in keeping with repentance' (Matthew 3:8). The symbolic act of baptism would mean nothing if it was not matched by a change of life.

We dare not miss one other note: the people in Joel's day were to repent *'even now'*. The call to repentance was not only important but urgent, because an even greater disaster than the invasion of locusts was imminent. God's call to repentance—now as then—is always urgent. Delayed obedience is disobedience. The person who puts off repentance even for a day has one day more to repent of and a day less in which to do so.

It is common to think of the call to repentance as something to be preached to unbelievers, but most of the calls for repentance in the Bible are addressed to those who at least nominally belong to the family of faith. To fine-tune this in New Testament terms, godly sorrow for sin is one of the signs of being a true Christian. Jesus made this clear in the Sermon on the Mount, when he said, 'Blessed are those who mourn, for they shall be comforted' (Matthew 5:4). The word 'mourn' is a present active participle, and we could translate Jesus' statement to read, 'Blessed are those who are continuing to mourn.' This does not mean having a poor self-image, or always seeing the blackest side of things. The blessing Jesus promises is to those believers whose hearts are so tenderized by the Holy Spirit that they grieve whenever he makes them aware of sin in their lives. The American preacher Samuel Logan Brengle, who became a leading figure in the Salvation Army in the eighteen-nineties, said, 'I have carried a penitent form around in my heart for half a century or more, and if there is ever any need, instantly I fly there. Jesus waits, loves, pities and never turns away the seeking soul.' In saying this, Brengle was testifying to the truth of God's promise, 'If we confess our sins, he is faithful and just to forgive us our sins and to cleanse us from all unrighteousness' (1 John 1:9).

Calling on God's name

Our 'major point' applies to everyone who 'calls on the name of the LORD', but what does this mean? As with repentance the key thing to grasp is that *it calls for reality, not formality.* There is more to calling on the name of the Lord than merely using his name when we pray. One of the most sobering passages in the entire Bible is in the Sermon on the Mount, when Jesus warned his hearers, 'Not everyone who says to me, "Lord, Lord", will enter the kingdom of heaven, but the one who does the will of my Father who is in heaven' (Matthew 7:21). A little later he identified Pharisees and scribes as hypocrites who fulfilled Isaiah's prophecy, 'This people honours me with their lips, but their heart is far from me' (Matthew 15:8). There is more to worship than words and as far as these people were concerned their words were a cover-up for self-serving motives. As the seventeenth-century British preacher and Bible commentator Matthew Henry quaintly put it, their piety was 'from the teeth outwards'. What we are in public will never blind God to what we are in private. David acknowledged that God requires 'truth in the inward being' (Psalm 51:6) and Jesus emphasized that 'God is spirit, and those who worship him must worship in spirit and truth' (John 4:24).

True repentance before God is an earnest cry from the heart, not a superficial repetition of pious words, and the British preacher John Stott (news of his death was announced as I was writing this chapter) warned of an obvious danger: 'Some people weave around them such a tissue of lies that they can no longer tell which part of them is real and which is make-believe.' Yet hypocrisy and half-heartedness fall away when God brings his chosen people—those 'whom the LORD calls' (2:32)—to true repentance. As O. Palmer Robertson notes, 'Human responsibility and divine sovereignty could not be balanced more perfectly. The "whosoever" of the gospel opens the door to all men; and those who come are the ones the Lord has sovereignly called to himself.'

What does it mean to call 'on the name of the Lord'? In the Bible a person's name often means that person's essence, nature and character. To take the best example of all, the name 'Jesus' means 'Jehovah is salvation', which is exactly why before the baby's birth the angel told Joseph, '... you shall call his name Jesus, for he will save his people from their sins' (Matthew 1:21). To call on the name of the Lord is to call on his nature, in other words to appeal to him on the basis of who he truly is and in the confidence that he will respond in a way that will show that he is 'gracious and merciful, slow to anger, and abounding in steadfast love' (2:13). Calling on the name of the Lord means genuinely trusting that he will be true to his word.

Salvation

The promise God makes to all who call upon him in this way is that 'they shall be saved'. As far as Joel's hearers were concerned, this would mean a complete reversal of their desperate plight. God promised, 'I will restore to you the years that the swarming locust has eaten, the hopper, the destroyer, and the cutter' (2:25). He specifically mentioned sending 'the early and the latter rain, as before' (2:23), so that at harvest time 'the threshing floors shall be full of grain; the vats shall overflow with wine and oil' (2:24). The people were told that as a result of God's gracious response to their repentance, 'You shall eat in plenty and be satisfied, and praise the name of the LORD your God, who has dealt wondrously with you' (2:26). This was all perfectly in tune with God's promise elsewhere: '... if my people who are called by my name humble themselves, and pray and seek my face and turn from their wicked ways, then I will hear from heaven and will forgive their sin and heal their land' (2 Chronicles 7:14). Commenting on Joel's prophecy, the modern American theologian David Allan Hubbard writes, 'Good crops, brimming vats, full stomachs are not ends in themselves but are signs that God, who had seemed to abandon the people to the misery of their disaster and the mocking of their enemies, has now intervened on their behalf.'

God's promise to deal graciously with his people was the outworking of his covenant love for them, which runs like a golden thread throughout the Old Testament and is beautifully expressed in the assurance given to the prophet Jeremiah: 'I have loved you with an everlasting love; therefore I have continued my faithfulness to you' (Jeremiah 31:3). Mingled with God's assurance that he would punish their enemies was the equally firm assurance that his people would 'never again be put to shame' (2:26–27). Visiting a farm one day, C. H. Spurgeon noticed that the owner had placed the text 'God is love' on a weathervane on the roof of a farm building. Although glad to see it there, Spurgeon suggested that it might be taken to mean that God's love was as changeable as the wind. 'No', the farmer replied, 'I put it there to show that God is love whichever way the wind is blowing.' In Joel's day even the invasion of locusts was linked to God's love. It was a dramatic way of warning his people of a greater danger to come and of leading them to the repentance that would not only avert the looming disaster but open the door to greater blessing than they had ever known. God's love for his people never fluctuates; it is infinite, immeasurable, unchangeable and unconditional. As J. A. Motyer explains, 'The love of God is anchored to his character. He can only love in ways that are suitable to the kind of person he is.'

In Joel's day the promise to restore the locust-eaten years clearly referred in the first place to crops, cattle and vegetation, but James Montgomery Boice speaks for countless commentators when he also applies it as a contemporary spiritual promise to all who put their trust in God: 'We cannot undo what is done. Sin is sin, and the effects of sin often continue for long periods. But God can restore what the locusts have eaten... God can break the power of sin and restore a personal holiness and joy that would not have been dreamed possible in the rebellion.'

A neat statement speaking of the unity of the Bible's Old and New Testaments says, 'The New is in the Old concealed; the Old is in the New revealed.' Joel's prophecies about 'the day of the LORD' endorse this, as it is impossible to see the fuller meaning of his words until we see them quoted centuries later. On the Day of Pentecost the house in Jerusalem in which the disciples were meeting was filled with a sound from heaven 'like a mighty rushing wind' and 'tongues as of fire appeared to them and rested on each one of them' with the result that 'they were all filled with the Holy Spirit and began to speak in other tongues as the Spirit gave them utterance' (Acts 2:1–4). Later that day, when Peter was preaching to the crowds in the city he told them the disciples speaking in other languages was a fulfilment of 'what was uttered through the prophet Joel' (Acts 2:16). He then quoted the prophet's words, ending with our 'major point', '... everyone who calls on the name of the Lord shall be saved' (Acts 2:21). He had no hesitation in taking an Old Testament passage referring to Jehovah and applying it to Christ.

In the same sermon Peter also quoted God's promise to Joel: 'I will pour out my Spirit on all flesh' (Acts 2:17). This gave a dynamic new impetus to God's message of salvation. This was the first time Joel mentioned spiritual rather than merely material blessing and Peter's reference to it enables us to interpret what the prophet meant. The Holy Spirit would no longer be confined to a restricted number of people such as prophets, priests, kings and judges (as in Old Testament days) but would be given to all who cried out to God for salvation. Joel prophesied that the Spirit would be poured out on 'all flesh', then identifies 'sons', 'daughters', 'old men', 'young men' and 'male and female servants' as an indication that nobody would be excluded.

The Holy Spirit indwells every Christian without exception. Paul told the Christians at Rome that they were 'in the Spirit, if in fact the Spirit of God dwells in you', and added, 'Anyone who does not have the Spirit of Christ does not belong to him' (Romans 8:9). The essence of salvation is deliverance *from* things, and everyone who calls on the name of the Lord for salvation is delivered from the guilt of sin, and by the indwelling power of the Holy Spirit delivered from a life governed by their sinful nature.

Joel's final words—'Judah shall be inhabited for ever, and Jerusalem to all generations' and 'the LORD dwells in Zion' (3:20–21) look far beyond earthly locations. These will all disappear when the final day of the Lord comes and 'the heavenly bodies will be burned up and dissolved' (2 Peter 3:10). On that day all who have truly called on the name of the Lord will be delivered from this indescribable holocaust and rejoice for ever 'before the throne of God', where they will 'serve him day and night in his temple; and he who sits on the throne will shelter them with his presence' (Revelation 7:15).

A modern version of a hymn written by the twelfth-century monk Bernard of Cluny puts it well:

How lovely is that city!
The home of God's elect;

How beautiful the country
That eager hearts expect!
Jesus in mercy bring us
To that eternal shore
Where Father, Son and Spirit
Are worshipped evermore.

AMOS

As we saw in the Introduction, the books written by the Minor Prophets were not compiled in the order in which they now appear in the Bible. However, in previous arrangements Hosea has always come first, perhaps because of its extensive treatment of some of the Minor Prophets' major themes. Joel distils many of these, while Amos (who may date over two centuries before Joel) complements the other two books by emphasizing the devastating social consequences of corrupt worship. This may explain the consistent order of the first three books, as they set the scene for the other nine prophets.

Amos prophesied 'in the days of Uzziah king of Judah and in the days of Jeroboam the son of Joash, king of Israel' (1:1). Uzziah (also known as Azariah) was crowned king of Judah as a teenager and ruled from 792 to 740 BC, while Jeroboam (to be precise, Jeroboam II) ruled Israel from 793 to 753 BC). This gives us a window of about forty years during which the book of Amos could have been written. There is another tantalizing clue, though it still leaves us guessing. The prophet tells us that God's word came to him 'two years before the earthquake' (1:1). This was clearly a major event, as Amos calls it '*the* earthquake', but gives us no indication as to when it happened. Some 250 years later the prophet Zechariah reminded his contemporaries that their predecessors 'fled from the earthquake in the days of

Uzziah king of Judah' (Zechariah 14:5), but again he gives no date for the event.

As to Amos himself, we know nothing about his family, but he begins by telling us that he was 'among the shepherds of Tekoa' (1:1), a Judean town in a bleak part of the country about twenty miles south of Jerusalem and some eighteen miles west of the Dead Sea. Later, we learn that he was 'a herdsman and a dresser of sycamore figs' (7:14). The difference between a shepherd and a herdsman was that one tended sheep and the other cattle, while dressing figs meant slitting the fruit to encourage its ripening. This may all point to his having been a general farm labourer, a 'jack-of-all trades'. His work as a shepherd would have put him in the social basement, as some rabbis rated a shepherd no higher than a heathen. Any gift a shepherd tried to put into a synagogue's offering box would be thrown back at him, while there were cases in which a synagogue was off-limits to a shepherd. Yet the book of Amos is not what we might expect from an uneducated farmhand. David Allan Hubbard goes so far as to say that 'his polished skills in debate and his familiarity with a host of literary forms all mark him as a man of uncommon experience, opportunity and sensibility, fully equipped by personal background as well as divine command to carry out his mission'.

Punishing the ungodly

Although Amos lived in the southern kingdom of Judah, his primary mission was to the northern kingdom; God sent him to 'prophesy to my people Israel' (7:15). Gareth Crossley suggests, 'It would be like a farm labourer from Scotland standing on the steps of St Paul's Cathedral in the city of London and prophesying against England.' However, when Amos reached Israel he began by pronouncing judgement on six neighbouring heathen nations: Damascus, Gaza, Tyre, Edom, Ammon and Moab. God's message to each of these began with the phrase, 'For three transgressions of *(name of nation)*, and for four, I will not revoke the punishment...' (1:3, 6, 9, 11, 13; 2:1). This was an idiomatic way of saying that God was judging them not for merely three or four offences but for many, committed over a long period of time—though for each nation just one appalling sin is pinpointed, all of them gross violations of human rights. In the case of Damascus (representing Syria) it was sickening cruelty; it had 'threshed Gilead with threshing sledges of iron' (1:3), massacring thousands of its enemies and making them 'like the dust at threshing' (2 Kings 13:7). In the case of Gaza (the capital of Philistia) it was the violation of human rights in selling prisoners of war; it 'carried into exile a whole people to deliver them up to Edom' (1:6). Tyre had been guilty of the same atrocity; it had 'delivered up a whole people to Edom' (1:9). In the case of Edom, which had historical links with Israel, its sin was ongoing hatred of God's people; 'he pursued his brother with the sword and cast off all pity, and his anger tore perpetually, and he kept his wrath for ever' (1:11). Ammon was guilty of vicious cruelty; in the course of extending its own borders, it 'ripped open pregnant women in Gilead' (1:13). Moab violated the commonly-held principles about how to treat the corpse of a royal enemy and 'burned to lime the bones of the king of Edom' (2:1).

As we can see in Chapter 1 and the beginning of Chapter 2, Amos prophesies that God would severely punish these heathen nations in ways that would reflect these particular sins. The fact that they were not among God's covenant people was immaterial. As James Montgomery Boice explains, 'Although they are not Israel and have not received Israel's blessing, they are nevertheless responsible for their violation of the law of God implanted in every mind and conscience.'

Before turning specifically to Israel, Amos adds a short, sharp warning to Judah, whose people had 'rejected the law of the LORD and have not kept his statutes' (2:4). The overriding law of God called for his exclusive worship, but as we learn elsewhere Judah had violated this and been dragged down into apostasy and idolatry. While the heathen nations had sinned in ignorance of God's written law, Judah had deliberately sinned despite knowing it, making their guilt even worse. Several hundred years later Jesus emphasized this principle when applying a parable about masters and servants: 'Everyone to whom much was given, of him much will be required, and from him to whom they entrusted much, they will demand the more' (Luke 12:48).

Israel's movers and shakers would have been happy to applaud all that Amos had to say against their neighbours (and against Judah, for that matter) but when he turned his focus on their own nation they quickly changed their tune. An influential priest called Amaziah warned King Jeroboam, 'The land is not able to bear his words' (7:10) and then (presumably on the king's authority) told Amos, '... flee away to the land of Judah, and eat bread there, and prophesy there, but never again prophesy at Bethel' (7:12–13). In reply, Amos told Amaziah, 'I was no prophet, nor a prophet's son ... But the LORD took me from following the flock, and the LORD said to me, "Go, prophesy to my people Israel"' (7:14–15). He backed that up by adding, 'Now therefore hear the word of the LORD' (7:16). Amos was not on a charm offensive, nor did he have upwardly mobile ambitions. Instead, he preached with the conviction that he was God's ambassador and that neither priest nor king had any right to silence him.

This comes across powerfully at the very beginning of his book, which is introduced as being, 'The words of Amos ... which he *saw* ...' (1:1, emphasis added). There is more to the word 'saw' than meets the eye, as it is a particular verb that only genuine prophets seem to have used. Jeremiah identified false prophets by asking the rhetorical question: '... who among them has stood in the council of the LORD *to see and to understand his word...*?' (Jeremiah 23:18, emphasis added). As we saw in the Introduction, the prophets were 'seers' before they were 'sayers'. Instead of resisting Amos, it was the Israelites' urgent responsibility to hear what God was saying through him. We have the same responsibility today whenever we come to 'the living and abiding word of God' (1 Peter 1:23), either in our private devotions or when we gather for public worship. Those who pay only scant attention when the Bible is read in church (often having failed to bring their own) and then casually drift in and out of concentration during the sermon are dishonouring God and reducing the exposition of his Word to the level of muzak.

When Cornelius, a God-fearing Roman centurion, invited Peter to speak to people crowded into his home he told him, '… we are all here in the presence of God to hear all that you have been commanded by the Lord' (Acts 10:33). All congregations should be able to say the same!

The woes of the wealthy

King Jeroboam had led the nation to great prosperity and prestige, largely through trade, agriculture and the reclamation of land from its enemies, but its material triumph had been more than matched by spiritual tragedy and the Bible's verdict on Jeroboam's forty-one-year reign is simple and shameful: '… he did what was evil in the sight of the LORD' (2 Kings 14:24). The effect on the nation was catastrophic and God's message through Amos specifies details of this with laser-like precision.

Ironically, it was Israel's material prosperity that sowed the seeds of its spiritual poverty. Amos drew attention to people who owned both a 'winter house' and a 'summer house', to others who had 'houses of ivory' (presumably custom-built and inlaid with ivory) or 'great houses' (3:15) and to others who had 'built houses of hewn stone' (5:11). The phrase 'great houses' may be better rendered 'many houses', another indication of excessive luxury at a time when many people were struggling to survive financially.

Later, Amos focuses on those who were 'at ease in Zion' and who felt 'secure on the mountain of Samaria' (6:1). In another passionate passage he says, 'Woe to those who lie on beds of ivory and stretch themselves out on their couches, and eat lambs from the flock and calves from the midst of the stall, who sing idle songs to the sound of the harp and like David invent for themselves instruments of music, who drink wine in bowls and anoint themselves with the finest oils' (6:4–6). Nor was the prophet concerned to be politically correct. He refers to the luxury-loving wives of the wealthy as 'you cows of Bashan' (4:1), not in a crudely insulting way, but in comparison to a well-fed breed of cattle in a fertile part of Gilead.

Many people with a flimsy grasp of what it says believe the Bible teaches that money is the root of all evil, but this is not the case. What the Bible says is: '… *the love of money* is a root of all kinds of evils' (1 Timothy 6:10, emphasis added), which is a very different matter. Those who claim that God has 'a bias to the poor' are equally wide of the mark. The idea that as the poor are denied so many material possessions in the present world they can be assured of eternal riches in the world to come has no biblical basis. God's final judgement of humankind will not depend on poverty or wealth. That said, material riches can often blind people to spiritual realities. C. S. Lewis once claimed, 'Prosperity is good campaigning weather for the devil' and the people Amos was attacking were tragic examples of this truth. Many years later Jesus taught, 'Only with difficulty will a rich person enter the kingdom of heaven' (Matthew 19:23), his point being that wealth can sometimes get so much of a rich man's attention that he neglects or ignores spiritual issues and has no concern to get right with God. There is a tragic madness in materialism.

On the other hand there are notable cases in the Bible of people honouring God as the giver of their great wealth. The great patriarch Abraham was 'very rich in livestock, in silver, and in gold' (Genesis 13:2) yet God referred to him as 'Abraham, my friend' (Isaiah 41:8). As part of God's blessing on him, Isaac 'became rich, and gained more and more until he became very wealthy' (Genesis 26:13). In Israel's exceptionally wealthy King David, God found 'a man after his own heart' (1 Samuel 13:14), while his successor King Solomon was even wealthier. Job was 'blameless and upright, one who feared God and turned away from evil', yet he was 'the greatest of all the people of the east' (Job 1:1, 3). In the New Testament, the believer who laid the body of Jesus in his own tomb, was 'a rich man from Arimathea, named Joseph' (Matthew 27:57). What the prophet Amos condemns is not people's wealth, but its relation to their wickedness, which he exposes in several areas

They used heartless means to become rich. They had become wealthy by stealing from 'the oppressed' (3:9) and at least some of their treasured wealth came from 'violence and robbery' (3:10). Amos identified those who 'trample on the needy and bring the poor of the land to an end' (8:4). As the nineteenth-century Bible scholar Thomas Nelson said, 'The book of Amos stands as an eloquent witness against those who subordinate human need and dignity to the pursuit of wealth and pleasure'.

They were ruthless in their business dealings. Bribery and corruption were common currency for these people and they were prepared to 'deal deceitfully with false balances' (8:5) and to 'buy the poor for silver' (8:6). Sharp practice ran in their DNA.

They were addicted to making money. They went through the formality of observing the prevailing religious customs, but longed for them to finish so that they could get down to business: 'When will the new moon be over, that we may sell grain? And the Sabbath, that we may offer wheat for sale …? (8:5). As far as they were concerned, the main business of the Sabbath was the same as on any other day—making more money.

Their judicial dealings were corrupt. Amos singles out those 'who turn justice to wormwood and cast down righteousness to the earth' (5:7). Dishonest and ruthless judges used to 'exact taxes of grain' (5:11) from people before handing down judgement in their favour. Court cases were heard near city gates and judges were prepared to 'take a bribe, and turn aside the needy in the gate' (5:12).

James Montgomery Boice warns, 'There is no seeking after God that is not at the same time a seeking after justice. Anything else is hypocrisy.' Amos had no hesitation in 'naming and shaming' those who were dishonestly and viciously feathering their own nests at the expense of the poor, who had no means of resisting them.

Rotten religion

No book in the Bible speaks more bluntly and powerfully against the sin of social injustice, but God used Amos to condemn another evil that had gradually seeped into Israel, that of lifeless and polluted religion. Two of the country's main religious centres were Bethel and Gilgal. Both were of significant importance in the nation's spiritual history, but their religious shrines had been grossly corrupted. Droves of people flocked there to go through countless rituals and ceremonies, fondly imagining that these were pleasing to God and entitled them to live as they liked. They could not have made a more terrible mistake, as we can discover from two passages in Amos.

In the first, Amos uses devastating sarcasm: 'Come to Bethel, and transgress; to Gilgal, and multiply transgression; bring your sacrifices every morning, your tithes every three days; offer a sacrifice of thanksgiving of that which is leavened, and proclaim freewill offerings, publish them; for so you love to do, O people of Israel' (4:4–5). These people thought that by going through their religious rituals (especially in Bethel and Gilgal) they were meeting their spiritual obligations, but by this time their religion had become so polluted that going through the motions only added to the worshippers' sins. In the modern American preacher Anthony Selvaggio's vivid phrase, 'They had domesticated God in their minds and hearts, relegating him to the temple as if it were a cage.' What is more, like the New Testament Pharisee in Luke 18, who stood on the temple premises in Jerusalem and prided himself on his virtues, these people loved to let others know about the offerings they had given.

God's verdict on their behaviour was very different: 'I hate, I despise *your* feasts, and I take no delight in *your* solemn assemblies. Even though you offer me *your* burnt offerings and grain offerings, I will not accept them; and the peace offerings of *your* fattened animals, I will not look upon them. Take away from me the noise of *your* songs; to the melody of *your* harps I will not listen' (5:21–23, emphasis added). The emphasized words tell us everything we need to know. Rather than the pure worship of God, their ceremonies were grossly self-centred. They were indulging in what Gareth Crossley calls 'a perverted religion formed of a mishmash of pagan ceremonies and a corrupted form of Jehovah-worship'. God hates religion that is merely a performance but not a living experience. The twentieth-century American preacher A. W. Tozer was right to say, 'For the true Christian the one supreme test for the present soundness and ultimate worth of everything religious must be the place our Lord occupies in it.'

It is difficult to imagine modern Christian churches sinking to these depths, but there are times when church programmes fall a long way short of biblical principles and standards. While preaching in the United States, I heard of a church in California that had a football autographed by team members of the local NFL franchise placed in the home of a non-Christian family and then organized a massive visitation programme. In every home the visitors asked whether the football was there and when it was eventually unearthed the leader of the team that found it was allowed to simulate kicking a field goal during the next Sunday morning service. This may sound extreme, but it should raise some warning flags. The drive for greater attendances will always open the door for unworthy methods, but even when crowds of people have been persuaded to attend we need to remember the twentieth-century British Methodist preacher W. E. Sangster's warning: 'A crowd is not an achievement; it is only an opportunity.'

In the planning and structuring of our church services and other events, in our music, in our special presentations, and especially in our preaching, we should be driven by one constant concern: *what would glorify God?* The current trend towards 'user-friendly' services sometimes misses the crucial point that our worship should first and foremost be aimed at glorifying God, not at pleasing his friends—let alone his enemies. Entertainment is no substitute for worship, tickling people's ears is no substitute for touching God's heart, and amusing ourselves is no substitute for delighting him. In a 1968 report produced by the Evangelical Alliance, Colin Chapman asked these penetrating questions: 'Could it be that what some of the audience hear is not so much a challenge to come to terms with the God who had made them and to whom they are accountable for their lives, but rather an invitation to fall in love with Jesus? … But would we not be more faithful to the gospel if we said that it is our refusal to love God which constitutes the compelling need for us to come to terms with God?' Paul even warned Christians at Corinth that there were times when they came together 'not for the better but for the worse' (1 Corinthians 11:17). Sadly, he would say the same of many congregations today.

None of the above is any excuse for dull, lifeless, stereotyped and predictable services producing the kind of atmosphere that once made a preacher friend of mine come away from church saying, 'It was so cold I could have skated down the aisle'. The Bible tells us how and why we should gather together for God's worship: 'Enter his house with thanksgiving, and his courts with praise! Give thanks to him; bless his name! For the LORD is good; his steadfast love endures for ever, and his faithfulness to all generations' (Psalm 100:4–5). Our services should be a worthy response to God and geared to the faithful declaration of his Word, not designed to massage the worshippers' egos or emotions.

Visions

In the second passage, which takes in parts of Chapters 7–9, Amos records five visions that together drive home the warning that God was not about to ignore Israel's sin, but would bring terrible judgement upon it. Israel was corrupt from top to bottom and, as David Allan Hubbard puts it, 'The divine Judge was to rap the gavel with a bang that would collapse both altar and palace.'

The first vision: 'This is what the Sovereign LORD showed me: He was preparing swarms of locusts after the king's share had been harvested and just as the second crop was coming up' (7:1, NIV). There have been two very different explanations of what this vision meant. The first says that the timing of this particular plague would be especially terrifying, as the king had already exercised his right to the first crop of cattle-feed as a tax on the land of the farmers. Coming after this, and before the second crop, locusts would leave the entire population staring disaster in the face. A second explanation sees the king as Jehovah and 'the king's share' as the judgements which had already fallen on the nation. In this picture, the second crop represents prosperity which had followed those judgements; yet even after that, a further spiritual relapse had resulted in the dreadful plague of locusts.

The second vision. This showed God 'calling for a judgement by fire' which 'devoured the great deep and was eating up the land' (7:4). Hosea had used similar language in warning Israel that because they had deliberately turned their backs on God he would 'send a fire upon his cities, and it shall devour her strongholds' (Hosea 8:14). The holocaust in the vision Amos saw, coming after the locusts had done their worst, would have completed a horrifying 'double whammy', drying up the underlying water table vital to the potential recovery of any scraps of vegetation the locusts had left.

The third vision. In this, Amos saw God standing by a wall with a plumb line in his hand. A plumb line consists of a heavy object suspended at the end of a flexible line (such as rope or string) to determine whether something built or placed alongside it is vertical. Amos quickly got the message: compared to the plumb line of God's righteousness reflected in the covenant he had made with them, the Israelites had become crooked and corrupt. This exposed them to God's holy anger, leading him to declare, 'I will never again pass by them; the high places of Isaac shall be made desolate, and the sanctuaries of Israel shall be laid waste, and I will rise against the house of Jeroboam with the sword' (7:8–9). This seems to have been the tipping point for the priest Amaziah who, as we saw earlier, reported Amos to King Jeroboam and had what amounted to a deportation clamped on the prophet. But God had more to say.

The fourth vision. God next showed Amos 'a basket of summer fruit' (8:1)—some translations have 'ripe fruit'—and told him, 'The end has come upon my people Israel; I will never again pass by them. The songs of the temple shall become wailings in that day' (8:2–3). The devastating message was that Israel was ripe for judgement and that there would be no reprieve.

The fifth vision. Finally, Amos 'saw the LORD standing before the altar' (9:1). This is the most disturbing of all the visions, as in it God spells out in chilling detail some of the ways in which his righteous anger would be shown. Nobody entrenched in their rebellion against God would be spared: '… not one of them shall flee away; not one of them shall escape' (9:1). The vision ended with a terrifying warning to those who felt that they could go on ignoring God without danger: 'All the sinners of my people shall die by the sword, who say, "Disaster shall not overtake or meet us"' (9:10).

The new Israel

It is impossible to escape what has been called the 'unrelenting movement towards judgement' as Amos faithfully warns rebellious, self-centred and arrogant Israelites of their appalling fate, yet he ends by looking even further ahead to a time of restoration, prosperity and security. Centuries of Bible scholars have in various ways applied the final five verses of Amos to the temporal nation of Israel, though in trying to fine-tune the details they have often run up against biblical and historical difficulties. What is clear is that the passage concerned is also Messianic, full of glorious truth for all who put their trust in the Lord Jesus Christ and are elsewhere called 'the Israel of God' (Galatians 6:16). Paul assured Galatian believers, 'if you are Christ's, then you are Abraham's offspring, heirs according to promise' (Galatians 3:29). We have space here for just four ways in which this is developed the book of Amos.

Firstly, God promised, 'I will raise up the booth of David' (9:11). In other Bible versions, 'booth' is rendered as 'tabernacle', 'shelter' or 'tent', but the fundamental promise is that the spiritual kingdom of David (which when Amos wrote was like a ruined building) would be restored. God had previously gone even further and promised David, '... your house and your kingdom shall be made sure for ever before me. Your throne shall be established for ever' (2 Samuel 7:16). This points to David's supreme successor, the promised Messiah. Isaiah called him the one who would reign 'on the throne of David and over his kingdom, to establish it and to uphold it with justice and with righteousness from this time forth and for evermore' (Isaiah 9:6). The leaders of the early church saw this prophecy in relation to the drawing in of Gentiles (see Acts 15:15), while the ultimate fulfilment of what Amos and Jeremiah prophesied is seen in the fact that Jesus the Messiah is now seated at God's right hand 'in the heavenly places, far above all rule and authority and power and dominion, and above every name that is named, not only in this age but also in the one to come' (Ephesians 1:20–21).

Secondly, Amos prophesied that God's restored and redeemed people would possess 'the remnant of Edom and all the nations who are called by my name' (9:12), an indication that Messiah's rule would extend far beyond one nation. Speaking to church leaders at Jerusalem, James quoted Amos when confirming that Gentiles who became Christians should not be bound by Jewish ceremonial law but be received as spiritual equals. This was because in terms of salvation God 'made no distinction between us and them' and had taken from the Gentiles 'a people for his name' (see Acts 15:1–21). The citizens of God's eternal kingdom are drawn from 'every tribe and language and people and nation' (Revelation 5:9).

Thirdly, God promised his people complete satisfaction and fulfilment (see 9:13–14). Drawing on his agricultural background, Amos said, '… the ploughman shall overtake the reaper and the treader of grapes him who sows the seed' (9:13). This extravagant metaphor pictures a constant and never-ending harvest in which the normal times of sowing and reaping are set aside. In his vision of heaven, the apostle John was also given a picture of abundant provision when he was shown 'the river of the water of life, bright as crystal, flowing from the throne of God and of the Lamb through the middle of the street of the city; also, on either side of the river, the tree of life, with its twelve kinds of fruit, yielding its fruit each month' (Revelation 22:1–2). As the twentieth-century British theologian Ernest F. Kevan put it, 'Heaven will mean the realization of all the things for which man was made and the satisfaction of all the outreaching of his heart.' It is impossible for us to put into words all the fullness of joy that God's people will experience throughout eternity, but the Bible sums it up in the sublime statement that they will be 'with Christ, for that is far better' (Philippians 1:23).

Fourthly, God promised his people eternal security. Israel's history had ebbed and flowed between triumph and disaster, victory and defeat, but God's final promise to Amos was, 'I will plant them on their land, and they shall never again be uprooted out of the land that I have given them' (9:15). As we are all painfully aware, life is fragile and fragmented and full of changes and uncertainties. It is literally true that we 'do not know what tomorrow will bring' (James 4:14) and as long as we live we are faced with the possibility of pain, loss, uncertainty, doubt and fear. Even if we feel relatively secure, here on earth 'we have no lasting city' (Hebrews 13:14). Things will be very different in heaven, when God's redeemed people will enjoy 'an inheritance that is imperishable, undefiled, and unfading' (1 Peter 1:4) and will 'reign for ever and ever' (Revelation 22:5). Small wonder that Calvin wrote, 'No man has made much progress in the school of Christ who does not look forward to the day of death and final resurrection'!

Major point—major problem?

Many statements in Amos could be identified as 'major points', but we will focus on one that should get the attention of any thoughtful reader. In commenting on the meaning of the first two visions I deliberately bypassed how Amos reacted to them and—more importantly—God's response to what the prophet did. After seeing the first vision about locusts, Amos cried out, 'O Lord GOD, please forgive! How can Jacob stand? He is so small!' (7:2). Other than calling out 'please cease' instead of 'please forgive' Amos used identical words after seeing the vision about fire (see v.5) and as God's response to both prayers was the same we will concentrate on the first one.

The prophet's reaction to God's warning should hardly surprise us. Any believer whose country is in a moral and spiritual tailspin should pray that God would change the hearts of leaders and followers and reverse the downward trend—for the bedrock biblical reason that 'Righteousness exalts a nation, but sin is a reproach to any people' (Proverbs 14:34). What should now get our close attention as a 'major point' is God's response to the prophet's plea:

The LORD relented concerning this: 'It shall not be,' said
the LORD.   (7:3)

Instead of sending the devastating plague of locusts and the
scorching fire, God withheld both. What can this mean? Did
God abandon Plan A in favour of Plan B? That can hardly be
the case, as it would mean that Plan A was flawed, whereas
'The LORD is righteous in *all* his ways' (Psalm 145:17, emphasis
added). Then did he suddenly decide to ignore Israel's rebellion?
This idea can also be rejected, as God 'cannot look at wrong'
(Habakkuk 1:13), let alone shrug his shoulders or sweep it under
the carpet. We can be sure of this because of what God revealed
to Amos in the third vision. He had graciously answered the
prophet's prayers and set aside the punishments of locusts and
fire threatened in the first two visions, but in the third he drove
home the undeniable fact that Israel had grossly deviated from
God's standard of righteousness (represented by the plumb line)
and that there would be consequences. This lies at the very heart
of the message that Amos was told to bring. A holy, covenant-
keeping God was being rejected by an unholy, covenant-breaking
nation—and there would be a price to pay. We have no record
of Amos praying for God to stay his hand over the catastrophes
predicted in the other three visions, but God knew perfectly well
judgement would fall in Israel exactly as he warned.

The fact that God answered the prophet's prayers and set
aside the judgements threatened in the first two visions raises
a question that has often engaged and baffled many Christians:
does God sometimes change his mind? Anyone reading the Bible
from start to finish runs into the issue very early on: 'The LORD
saw that the wickedness of man was great in the earth, and
that every intention of the thoughts of his heart was only evil
continually. And the LORD was sorry that he had made man on
the earth, and it grieved him to his heart' (Genesis 6:5–6). Later,
we read, 'The LORD relented from the disaster that he had spoken
of bringing on his people' (Exodus 32:14). These are very striking
statements, but God's perfection tells us that his sorrow cannot
mean that he had made a mistake in creating man. Instead, it
expresses the response of a holy God to man's sinful rebellion.

As we know that God 'cannot deny himself' (2 Timothy 2:13)—that is, he can never do anything that is out of character—the right way to begin answering the question is by establishing two of God's attributes. The first is his *immutability*, that is, his changelessness. He himself says, 'I the LORD do not change' (Malachi 3:6). With God 'there is no variation or shadow due to change' (James 1:17). This attribute is fine-tuned when we are specifically told, 'God is not man, that he should lie, or a son of man, that he should change his mind' (Numbers 23:19), while elsewhere we read, 'The counsel of the LORD stands for ever, the plans of his heart to all generations' (Psalm 33:11).

God's changelessness is obviously related to his moral perfection, which the Bible underlines by stating that 'God is light, and in him is no darkness at all' (1 John 1:5). As the modern Scottish theologian Bruce Milne explains, 'His very being is the outshining and outpouring of purity, truth, righteousness, justice, truth, goodness and every moral perfection.' Since God is eternally and absolutely perfect he cannot change for the better; nor can he change for the worse as this would mean him becoming less than perfect. His knowledge, principles, thoughts, motives, promises and plans are unchanged and unchangeable.

Yet to say that God is immutable is not to say that he is *immobile* and so incapable of any movement. The Bible's opening words—'In the beginning, God created the heavens and the earth' (Genesis 1:1)—show God in unimaginably powerful action. Before that chapter ends we are told that 'God created man in his own image, in the image of God he created him; male and female he created them' (Genesis 1:27) and the Bible teems with evidence that an unchanging God is constantly engaged in a dynamic relationship with humankind, acting and reacting for his eternal glory and his people's eternal good.

The second of God's attributes that relates directly to our question is his *omniscience*, his perfect knowledge of everything, past, present and future. Nothing shocks him, takes him by surprise, forces him to change tack, or leaves him uncertain as to how everything will work out. God never 'learns' or 'discovers' anything. Using the prophet Isaiah as his mouthpiece, God challenges false gods, 'Tell us what is to come hereafter, that we may know that you are gods' (Isaiah 41:23), and of course they could do no such thing. In total contrast, the entire future is an open book to God.

Some theologians say that as God never changes he must be *impassable*, that is, without passions or emotions, but this hardly ties in with God being 'sorry' and 'grieved' in his heart. When he joined Martha and Mary in mourning the death of their brother Lazarus, Jesus, the God-man, was 'deeply moved in his spirit and greatly troubled' (John 11:33). He 'wept' (Luke 19:41) over the impending doom of Jerusalem and 'rejoiced' (Luke 10:21) when his disciples reported on a particularly successful mission. The Bible is rich in language reflecting God's emotional involvement in everything that happens in the world, without ever suggesting that his emotions take over (as ours often do).

The modern American theologian Kevin Vanhoozer gets it right: 'God feels the force of human experience without suffering in his being, will or knowledge. Impassibility does not mean that God is unfeeling, but that God is never overcome or overwhelmed by passion... God genuinely relates to human persons via his communicative action, but nothing humans do conditions or affects God's communicative initiatives and God's communicative acts.'

To a greater or lesser degree all human beings are prone to be emotionally unstable at times. Yet, as we have just seen, 'God is not man' and we must view him differently. The most straightforward way to do this when faced with the question, 'Does God sometimes change his mind?' is to see phrases such as 'the Lord relented' and 'the Lord was sorry' as examples of what theologians call 'anthropopathism'. This is quite a mouthful (and my computer's spell-check feature refuses to accept it!) but we can easily break it down: *anthropos* is the Greek word for 'human' and *pathos* is the Greek word for 'emotion'. Anthropopathism means speaking about God in words we use when speaking about human emotions, but without in any way implying that God shares our limitations and weaknesses. It means speaking of God acting in ways that, *were he human,* would have been the result of his emotional reaction to circumstances over which he had no control.

Anthropomorphism is a similar form of language and is often used in the Bible to help us understand God's actions. It says, 'The eyes of the LORD are towards the righteous and his ears towards their cry' (Psalm 34:15); and that the Ten Commandments were written with 'the finger of God' (Exodus 31:18); while God tells Isaiah, '... the earth is my footstool' (Isaiah 66:1). Yet as 'God is spirit' he does not have eyes, ears, feet or any other physical features. In these verses God is stooping to our weakness and leading the biblical authors to use language we can easily understand in order to convey truth that would otherwise elude us.

A compromise?

One attempt to settle the question goes under the name of Open Theism (or Neotheism). This says that if God knows every detail of what will happen in the future, man's freedom to respond to responsibility and to make choices has no real meaning. It claims that God's omniscience covers only that which is knowable, and that as man's future choices are all options and not certainties they cannot be known. It accepts that God can influence these choices by precepts, warnings and promises, but says that options became certainties (and therefore knowable, even by God) only after man makes his choices. It also claims that God's intentions are influenced by human behaviour in such a way that he adjusts his plans and acts differently when he learns something new.

There are biblical statements that at first glance seem to give Open Theism some kind of credibility, but the theory runs headlong into the fact that God 'works all things according to the counsel of his will' (Ephesians 1:11). Nothing could be more inclusive—or conclusive—than 'all things', which must by definition include wrong attitudes, decisions and actions. God said of Pharaoh, 'I will harden his heart, so that he will not let the people go' (Exodus 4:21) and we are told of the pagan king Sihon, 'God hardened his spirit and made his heart obstinate' (Deuteronomy 2:30). When Samson wrongly negotiated marriage with a Philistine, 'it was from the LORD' (Judges 14:4). God asked through Amos, 'Does disaster come to a city, unless the LORD has done it?' (3:6). We are specifically told that even the worst sin ever committed—the brutal murder of Jesus—was 'according to the definite plan and foreknowledge of God' (Acts 2:23) and that the death of the Son of God was 'foreknown before the foundation of the world' (1 Peter 1:20). As J. I. Packer says, 'Even the Son on his cross ... was suffering by his and the Father's conscious foreknowledge and choice, and those who made him suffer, however free and guilty in their action, were real if unwitting tools of divine wisdom and agents of the divine plan.'

God has not deserted his creation, but is actively governing his universe and knows precisely how people will behave. When Peter swore that he would never desert Jesus, he was told, 'Truly, I tell you, this very night, before the cock crows, you will deny me three times' (Matthew 26:34). God controls even random events that seem to rely on chance or luck: 'The lot is cast into the lap, but its every decision is from the LORD' (Proverbs 16:33). As we shall see in a later chapter, Jonah's amazing story includes a key moment when sailors cast lots to see who was responsible for the storm that threatened to sink their ship and 'the lot fell on Jonah' (Jonah 1:7). God knew that this would happen, just as he knows the result of every lottery before the balls, tickets or tokens are ever drawn.

In becoming Christians, people exercise repentance and faith, which on the surface seem to be purely personal choices, yet when people repent they do so only because 'God has granted repentance that leads to life' (Acts 11:18), while faith is 'the gift of God, not as a result of works, so that no one may boast' (Ephesians 2:8–9).

The issue becomes clearer when we realize that God's will includes conditional and unconditional elements, leaving him free to treat people differently without compromising his own consistency. God told the prophet Jeremiah: 'If at any time I declare concerning a nation or a kingdom, that I will pluck up and break down and destroy it, and if that nation, concerning which I have spoken, turns from its evil, I will relent of the disaster that I intended to do it. And if at any time I declare concerning a nation or a kingdom that I will build and plant it, and if it does evil in my sight, not listening to my voice, then I will relent of the good that I had intended to do to it' (Jeremiah 18:7–10). Men can and do change, but God does not. Nothing that happens forces him into a U-turn or changes his eternal intentions.

God's perfection inevitably means that he treats people differently, yet always in ways perfectly suited to their position, while being entirely consistent with his divine nature and in tune with his sovereign and eternal purposes. To give one of many obvious examples, 'God opposes the proud, but gives grace to the humble' (James 4:6). God's eternal purposes are not shuffled around when he reacts to changes in people's response to his dealings with them. While God is not impervious to human pain or unmoved by human sorrow, none of the pain, sorrow, sin (or any other human conditions or circumstances) surprise him, force him to alter course or make him react in ways that he had not anticipated. The nineteenth-century American theologian Augustus H. Strong applied this to God's dealings with his people: 'God's immutability itself renders it certain that his love will adapt itself to every varying mood and condition of his children, so as to guide their steps, sympathize with their sorrows, answer their prayers.'

Open Theism belittles God and bloats man and in doing so seriously distorts what the Bible teaches. As someone has said, the theory ends up with 'a weakened deity who is finite in power and knowledge, makes mistakes for which he may even have to apologize, is often frustrated and disappointed and cannot assure us of a triumphant outcome to history.' But if God does not know the entire future, we are left with our spiritual fingers crossed, vaguely hoping that things will eventually turn out as God wishes. J. I. Packer is right: 'What [God] does in time, he planned from eternity. And all that he planned in eternity he carries out in time.'

When we read in the Word of God that God was sorry, or

that he relented or changed his mind, we must accept that it is expressing truth we could never begin to grasp were it not couched in the kind of language we commonly use of human emotions and actions. Applying this to the book of Amos, there was nothing phoney in the prophecy about locusts. Amos took it very seriously and cast himself upon God's mercy, crying out for him to intervene and to spare his people. With centuries of hindsight, we see the prophecy, the prayer and the pardon in chronological order, but God—for whom 'one day is as a thousand years, and a thousand years as one day' (2 Peter 3:8)— saw all three as a whole. God is outside of time, not hemmed in by it. Before he was even 'forming the locusts' he knew that Amos would cry out for mercy and that he would grant the prophet's prayer.

God's word to Isaiah clinches the matter: 'I am God, and there is none like me. *I make known the end from the beginning, from ancient times, what is still to come*' (Isaiah 46:9–10, NIV, emphasis added).

After he had gone through very testing times, the nineteenth-century British lay preacher and poet Josiah Conder wrote a hymn that included these rhetorical and unanswerable questions:

> The Lord is King! Who then shall dare
> Resist his will, distrust his care,
> Or murmur at his wise decrees,
> Or doubt his royal promises?

OBADIAH

The first and obvious thing to say about the book of Obadiah is that it is the shortest of the books written by the Minor Prophets. It is also, and by a big margin, the shortest book in the Old Testament. Its twenty-one verses can be read without hurrying in just three minutes, yet as we saw in the Introduction this does not mean that Obadiah has little to say to us. The opening verse declares, 'Thus says the Lord GOD'—and God has no small talk. The book of Obadiah is as powerful and relevant as the major books of Isaiah or Jeremiah, or any other part of the Old or New Testaments.

Not only is this particular prophecy inconspicuous, it may also be anonymous, as it is not certain that the writer was somebody called Obadiah. In the Old Testament, people's names often have theological significance. We can see this as far back as Genesis, where 'Adam' means 'man' or 'mankind'. As the word 'Obadiah' means 'the servant (or worshipper) of Jehovah', its use here may be a reference to the writer's ministry, not his name. That said, 'Obadiah' was a common Israelite name and there are twelve others in the Old Testament, the first being mentioned in 1 Kings 18 and the last in Nehemiah 12. The book we are now examining in this chapter may well have been written by a man called Obadiah, but if so that is all we know about him. We have no clue as to his background, his family, his location or his primary occupation.

It is just as difficult to be sure exactly when this particular book was written. The strongest clue we have is that it mentions the sacking of Jerusalem, but as the city was sacked four times this hardly provides us with much help. However, most of the experts who have tried to tie Obadiah's prophecy into his nation's history suggest that it points towards what happened when the Babylonians (the Chaldeans) ravaged Jerusalem in 586 BC, as recorded in 2 Kings 25. The arguments for and against other possible dates are fascinating, especially those that have to do with the language that was used in describing the events concerned. After centuries of investigation the jury is still out, but we will assume that Obadiah has 586 BC in mind.

The seer

In the Introduction we noted that prophets were 'seers' before they were 'sayers'. Obadiah fits this description, calling his book 'The vision of Obadiah' (v.1), indicating that he had been granted a supernatural revelation of the message God ordained him to announce. Obadiah was not freelance; he was an instrument chosen by God to bring a specific message about a specific situation at a specific time. Several of the Bible's human authors emphasized the supernatural nature of their calling, showing that God did not look around to find suitably articulate candidates. God told Jeremiah, 'Before I formed you in the womb I knew you, and before you were born I consecrated you; I appointed you a prophet to the nations' (Jeremiah 1:5). There is a parallel statement in the New Testament, where the apostle Paul claimed that God 'set me apart before I was born and … called me by his grace' and 'was pleased to reveal his Son to me, in order that I might preach him among the Gentiles' (Galatians 1:15–16).

Paul's testimony underlines the principle of grace in all of this. None of the prophets, Major or Minor, could claim any credit for exercising their ministry. We have no biblically-qualified prophets today (not even those who decorate themselves with the name) but the same principle applies to any true preacher of the Word of God. A man can no more claim credit for being a preacher than he can for being a Christian. It is by grace alone that any preacher is saved, called and equipped—and it is only by grace that any service rendered bears genuine fruit. C. H. Spurgeon used to tell candidates for the ministry, 'Prepare yourselves my young brethren to become weaker and weaker. Prepare yourselves for sinking lower and lower in self-esteem. Prepare yourselves for self-annihilation and pray God to expedite the process!' Obadiah would have qualified.

The feud

Although it contains a message of great hope for God's people, the main thrust of the book is a dire prophecy of God's judgement 'concerning Edom' (v.1), a land to the south-east of Israel. The reason for God's anger against the people of this particular country is rooted in many years of tangled history, which began to take shape with a fascinating event recorded in Genesis:

> These are the generations of Isaac, Abraham's son: Abraham fathered Isaac, and Isaac was forty years old when he took Rebekah, the daughter of Bethuel the Aramean of Paddan-aram, the sister of Laban the Aramean, to be his wife. And Isaac prayed to the LORD for his wife, because she was barren. And the LORD granted his prayer, and Rebekah his wife conceived. The children struggled together within her, and she said, 'If it is thus, why is this happening to me?' So she went to enquire of the LORD. And the LORD said to her, 'Two nations are in your womb, and two people from within you shall be divided; one shall be stronger than the other, the older shall serve the younger.' When her days to give birth were completed, behold, there were twins in her womb. The first came out red, all his body like a hairy cloak, so they called his name Esau. Afterwards his brother came out with his hand holding Esau's heel, so his name was called Jacob. Isaac was sixty years old when she bore them.
> (Genesis 25:19–26)

Esau, the first to be born, was later called 'Edom' (Genesis 36:1) and at one point God told Jacob, 'Your name shall no longer be called Jacob, but Israel' (Genesis 32:28). The story of the twins' birth makes it appear that they were at odds even before they were born, and from then on their history is a catalogue of conflict.

Coached by his mother, Jacob took advantage of his father's poor eyesight and cheated his brother out of the blessing due to the first-born son. Furious that he had been robbed of what was rightfully his, Esau vowed to kill his younger brother, but Rebekah warned Jacob of the danger and he escaped into exile for twenty years.

Peace was restored between them some time later, but after they had become the founders of separate nations the old enmity resurfaced. Centuries later Jacob's descendants were taken into slavery in Egypt for over 400 years, until the Exodus, when they were miraculously delivered by God and began their forty-year trek through the desert to the land promised to their forefather Abraham. When they reached the borders of Edom they asked for permission to shorten their journey by passing through the land (and even to pay for any water their people or animals used) but the king of Edom turned them away and threatened to kill them if they so much as set foot in his territory (see Numbers 20:14–21).

On another occasion Edom joined with the Moabites and Ammonites in attacking Judah (the two southern tribes of Benjamin and Judah that became separated from the ten northern tribes that retained the name of Israel), but were routed when God intervened (see 2 Chronicles 20:1–2). Another attack was more successful and the Edomites 'defeated Judah and carried away captives' (2 Chronicles 28:17).

The bitter enmity broke out again and again, sometimes at a personal level. When an Edomite by the name of Doeg persuaded Israel's first king, Saul, that a priest called Ahimelech had betrayed Saul by helping one of his enemies, Saul's soldiers balked at the king's command to kill Ahimelech and his fellow priests, but Doeg had no such qualms. He not only killed eighty-five priests, but wiped out the entire village in which they lived; 'both man and woman, child and infant, ox, donkey and sheep, he put to the sword' (1 Samuel 22:19).

The last straw

By Obadiah's time Edom's feud with Israel and Judah had lasted for some 800 years; now it spilled over in a series of events that finally sealed its fate. In 586 BC Nebuchadnezzar, the king of the Babylonians, mounted a massive attack against Judah, concentrating his fiercest fire on Jerusalem:

> [He] killed their young men with the sword ... and had no compassion on young man or virgin, old man or aged... And all the vessels of the house of God, great and small, and the treasures of the house of the LORD, and the treasures of the king and of his princes, all these he brought to Babylon. And they burned the house of God and broke down the wall of Jerusalem and burned all its palaces with fire and destroyed all its precious vessels. He took into exile in Babylon those who had escaped from the sword ...
>
> (2 Chronicles 36:17–20)

In the face of this onslaught, Judah desperately needed help, but God directed Obadiah to remind the Edomites, their nearest neighbours, that they had done exactly the opposite.

'... *you stood aloof on the day strangers carried off his wealth and foreigners entered his gates and cast lots for Jerusalem*' (v.11). With historical ties dating right back to Jacob and Esau, the Edomites could have thrown their weight behind their neighbours. Instead, they opted to sit on their hands and let the Babylonians do their worst.

'... *you were like one of them*' (v.11). By not helping Judah the Edomites were as guilty as those who were savaging Jerusalem. Years later, a psalmist records that while Jerusalem was under attack, the Edomites shouted, 'Lay it bare, lay it bare, down to its foundations!' (Psalm 137:7). No doubt many of them felt that Judah was getting its comeuppance for its own wrongdoing against them centuries earlier, but God was not about to accept that as an excuse for their standing by while Judah was being savaged.

'... *do not gloat over the day of your brother in the day of his misfortune; do not rejoice over the people of Judah in the day* of their ruin; do not boast in the day of distress' (v.12). While Judah was reeling the Edomites were rejoicing, cheering on the Babylonians as they tore the sacred city apart.

'... do not loot his wealth in the day of his calamity' (v.13). Even worse, the Edomites slipped into Jerusalem and joined in the wholesale looting that went on when the population was being swept away into captivity.

'Do not stand at the crossroads to cut off his fugitives; do not hand over his survivors in the day of distress' (v.14). Worst of all, when Judeans tried to escape, the Edomites cut them off and handed them over to the Babylonians, who hauled them away into slavery.

It is against this background that Obadiah prophesied. Although his prophecy was not directly addressed to either Edom or Judah it spoke to both. The message to each of them had as its foundation a massive truth that we can properly call Obadiah's 'major point' and this can be identified by combining words from his first and last sentences:

Thus says the Lord GOD ... the kingdom is the LORD's.

(vv. 1, 21)

These two phrases bracket the entire prophecy and form its overriding theme. They lay down the universal and unshakeable sovereignty of a just and holy God, a truth that finds its focus in two powerful prophecies—*disaster for those who oppose God and deliverance for those who trust him.*

Disaster

We begin by looking at the meaning and relevance of the first prophecy to those who were on the receiving end at the time. As we shall see shortly, punishment for Edom's sin was to be fearsome and fatal, but before spelling that out in detail God's word through Obadiah cuts right to the chase and pinpoints the root cause of their depravity—'The pride of your heart has deceived you' (v.3).

Of all the sins catalogued in Scripture, none is said to be

more obnoxious to God than pride: 'Everyone who is arrogant in heart is an abomination to the LORD' (Proverbs 16:5). Why is pride singled out in this way? The answer is obvious—because it dethrones God and replaces him with man. Pride is not only a sin against God's law, it is a sin against his sovereignty. We need to bear this in mind in today's rampantly self-centred 'me-first' society in which humility is often seen as weakness. Even committed Christians are far from being immune to the danger of getting sucked in to the spirit of the age and we can easily find pride worming its way into our thinking. We can be proud of our education, our ability, our achievements, our possessions, our homes, our children or our position in the church. We can be proud of our doctrinal position, our Bible knowledge, our Christian service, our giving or our prayer life—even when there is no cause for boasting. There is no part of life that is ring-fenced against pride. It is even possible to be proud of one's supposed humility! The Puritan leader Thomas Hooker confessed, 'Pride is a vice which cleaves so fast unto the hearts of men, that if we were to strip ourselves of all faults, one by one, we should undoubtedly find it the very last and hardest to put off.'

Turning directly to Edom, we are told of several areas in which its people's arrogance was expressed.

They were proud of their geography. They are described as 'you who live in the clefts of the rock, in your lofty dwelling' (v.3). The land of Edom (today part of Jordan) was also known as 'the land of Seir' (Genesis 32:3) and occupied a high plateau to the south and south-east of the Dead Sea. The land straddled the Arabah rift valley and in places was over 5,000 feet above sea level. This made the Edomites think that they were so secure from enemy attack that they arrogantly asked, 'Who will bring me down to the ground?' (v.3).

They were proud of their diplomacy. Obadiah mentioned, 'All your allies' (v.7), which tells us that Edom had established a network of allies among the surrounding nations. They knew how to make friends and influence people, or at least to come to some understanding with their neighbours that would create a buffer zone as a second line of defence against attack. The Edomites were proud of the way they could manipulate things to their own advantage.

They were proud of their philosophy. Obadiah refers to 'the wise men out of Edom' (v.8), a feature for which it was noted. Elsewhere in the Old Testament we are told that the most able of Job's advisers was 'Eliphaz the Temanite' (Job 2:11)—and Teman was a town in Edom. Eliphaz's speeches show a wide range of thinking, though at times they are fatally flawed by humanistic philosophy and we read that eventually, 'The LORD said to Eliphaz the Temanite: "My anger burns against you ... for you have not spoken of me what is right"' (Job 42:7). Edomites boasted of what they believed was their superior knowledge and wisdom, but as the Puritan preacher Thomas Adams put it, 'He who is proud of his knowledge has gout in the wrong end.'

The distinguished twentieth-century German-American theologian and philosopher Paul Tillich admitted, 'Every day, and in a thousand ways, I'm tempted to make myself the centre of the universe.' There are echoes of that in us all! Whenever we become proud of our education, our qualifications, our titles, our ability, our possessions, our positions in business, society or the church, our influence, our achievements (or anything else) we are putting ourselves in harm's way. In four of the clearest words in the Bible we are told, 'God opposes the proud' (James 4:6). The Greek verb here is *antitassetai*, a military term used of arranging an army in battle order against an enemy. When used of God the picture is vivid and terrifying, as he is 'the LORD of hosts' (Psalm 46:7). In opposing the proud God can deploy every living being in heaven and on earth, every law of physics and every atom in the cosmos in any way he chooses to frustrate and humiliate the proud. We dare not forget this sobering fact!

Retribution

Gareth Crossley is not exaggerating when he writes, 'Edom was full of pride. Like their forefather Esau, they had no interest in the promises and purposes of God. They were an independent, arrogant people, so independent that they thought they could do without God.' They were to pay a fearful price for this, and part of their punishment for double-crossing Israel would be that their own allies would desert them at a time of great need.

For 1,300 years Edom had flaunted itself in God's face and time and again persecuted his chosen people of Israel and Judah. Now, it was as if God said, 'Enough is enough.' Edom had every opportunity to turn from its wickedness, throw in its lot with God's people, accept his providential dealings with them and share in the blessings of the faithful, but it chose not to. It was now to suffer for its stubborn arrogance and find out to its horrendous cost that all sin is sin against God and that no sin goes unpunished.

The important lesson to learn here is that while God's patience is amazing, it is not unending. The apostle Paul's testimony that although he had been the 'foremost' of sinners he had been shown 'perfect patience' (1 Timothy 1:16) is not saying that God's patience will give even the worst of sinners endless opportunities to repent. It is testifying that God can save the worst of sinners. This is why we are urged to 'Seek the LORD *while he may be found*' and to 'call upon him *while he is near*' (Isaiah 55:6, emphasis added). The person who presumes on the patience of God is a fool. God's patience is lasting, but nowhere in the Bible are we told that it is everlasting. This does not mean that God loses his patience (in the way that we can so easily do) then flies off the handle and acts impulsively, impetuously or unjustly. Instead, it means that God's patience is balanced by his perfect justice and always exactly suited to its purpose. Isaiah made this clear when speaking to the people of Israel: '... the LORD waits to be gracious to you, and therefore he exalts himself to show mercy to you. For the LORD is a God of justice; blessed are all those who wait for him' (Isaiah 30:18). To assume that because God's patience is perfect it is permanent is to make a serious and potentially costly mistake. Paul warned people about playing fast and loose with God's patience: '... do you presume on the riches of his kindness and forbearance and patience, not knowing that God's kindness is meant to lead you to repentance?' (Romans 2:4).

In Edom's case God determined that the time had come to bring his perfect justice to bear on those who had refused to listen to his voice, and to do so in ways that exactly reflected their specific sins: 'As you have done, it shall be done to you; your deeds shall return on your own head' (v.15). This principle is underlined in the New Testament: 'Do not be deceived: God is not mocked, for whatever one sows, that will he also reap (Galatians 6:7). God's word to Obadiah gives details of some of the ways in which his fearful prophecy was fulfilled to the letter.

As we saw earlier, Edom prided itself on its geographical position, high up in a mountain range that rendered it virtually impregnable; but God said, 'Though you soar aloft like the eagle, though your nest is set among the stars, from there I will bring you down' (v.4).

The lower parts of Edom were on a major trade route bringing goods from India and Arabia to the Mediterranean coast and Egypt along the 'King's Highway' (Numbers 21:22). Edom boasted in the wealth this produced; but God said, 'If thieves came to you, if plunderers came by night—how you have been destroyed!—would they not steal only enough for themselves? If grape gatherers came to you, would they not leave gleanings?' (v.5).

The point God is making is that when thieves break into a house they do not usually take everything. They choose what is likely to be of most value to them and leave the rest behind. My wife and I had our house broken into three times. The last occasion was the worst and took place while we were in Guernsey at my dying step-mother's bedside. Despite making a dreadful mess, the thieves took only certain items and thankfully left many things of sentimental value behind. Obadiah uses the same kind of illustration with regard to thieves raiding a vineyard; they would not remove every single grape. By stark contrast, Edom was facing devastation so certain and complete that Obadiah was able to write about it in the past tense: 'How Esau has been pillaged, his treasures sought out!' (v.6). As we are told elsewhere, Edom was 'doomed to be destroyed' (Psalm 137:8).

There were parts of Edom, particularly in the north-east, where farming could be undertaken and herds of animals grazed. This helped to make Edom proud of its independence; but God said that 'the house of Esau' would become 'stubble' (v.18).

All these fearful forecasts were capped by one final prophecy: '… there shall be no survivor for the house of Esau, for the LORD has spoken' (v.18). This, too, was fulfilled to the letter. Five years after the sacking of Jerusalem the Babylonians crushed the Edomites on their way to Egypt. Years later the Persians conquered the country and slaughtered thousands of its citizens. In 120 BC the Maccabees, a Jewish rebel army, added to the slaughter. Another Jewish leader, John Hyrcanus, forced the Edomites into becoming nominal Jews and into accepting circumcision. Yet there was worse to come—and it followed a final outrage.

The last throes

Long after Obadiah wrote his prophecy Judea became combined with other territories to form a Roman province under the empire's first Emperor, Caesar Augustus, with the Roman Senate eventually appointing Herod the Great as its client king over the region. He took the title 'King of the Jews' and as such acquired a notorious place in biblical history. When Jesus was born in Bethlehem, 'wise men from the east came to Jerusalem, saying, "Where is he who has been born king of the Jews?"' (Matthew 2:1–2). Herod asked them to find the newborn child, then report back to him 'that I too may come and worship him' (Matthew 2:8), but when God warned them that they were being conned they ignored Herod and went back to their own country. Furious that he had been outwitted, Herod 'killed all the male children in Bethlehem and in all that region who were two years old and under, according to the time that he had ascertained from the wise men' (Matthew 2:16).

The reason for recording this in our study of Obadiah's prophecy is that *Herod was an Edomite!* Many centuries after Esau threatened to kill Jacob, his most notorious descendant tried to eliminate the real King of the Jews (who was born into Jacob's line) and was prepared to slaughter countless innocent children in order to be sure he had done so. Even this ruthless ploy failed and ironically Herod died of chronic renal failure before Jesus became a teenager.

Edom was then in its death throes and in the course of the campaign in which they captured Jerusalem in AD 70, the Romans wiped out the remaining Edomites. It had remained boastful in spite of its many setbacks, but Edom was finally eliminated and from that time on has ceased to exist as a nation. This appalling fate fulfilled a powerful prophecy by another of the Minor Prophets: 'If Edom says, "We are shattered but we will rebuild the ruins," the LORD of hosts says, "They may build, but I will tear down, and they will be called 'the wicked country,' and 'the people with whom the LORD is angry for ever"'' (Malachi 1:4). Edom may have thought that it was invincible, but God is 'the Judge of all the earth' (Genesis 18:25) and no power on earth can evade his sovereign justice. We dare not read Obadiah's prophecy without reflecting that the proud rejection of God's word always leads to eternal loss, as it did for Edom.

Deliverance

The second part of Obadiah's prophecy in which his 'major point' is shown is in God promising deliverance to his battered and bewildered people in Judah, who at the time Obadiah wrote were in exile in Babylon. The terrible warnings to Edom were given in the context of the assurance to God's people that 'the day of the LORD is near upon all the nations' (v.15) and the promise to Judah is part of the same turning of the tide.

The clearest expression of its deliverance is the statement 'But in Mount Zion there shall be those who escape, and it shall be holy, and the house of Jacob shall possess their own possessions' (v.17). To those who could understand what was being said at that time, this would come as amazing and wonderfully welcome news. As a result of the Babylonians' *blitzkrieg* Jerusalem was in ruins, the temple was reduced to ruins and the citizens had been forced into exile, losing their national and religious identity. Yet God had not reneged on his covenant with their forefathers, and would fulfil it to the letter, bringing terrible punishment to their (and his) enemies while restoring them to their beloved Mount Zion. For God's people 'their own possessions' were Jerusalem and the entire Promised Land. This would be a marvellous fulfilment of the promise made to Moses while God's people were still in captivity in Egypt: 'I will bring you into the land that I swore to give to Abraham, to Isaac, and to Jacob. I will give it to you for a possession. I am the LORD' (Exodus 6:8).

The way in which God fulfilled his promise is breathtaking. As we saw in an earlier chapter he moved Cyrus, the pagan king of Persia (who had conquered Babylon), to make a declaration allowing exiles from Judah to return to their own country. Zerubbabel led the first 50,000 expatriates back to Jerusalem, where he reinstituted national worship and helped to lay the foundations of the replacement temple. Another Old Testament writer's description of the scene tells us exactly what it meant to those who were there: 'And all the people shouted with a great shout when they praised the LORD, because the foundation of the house of the LORD was laid. But many of the priests and Levites and heads of fathers' houses, old men who had seen the first house, wept with a loud voice when they saw the foundation of this house being laid, though many shouted aloud for joy, so that the people could not distinguish the sounds of the joyful shout from the sound of the people's weeping, for the people shouted with a great shout, and the sound was heard far away' (Ezra 3:11–13). It took twenty-two years (until 515 BC) to complete the rebuilding and seventy years to rebuild the walls of Jerusalem.

There were still further elements in the fulfilling of God's promise to his people. Far from being subdued and humiliated by the arrogant Edomites, they were to be one of God's instruments in bringing about their destruction: 'The house of Jacob shall be a fire, and the house of Joseph a flame, and the house of Esau stubble' (v.18). 'Jacob' may represent Judah and 'Joseph' the other ten tribes. All God's people, those (Israel) taken into captivity in Assyria and those (Judah) taken into captivity in Babylon would combine in Edom's final downfall. The words 'fire' and 'flame' represent God's wrath, as they do in the Bible's description of hell as 'the lake of fire' (Revelation 20:15), virtually the last thing the Bible has to say about the fate of the ungodly. God's people, so often attacked and ill-treated by Edom, would be used by God to help in wiping their vicious enemy from the face of the earth.

The day of the Lord

As he moves towards the end of his prophecy Obadiah links what he has said to 'the day of the LORD' (v.15), an expression he and other prophets use to describe various events, culminating in a day when God moves decisively to fulfil his prophecies of disaster for his foes and triumph for his followers. As we saw in the chapter on Joel, the phrase is often used in the Old Testament with reference to events that would take place in the relatively near future. In the New Testament it is used four times, referring always to what Peter calls 'the great and magnificent day' (Acts 2:20) when at the end of time the terror of the ungodly and the triumph of the godly will be complete.

Although Jesus made it clear that as far as the timing was concerned, 'no one knows' (Matthew 24:36) countless people have claimed to have 'inside information'. In 1533 Michael Stifel, a German associate of Martin Luther, persuaded some of his followers to sell their property immediately as the world would end very soon. Followers of an American preacher William Miller predicted that it would do so on 22 October 1844. Jehovah's Witnesses have so far backed several losers, including 1874, 1914, 1915 and 1975. The modern American evangelist and author Hal Lindsey wrote a best-seller entitled *The Late Great Planet Earth*, which claimed it would happen within one generation of 1948. In 1988 ex-NASA engineer Edgar Whisenant published a book listing eighty-eight reasons why the world would end in 1988 and claimed, 'Only if the Bible is in error am I wrong.' The book sold 4.5 million copies, but later titles revising the date to 1989, then 1993, then 1994 failed to make the charts. Many cults forecast that the world would coincide with the turn of the millennium in December 1999–January 2000. More recently, the American radio broadcaster Harold Camping, who had previously predicted that the world would end in 1994, confidently went on air to predict that this would happen on 11 May 2011 and his radio station spent $100 million advertising the fact. He said that he would not do any media interviews should it not happen (and of course would not have been available to do any if it did!). On 22 May he said he was 'flabbergasted' that he was still living on the earth and later revised his prediction to 21 October in the same year.

The simple truth is that nobody on earth is qualified to give us details of the world's terminal timetable, and all claims to do so are based on human speculation, not on divine revelation. This is what C. H. Spurgeon had in mind when he said, 'There are two great certainties about things that shall come to pass— one is that God knows, and the other is that we do not know.' What we *can* be certain of is the fulfilment of God's promise that the final 'day of the LORD' will assuredly come, bringing unspeakable horror to those who reject him and unspeakable joy to those who trust him. On his ninetieth birthday George Bernard Shaw said, 'Our conduct is influenced not so much by our experience as by our expectations.' There is a measure of truth in this, and the certainty of the Second Coming of Messiah should profoundly affect those who trust him for their salvation. The Puritan preacher John Trapp went so far as to say, 'This is pinned as a badge to the sleeve of every true believer—that he looks and longs for Christ's coming to judgement.'

Obadiah then added a third dimension to 'the day of the LORD'. He sees God at work not only in the relatively near future and finally at the end of time but also in the lives of God's people at all times, as we can see from the following examples:

In its immediate context 'Mount Zion' meant the holy city of Jerusalem and the surrounding land, but in the New Testament we are told that all Christian believers 'have come to Mount Zion and to the city of the living God' (Hebrews 12:22). Even while still living on earth Christians have already entered a spiritual city. There, they have 'escaped from the corruption that is in the world' (2 Peter 1:4), having previously been in the clutches of the devil, where they had been 'captured by him to do his will' (2 Timothy 2:26). What is more, Christians may know that they now belong to 'the heavenly Jerusalem' and that their names are already 'enrolled in heaven' (Hebrews 12:22–23), where they will never again face the trials and traumas they battled against while on earth.

Obadiah says of the earthly Mount Zion to which the exiles returned that 'it shall be holy' (v.17). The phrase could be translated 'there shall be holiness', which would point to God's people committing themselves to a life of holiness, enabled by God's promised presence. In the same way, Paul told his fellow Christians, 'God did not call us to be impure, but to live a holy life' (1 Thessalonians 4:7, NIV) and millions can testify that they are experiencing a growing measure of God's gracious enabling to do so. Paul reminded Christians at Corinth whose lives had once been steeped in sin, 'But you were washed, you were sanctified, you were justified in the name of the Lord Jesus Christ and by the Spirit of our God' (1 Corinthians 6:11).

Although God is at work in the lives of all believers, their moral and spiritual transformation is not complete while they remain on earth. No Christian can validate a claim to have gained complete victory over sin (or complete victory over any sin). No Christian is perfect; C. H. Spurgeon said he had met only one 'perfect' man and he was a perfect nuisance! Yet as Paul testified, we are gradually being transformed 'from one degree of glory to another' (2 Corinthians 3:18)—and for every believer there is the glorious prospect of entering the heavenly Jerusalem. In J. I. Packer's words, 'There will be no sin in heaven, for those who are in heaven will not have it in them to sin any more.' Isaiah makes the perfect link between the earthly and heavenly fulfilment of the prophecy: 'And the ransomed of the LORD shall return and come to Zion with singing; everlasting joy shall be upon their heads; they shall obtain gladness and joy, and sorrow and sighing shall flee away' (Isaiah 51:11).

Obadiah prophesied that in returning to Jerusalem 'the house of Jacob shall possess their own possessions' (v.17). For them, this would mean the land promised to their forefathers centuries earlier. Christians, too, are in line for an inheritance. They are 'heirs of God and fellow heirs with Christ' (Romans 8:17). What is more, they already have 'the immeasurable riches of his grace' (Ephesians 2:7) as well as God's 'precious and very great promises' (2 Peter 1:4), assuring them that they are on their way to the full possession of 'an inheritance that is undefiled, imperishable, and unfading' kept in heaven for those 'who by God's power are being guarded through faith for a salvation ready to be revealed at the last time' (1 Peter 1:4–5).

Obadiah ends his prophecy by saying, 'Saviours shall go up to Mount Zion to rule Mount Esau, and the kingdom shall be the LORD's' (v.21). The immediate meaning would seem to be that when the exiles returned from captivity they would 'save' the nation by restoring its religious structure and go on from there to reign over what had previously been enemy-occupied territory. The contemporary fulfilment of the prophecy is seen in God working in the lives of his people in such a way that although far from perfect they bear clear testimony that they belong to his kingdom. Yet there is much more to come and Paul assures his fellow believers that even the worst of life's trials are 'preparing for us an eternal weight of glory beyond all comparison' (2 Corinthians 4:17).

The New Geneva Study Bible makes a fine point that Christians should bear in mind: 'When the church suffers at the hands of God's enemies, she needs to return to the prophecy of Obadiah and renew her faith in the just God revealed there. He cares for his persecuted people, and behind their circumstances he is always at work for them.'

Dudley Tyng was born in Pennsylvania in 1825 and in 1854 followed his father as the minister of a fashionable church in Philadelphia. His direct attacks on the evils of slavery upset the church leaders and he was forced out. By 1858 he had founded another church in the area and his passionate, Christ-centred preaching attracted thousands to hear him. But tragedy was soon to strike. While visiting his family he wandered into a barn, where his clothing got caught in machinery and he suffered terrible injuries. As he lay dying he asked his father to be sure to tell all his fellow ministers, 'Stand up for Jesus'. A few days later his close friend and fellow minister George Duffield wrote a poem beginning with Tyng's words, which was later to become a well-known hymn. A modern version of its last verse echoes the certainty of the final part of Obadiah's prophecy:

Stand up, stand up for Jesus,
The strife will not be long:
This day the noise of battle,
The next the victor's song.
To everyone who conquers
A crown of life shall be;
We with the King of glory
Shall reign eternally.

JONAH

The book of Jonah is different from the other Minor Prophets in that it is the only one of the twelve in which the prophet concerned comes across as an anti-hero, with attitudes and actions that stand as warnings and not examples.

Among the Bible's 'clean pages' Jonah usually shows at least some evidence of having been read from time to time, almost certainly because it is the most user-friendly. There are no complicated symbols or visions to interpret (as there are, for instance, in the book of Zephaniah), nor are there any long prophecies, oracles or sermons to work through. In the English Standard Version (which I am using almost exclusively in these studies) there are only eight words of prophecy. Instead of extended tracts of teaching, Jonah is a gripping, high-speed story. We could imagine it being reviewed as 'a page-turner' or 'unputdownable' or as having 'as many twists and turns as a mystery novel'. This is precisely why many critics dismiss it as being no more than a colourful yarn put together by somebody with a vivid imagination. Others take a slightly different position and say it is a parable—a fictional story told to convey a moral truth of some kind—but, as we shall see, we can take it that the book of Jonah records events that actually happened.

The runaway

All we know about Jonah's background is that he was 'the son of Amittai' (1:1) and that he lived in Gath-hepher (see 2 Kings 14:25), a village about three miles north-east of Nazareth. We are given no exact date as to when his remarkable story unfolds, but as 2 Kings 14 places him in the reign of Jeroboam II it was almost certainly in the latter part of the eighth century BC that God suddenly gave him a spine-chilling assignment: 'Now the word of the LORD came to Jonah the son of Amittai, saying, "Arise, go to Nineveh, that great city, and call out against it, for their evil has come up before me"' (1:1–2). This was a breathtaking commission. Nineveh, which was then the capital of Assyria and located in what we now know as northern Iraq, was rated the greatest city of the ancient Near East, surrounded by massive walls 100 feet high and wide enough to take three chariots abreast. It was also 500 miles north-east of where Jonah lived, so even getting there would have meant a long and dangerous journey. More to the point, it also had a well-earned reputation for paganism, idolatry, immorality and violence and its vicious leaders thought nothing of cutting off the fingers, lips and noses of those who opposed them.

One of the most impressive things about the Old Testament prophets is the way in which they obeyed God's commands— though a few tried to negotiate their way out of the particular commissions they were given. When Moses was called to liberate God's people from their captivity in Egypt by directly confronting Pharaoh, the nation's despotic ruler, his first reaction was to ask, 'Who am I that I should go ...?' (Exodus 3:11). He then tried to wriggle out of the assignment by protesting, 'I am not eloquent ... I am slow of speech and of tongue' (Exodus 4:10). Finally, he pleaded, 'Oh, my Lord, please send someone else' (Exodus 4:13)—*but eventually he went.* When Jeremiah was called by God to the prophetic ministry he cried, 'Ah, Lord GOD! Behold, I do not know how to speak, for I am only a youth' (Jeremiah 1:6)—*but eventually he went.*

Jonah's response was very different; when the going got tough, Jonah got going—but in the wrong direction. He turned God down out of hand and instead of beginning the 500-mile trek to the north-east he travelled sixty miles south-west and 'went down to Joppa' (1:3). The journey to the Mediterranean seaport of Joppa (now the modern Jaffa) would have taken him several days, giving him ample opportunity to think through what he was doing and to change his mind, yet he did no such thing. Even worse, Joppa was to be just the first step. Jonah's real intention was 'to flee to Tarshish from the presence of the LORD' (1:3). Tarshish is thought to have been Tartessus, a city west of the Straits of Gibraltar and on the Atlantic coast of southern Spain. People living in the Middle East knew of nothing beyond Tarshish; as far as they were concerned it was the end of the world. It was some 3,000 miles from Nineveh and it is not difficult to imagine Jonah scouring the docks in Joppa looking for a ship that would take him as far away from that city as possible.

Whatever the exact details, Jonah's actions were not only sinful but foolish, as his aim was to run away 'from the presence of the LORD'. Going as a one-man missionary to Nineveh may have been difficult, but running away from God was 'mission impossible'. It matches what Adam and Eve tried to do in the Garden of Eden, when after they had fallen into sin they 'hid themselves from the presence of the LORD God among the trees of the garden' (Genesis 3:8). This was an exercise in utter futility, not only because God had put all the trees there in the first place, but also because as he is omniscient he always knew exactly where they were. A good friend of mine used to be a captain on the staff of American Airlines, with long experience of piloting planes on intercontinental flights. Interviewing him in the course of a church service I asked him for his favourite Bible verse. He replied, 'Where shall I go from your Spirit? Or where shall I flee from your presence? If I ascend to heaven, you are there! If I make my bed in Sheol, you are there' (Psalm 139:7–8).

We can assume that Jonah would have known the psalm from which my friend quoted. The interesting question is to ask what the writer meant by 'Sheol'. This is the English transliteration of a Hebrew word that sometimes meant a deep place on earth, such as a cave, but, as we know from 1 Kings 19:9, the prophet Elijah tried in vain to hide from God in a cave. It sometimes meant death, but death does not remove a person from God's knowledge or presence; nobody can run away from God by dying. Yet the word 'Sheol' sometimes meant hell, the eternal destiny of the damned, and the Bible makes it clear that *God is there too*. The best-known symbol of hell is fire, which indicates God's unending anger against sin and the sinner. We will examine this more closely when we reach Zephaniah, but for the moment will settle on this comment by the nineteenth-century American preacher W. S. Plumer: 'Both in heaven and in hell is God's essential presence. In heaven they have his gracious presence and in hell they feel his wrathful presence.' All of this shows how foolish Jonah was to try to escape from God, who is all-knowing and ever-present. The Hebrew word for 'Jonah' is also the common noun 'dove' and another minor prophet writes, 'Ephraim is like a dove, silly and without sense' (Hosea 7:11). In trying to run away from God, Jonah lived up to this description. As O. Palmer Robertson says, 'Trying to get away from God is like trying to get away from air.'

The downward spiral

We are told that Jonah 'went *down* to Joppa'. This is literally correct as he not only went south-west but down from Gath-hepher, which was high in the foothills near Nazareth, to Joppa, which was obviously at sea level. After he had paid the fare and the ship sailed for Tarshish he was soon to go even further down. God sent 'a mighty tempest on the sea, so that the ship threatened to break up' (1:4). The crew members were terrified 'and each cried out to his god' (1:5). In order to lighten the ship (or perhaps to appease one of their pagan gods) they threw some of the cargo overboard, but while they were desperately trying to escape disaster 'Jonah had gone down into the inner part of the ship and had laid down and was fast asleep' (1:5).

Returning from the United States some years ago I recall flying across the area known as the Bermuda Triangle when the plane was suddenly hit by such a violent storm that when trying to make my way back to my seat from the toilet I was ordered to throw myself on the floor. In thousands of flights, it was the greatest turbulence I had ever known. Even if I had been seated and strapped in when the storm hit I am sure I would not have been fast asleep! Had I been on Jonah's ship I would have been green around the gills and doing everything I could to save my own skin. Then why was he fast asleep, especially with the ship being tossed around like a cork and the chaotic noise of shouting crew members hurriedly moving cargo?

There may be a clue elsewhere in the Bible. When Jesus was on the brink of being arrested in the Garden of Gethsemane, he returned from a time of private prayer to find his closest disciples 'asleep, exhausted from sorrow' (Luke 22:45, NIV). They may well have been physically tired, but it was the mental exhaustion of grief that swept them into sleep. Jonah was very likely physically tired after his three-day journey from Gath-hepher and emotionally worn out after searching for the right ship, but he was almost certainly stressed out with sorrow, shame and guilt at what he was doing in disobeying God. Fighting against the devil can be tiring at times, but fighting against God is utterly exhausting, which is why an unbeliever can often be happier than a backsliding Christian. An unbeliever can often sin without so much as a twinge of conscience and a hard-wired atheist can do so without any thought that they might be morally answerable for their behaviour. On the other hand, backsliding places a strain on the conscience, the emotions, the mind, the central nervous system and eventually on the whole human fabric. Backsliding is a 'dis-ease'. As C. H. Spurgeon put it, 'It may be hard going forward, but it is harder going back.'

Asleep on the lowest deck of the ship, Jonah had still not finished going down. Sharing his crew's panic, the captain woke Jonah up and told him to pray that God would deliver them. Meantime, the crew superstitiously felt that someone on board must have been responsible for the storm, so cast lots to find out who this was—and 'the lot fell on Jonah' (1:7). When they asked him what they should do Jonah replied that they should throw him into the sea, as he was to blame for the trouble they were all in. His earlier testimony to the crew that he worshipped 'the LORD, the God of heaven, who made the sea and the dry land' (1:9) must have rung hollow when he told them that he was running away from him. Now, mention of such a God threw the crew into an even greater panic. At first, they tried hard to row the ship to shore, but when this failed they did their best to pray to Jonah's God, and when that seemed futile they heaved the prophet overboard. Jonah then went even further down than the bottom deck of the ship; he went down into the sea.

One reason why Jonah's rebellion was so sinful is that God had been so gracious to him in the past. The only other Old Testament reference to Jonah tells us this:

> In the fifteenth year of Amaziah the son of Joash, king of Judah, Jeroboam the son of Joash, king of Israel, began to reign in Samaria, and he reigned for forty-one years. And he did what was evil in the sight of the LORD. He did not depart from all the sons of Jeroboam the son of Nebat, which he made Israel to sin. He restored the border of Israel from Lebo-hamath as far as the Sea of the Arabah, according to the word of the LORD, the God of Israel, which he spoke by his servant Jonah the son of Amittai, the prophet, who was from Gath-hepher.   (2 Kings 14:23–25)

In spite of Jeroboam's wickedness, his reign included a period when God prospered Israel, enabling her to recapture lost territory, exactly as Jonah had prophesied. This would have raised the prophet's profile, not only in the eyes of the people in general, but also in those of a godless king. Even the Assyrians, who had literally lost ground as Israel pushed them back, may well have heard of Jonah's part in the event. Be that as it may, Jonah had seen God's great power at work in a remarkable way at a national level, yet still he turned his back on him.

As we pick up Jonah's story we should learn the lesson that God's mercy is never at the expense of his justice. In the well-known New Testament parable Jesus told at Luke 15:11–32 it was one thing for the prodigal son to come to his senses, but another thing to return to his father. The irony in the case of Jonah is that although he had paid the fare he never got to Tarshish—and never got a refund! There is always a price to be paid for backsliding. It is rightly said that there is no such thing as cheap grace, but neither is there such a thing as cheap disgrace. Donald Grey Barnhouse commented, 'When you run away from the Lord you never get where you are going and you always pay your own fare.' Every step of disobedience is a costly step downhill.

For Jonah, the cost now included being thrown into the sea without any means of survival. Then came the event that turned the entire story around: 'And the LORD appointed a great fish to swallow up Jonah. And Jonah was in the belly of the fish three days and three nights' (1:17). This must have seemed beyond belief to Jonah, and it hardly needs a vivid imagination to see what a miracle it was. When we are told that God 'appointed' a great fish, does this mean that years earlier it was a tiddler which gradually developed into a fully-grown monster, and was then steered by God to ensure that it was in the right place, on the right day, at the right time, and with its mouth open at exactly the right angle to swallow the drowning prophet? We are not told. Perhaps God brought this particular sea monster into being for this one purpose. As the twentieth-century American theologian and apologist Bernard Ramm rightly says, 'If this means a special creature for a special purpose we need not search our books on sea creatures to find out the most likely possibility.'

For countless people the idea that Jonah could have been 'swallowed by a whale' (the usual way it is put) then regurgitated three days later is sufficient for them to discard the whole book. In fact, the Bible nowhere says that Jonah was swallowed by a whale but by 'a great fish', without specifying the species. Our modern rules of biological taxonomy (the arrangement of species) lists the whale as a mammal, not a fish, but as these rules were not in place in Jonah's day we need not rule out a whale. In the Septuagint, the creature concerned is described as *ketos*, which means 'a large sea monster'. This could either have been a whale or some other kind of huge sea creature. Sceptics anxious to airbrush miracles out of Jonah's story have even gone so far as to suggest (without a shred of evidence) that Jonah swam to shore and spent three nights in an inn called 'The Fish'!

The weed, the worm and the wind

Critics also identify an even bigger target in Chapter 4. With Jonah angry and exhausted (we will later see why) a huge plant suddenly sprang up and gave him shade from the burning sun, but at dawn the next day a worm attacked the plant so that it withered and died. Then when the sun rose a scorching east wind beat down on him so strongly that he wanted to die. For the sceptic who says that miracles never happen, the sudden appearance of the plant alone is sufficient to mean that the entire book of Jonah can be rejected.

The eighteenth-century Scottish thinker David Hume was so sceptical about miracles that he felt the only real one was that people could believe in any of them. Modern sceptics go further and say that as so-called miracles contradict known scientific law they can immediately be ruled out as being nothing more than fairy tales. Yet this approach is not only unscientific, but more than a little arrogant. To reject miracles because they clash with one's worldview is hardly a sensible way to go about things. As the nineteenth-century British author Charles Caleb Colson put it, 'He who believes only what he can comprehend must have a very long head or a very short creed.'

In 1984 the Bishop of Durham hit the headlines when he questioned the miraculous element in the Bible by saying, 'To believe in a Christian way, you don't necessarily have to have a belief that Jesus was born from literally a virgin mother, nor a precise belief that the risen Jesus had a literally physical body.' In the uproar that followed, Professor R. J. Berry, President of the prestigious Linnean Society, was joined by twelve other scientists in writing a letter to *The Times*, in the course of which they said, 'It is not logically valid to use science as an argument against miracles. To believe that miracles cannot happen is as much an article of faith as to believe that they can happen ... *miracles are unprecedented events ... science, based as it is on the observation of precedents, can have nothing to say on the subject*' (emphasis added). In *Quarks, Chaos and Christianity*, Sir John Polkinghorne, the distinguished theoretical physicist and one-time President of Queen's College, Cambridge, says much the same thing: 'The question of miracles is not primarily scientific but theological ... *Science cannot exclude the possibility that, on particular occasions, God does particular, unprecedented things'* (emphasis added).

Neither of these statements is meant to undervalue or denigrate science in any way. Instead, each one underlines the simple fact that science is an ongoing process of discovering truth in the *natural* world but has no authority or integrity in the *supernatural* world. The Bible records many miraculous events and when these appear to clash with scientific claims, we have 'the living and abiding word of God' (1 Peter 1:23) on one side and current human opinion on the other. If they cannot be reconciled, the Christian should know which to trust.

There is something sad about Christians running to the laboratory to check whether the Bible can be trusted. Let me illustrate by expanding the argument to look at a much larger issue than weeds, worms and wind—the existence of the universe in general and planet Earth in particular. If every scientist in the world came to the conclusion that the entire cosmos came into existence by an act of creation by a transcendent Being of infinite power, imagination and power, *this would prove nothing scientifically*, as creation by God is by definition miraculous and so impossible to express in scientific terms.

We can take the creation issue further. The Bible says, 'By faith we understand that the universe was created by the word of God, so that what is seen was not made out of things that are visible' (Hebrews 11:3). The only way we can come to a right understanding of creation is by faith. There were no eyewitnesses and no scientific instruments to record exactly when or how it happened. The Christian relies not on research but on revelation and believes creation took place because the Bible says it did. This is where the Christian goes for his epistemology (the nature and scope of his knowledge). The best that science can do—and often does brilliantly—is to provide secondary information that supports biblical truth.

One further point needs to be added. To say that the Bible is trustworthy because it says it is might be dismissed by sceptics as a circular argument. There is a sense in which it is—but if the Bible is the Word of God *where else could God get superior authentication of what he has said*? At this point John Calvin provides the perfect reason why the Christian believes what he does: 'Enlightened by [the Holy Spirit] we no longer believe, either on our own judgement or that of others, that the Scriptures are from God; but in a way superior to human judgement, feel perfectly assured—as much as if we beheld the divine image visibly impressed on it—that it came to us, by the instrumentality of men, from the very mouth of God.' The Bible's integrity is rooted in the identity and integrity of its divine Author.

Amazing grace

Jesus confirmed the authenticity of the book of Jonah some 500 years after it was written. When Pharisees asked him to show them a sign (that is, a miracle), he replied, 'An evil and adulterous generation seeks for a sign, but no sign will be given to it except the sign of the prophet Jonah. For just as Jonah was three days and three nights in the belly of the great fish, so will the Son of Man be three days and three nights in the heart of the earth' (Matthew 12:39–40). Jesus' death, burial and resurrection were to be historical events so momentous that the entire Christian faith came to stand on them, and it is inconceivable that Jesus would decorate this awesomely important teaching with a fairy tale. Accepting Jonah as historical is the only worthy position for those who accept the deity of Christ, for whom the book was part of the inspired Word of God. A book may be historically accurate and not be inspired, but it could not be inspired and historically inaccurate.

This historically accurate book is not merely, or even primarily, about Jonah; it is more importantly about God's gradually unfolding plan of salvation. Yet our 'major point' in this particular study is part of one sentence that sweeps Jonah's story towards its remarkable conclusion:

Then the word of the LORD came to Jonah the second
time.   (3:1)

If Jonah's disobedience is one of the lowest points in Scripture,
this is one of the highest. It is a glorious display of God's love,
mercy, grace and patience. Think of what had led up to it. When
Jonah was specifically commanded by God to go and preach in
Nineveh he flatly refused and headed in exactly the opposite
direction. Safely aboard the ship he must have thought that he
had got away with it—then God stepped in. As the sailors cast
lots to see who was responsible for the storm, the odds were
against them pointing to Jonah, but as we have already seen,
'The lot is cast into the lap, but its every decision is from the
LORD' (Proverbs 16:33). In a world under God's sovereign rule
there is no such thing as uncontrolled 'chance' and there was no
way Jonah could avoid being chosen, even though the lots were
cast by people who were pagans. When he was thrown into the
sea, that might have seemed like the last we would ever hear
of him, but God had other plans and 'appointed a great fish' to
be in the right place at exactly the right time to save him from
drowning. Finding himself inside this colossal creature may not
have struck Jonah as much of a deliverance, but yet again God
stepped in, kept him undigested and supplied with oxygen for
three days, then so controlled the monster that it 'vomited Jonah
out upon the dry land' (2:10).

It was while he was inside the great fish that Jonah made a
dramatic spiritual U-turn. Instead of running away from God, he
turned 180 degrees and began running towards him. The whole
of Chapter 2 records what happened next. To begin with, 'He
prayed to the LORD his God' (2:1), something he had probably
avoided doing for some time. Then he recognized God's sovereign
overruling of the sailors' actions in throwing him overboard:
'For *you* cast me into the deep, into the heart of the seas' (2:3).
He acknowledged that even the raging seas were in God's hands:
'... all *your* waves and *your* billows passed over me' (2:3). He had
reached the point when it seemed there was no escape from
death—'The waters closed in over me to take my life... I went
down to the land whose bars closed upon me for ever' (2:5-6)—

but God had further work for Jonah to do and delivered him just as he was 'fainting away' (2:7). Reading Jonah's testimony at this point it is difficult not to think of the other Old Testament writer who cried, 'Out of the depths I cry to you, O Lord! O Lord, hear my voice! Let your ears be attentive to the voice of my pleas for mercy!' (Psalm 130:1–2); Jonah may even have had that part of Scripture in mind. Looking gratefully back, Jonah told God, '... my prayer came to you, into your holy temple' (2:7). Rejoicing in this, he pledged, 'I with the voice of thanksgiving will sacrifice to you; what I have vowed I will pay' (2:9) before ending with the triumphant declaration, 'Salvation belongs to the Lord!' (2:9).

The modern Scottish preacher Gordon Keddie has a fine comment on this: 'The sins of the backsliding Christian have a peculiar bitterness to them, because they are sins against the light. Similarly, being brought back to the Lord, to receive again his forgiveness and renew faith in him, is a sweet restoration indeed—all the more because he has been faithful to his promises when we have broken ours. This emphatically demonstrates the sovereign love of the Lord towards his people and provides the most powerful motive for striving to be faithful to such a gracious and long-suffering God in the future.'

If Jonah's story ended there it would give us enough reason to stand in awe of God's stupendous sovereignty. He superintended Jonah's trek to Joppa, his choice of a ship, the gathering storm, the sailors' decisions, the casting of lots, the positioning of the great fish, the preservation of Jonah when he was swallowed and the fish's instinct to spew him out rather than chew him up. As we saw in an earlier chapter, God has no 'no-go' areas. He is the first and final cause of everything that happens in the entire universe and uses whatever secondary causes he chooses to bring about his purposes. We should also be in awe of his amazing grace that overcame Jonah's wilful, deliberate and determined disobedience and spared him from an appalling fate. The twentieth-century American evangelist Rolfe Barnard was right to say, 'Mercy is God's favour that holds back from us what we deserve. Grace is God's favour that gives us what we do not deserve.' Jonah received an abundance of both, though they were not handed to him on a plate. God chastened him, frustrated his plans, wore him out with sorrow, hurled him into the sea and into the belly of a great fish—*but he never abandoned him*. Jonah was taken a long way out of his comfort zone, but never allowed out of God's grip.

Christians should take heart from this. We may feel spiritually dry, or sense that we are no longer enjoying the close walk with God we once knew. We may feel that we are fruitless and virtually useless. We may have allowed our devotional life to wither and our Bible reading to become an almost reluctant duty rather than the delight we once knew it to be. We may even think that we are in a backslidden state with little signs of recovery. If so, we should read Jonah's story, especially his testimony in Chapter 2, and notice again that God never abandoned him. We should see that as soon as Jonah cried out to God from a full heart God responded in mercy and grace. It is impossible for anybody to take a step back towards God without God taking a step towards them—and God takes bigger steps.

There is a picture of this in the story of the Prodigal Son. The story is often preached evangelistically, but the prodigal was already a son when he turned his back on home and went his own headstrong way. He gradually slid further and further downhill and was reduced to eating pigswill before he came to his senses and decided to return home. We then read these wonderful words: 'But while he was still a long way off, his father saw him and felt compassion, and ran and embraced him and kissed him' (Luke 15:20) before laying on a lavish feast to celebrate his return. God's unfailing promise to those who have strayed is, 'Return to me ... and I will return to you' (Zechariah 1:3).

Reflecting on God's sovereignty and grace in Jonah's life should move us to adoration and worship—but there is more. God not only restored Jonah to the joy of his salvation, he also restored him to the privilege of service: 'Then the word of the LORD came to Jonah the second time, saying, "Arise, go to Nineveh, that great city, and call out against it the message that I tell you"' (3:1–2). This is not only a major point in Jonah's story, it is one that provides a memorable example of God's gracious dealings with his erring children. The patriarch Abraham, often referred to as 'the father of the faithful', was living in a pagan environment in Mesopotamia when he responded to God's call, 'Go from your country and from your kindred and your father's house to the land that I will show you' (Genesis 12:1). Led by his father Terah, Abraham responded, but only got as far as Haran, several hundred miles short of the Promised Land of Canaan, when for one reason or another he settled down for a considerable time. Yet after Terah's death and when Abraham was then seventy-five years of age, *God called him a second time.*

David was chosen by God to be Israel's king and became an outstanding and highly respected ruler, statesman, soldier and administrator. But when he was at the peak of his power he treacherously arranged the death of Uriah, a distinguished army captain, to cover up his own adultery with Bathsheba, Uriah's wife. *Yet God never abandoned him,* but led him to genuine repentance, as David powerfully expressed in the words of Psalm 51. In God's wisdom and justice, David was to know God's chastening for his appalling sin, yet his testimony was: 'Blessed is the one whose transgression is forgiven, whose sin is covered' (Psalm 32:1) and in his dying words David acknowledged God as having been to him 'like the sun shining forth on a cloudless morning, like rain that makes grass to sprout from the earth' (2 Samuel 23:4).

When Jesus was about to be arrested, the apostle Peter promised him, 'Lord, I am ready to go with you both to prison and to death' (Luke 22:33), but a few hours later, when challenged that he was one of Jesus' followers, Peter claimed, 'I do not know him' (Luke 22:57). *Yet Jesus did not abandon him* and after his resurrection re-commissioned him so that he became an early leader in the Christian church.

As Gordon Keddie says, 'The revealed will of God for our lives is not negotiable' and in Jonah's case the re-commissioning could not have been more definite or dramatic: 'Arise, go to Nineveh, that great city, and call out against it the message that I tell you' (3:2). This time, Jonah's response was immediate and committed—'So Jonah arose and went to Nineveh, according to the word of the LORD' (3:3). When he got there his message was uncompromising and urgent: 'Yet forty days, and Nineveh shall be overthrown!' (3:4). We can assume that he preached more than these eight words (just five in the original Hebrew) but his message was exactly the one God had committed to him. He made no attempt to spin God's words into something the Ninevites might find more user-friendly—and today's Christian preachers should follow his example and keep to the timeless truths of Scripture.

The effect of Jonah's preaching was astonishing: 'And the people of Nineveh believed God' (3:5). They had apparently heard of Jonah's amazing experience of being delivered from three days inside the sea monster, as Jesus told the people of his day, 'Jonah became a sign to the people of Nineveh' (Luke 11:30). Suddenly realizing that their gross wickedness had exposed them to God's wrath and that they needed to change their ways before judgement fell on them, the Ninevites put on sackcloth 'from the greatest of them to the least of them' (3:5). This does not necessarily mean every person in the city, but that people from every section of society did so. Considering the city had a reputation for being saturated with paganism, this mass confession of sin was a greater miracle than the sudden appearance of a sea monster to swallow Jonah.

When the king heard of this, 'he arose from his throne, removed his robe, covered himself with sackcloth, and sat in ashes' (3:6). What is more, he issued a proclamation saying, 'Let everyone turn from his evil way and from the violence that is in his hands. Who knows? God may turn and relent and turn from his fierce anger, so that we may not perish' (3:8–9). The outcome was astonishing: 'When God saw what they did, how they turned from their evil way, God relented of the disaster that he said he would do to them, and he did not do it' (3:10). As we saw in our study in the book of Amos, this does not mean that God changed his mind, as God remains 'the same' (Psalm 102:27) and 'does not change like shifting shadows' (James 1:17, NIV). The straightforward meaning is that God had warned of appalling disaster *if the Ninevites continued in their sinful ways,* but now he graciously stayed his hand. It would be going too far to claim that the Ninevites became true worshippers of the God of Israel (his definitive Old Testament name 'the LORD' is not even mentioned by them in Chapter 3) but there was undoubtedly a radical change in the city's moral tone, and the disaster Jonah said would happen in forty days' time did not take place. This ties in exactly with something that God told another prophet and that we saw in our study of Amos: 'If at any time I declare concerning a nation or a kingdom, that I will pluck up and break down and destroy it, and if that nation, concerning which I have spoken, turns from its evil, I will relent of the disaster that I intended to do to it' (Jeremiah 18:7–8). Far from this indicating a vacillating God whose word cannot be relied on at any given time, it reveals an utterly unwavering God whose warnings of punishment and promises of blessing can be trusted at all times.

The miracles in the book of Jonah did not end when the fish threw him up onto dry land, nor did evidence of God's grace. God rescued Jonah from the depths and lifted him up to the heights. Instead of putting an end to his prophetic ministry and relegating him to some minor role, he reinstated him as his mouthpiece to the world's greatest metropolis. Instead of the prophet being laughed at or attacked, God stopped countless Ninevites in their tracks and transformed their city.

Pride and prejudice

If the book of Jonah was a piece of fiction we might expect it to end by telling us that after the remarkable outcome of his preaching in Nineveh the prophet went on to exercise a dynamic and effective ministry for the rest of his life. In fact, the final chapter paints a very different picture and it begins by telling us exactly why Jonah tried to run away from God. As Nineveh was an evil, pagan city and no prophet in history had ever been sent to such a place, Jonah would have realized that he had been given a tough assignment. He may have been able to slip into the city unnoticed, but as soon as he announced why he had come the Ninevites would have thought nothing of killing him on the spot. Yet we saw that years earlier he had not been afraid to exercise his prophetic ministry when an ungodly king was on the throne, so we know that he was not a coward.

This makes what we next read come as a jolting surprise. When Nineveh was spared 'it displeased Jonah exceedingly, and he was angry' (4:1). He turned to God and admitted, 'That is why I made haste to flee to Tarshish; for I knew that you are a gracious God and merciful, slow to anger and abounding in steadfast love, and relenting from disaster' (4:2). Jonah's reason for refusing God's commission for him to go to Nineveh now becomes clear—and deplorable. All other prophets had been commissioned to preach to God's covenant people, either Judah or Israel, but Jonah was sent to a Gentile nation that had no covenant relationship with God. Proud of being an Israelite, he had an inbuilt aversion to pagan Gentiles, and a particular loathing of the Ninevites, who were sworn enemies of Israel. Knowing the power and grace of God, being sent to preach to Nineveh could mean only one thing—God intended to spare Nineveh the judgement that hung over its head. This so stuck in Jonah's craw that he set out on a journey far more hazardous (and five times as long) in an attempt to wash his hands of the whole business.

Jonah had lost sight of God's universal sovereignty and tried to squeeze it into his own narrow-minded nationalism. He was sure that God was the Sovereign Lord of Israel, but not of the whole world. This blind spot prevented him from seeing the significance of God's promise to Abraham that 'in you all the families of the earth shall be blessed' (Genesis 12:3). Jonah's view of God was partial, parochial and prejudiced and as a result he griped at God's goodness to the Gentiles. He failed to see that the universal and active sovereignty of God is the most liberating doctrine in Scripture, something that enables us to trust him even when we cannot trace him, and to acknowledge that all his ways are perfect. It enables us to rejoice at everything God does, even when we are unable to squeeze his ways into our personal agendas, restricted scenarios, sectarian prejudices, denominational boxes or cultural confines. In Jonah's case his deep-rooted prejudice meant he could not cope with the thought of God extending his mercy beyond his covenant people and he wanted no part in bringing this about. He resented the idea so deeply that he would sooner die than see it happen: 'Therefore now, O LORD, please take my life from me' (4:3).

When God responded by asking the pouting prophet, 'Do you do well to be angry?' (4:4) Jonah turned away and found a spot outside of the city where he could sit and sulk, perhaps even hoping that judgement might fall on Nineveh after all. He settled for being a spectator, yet again God dealt graciously with him: '... the LORD God appointed a plant and made it come up over Jonah, that it might be a shade over his head, to save him from his discomfort' (4:6). Jonah was 'exceedingly glad' for this (the only time in the entire story when he seemed to have been glad about anything!) but God had a further lesson to teach him: '... when dawn came up the next day, God appointed a worm that attacked the plant, so that it withered. When the sun rose, God appointed a scorching east wind' (4:7–8). As the Lord of hosts, God is in sovereign control of all nature's elements and it is worth noting that in dealing with Jonah he used those on land (the plant), in the sea (the great fish) and now in the air (the scorching wind). When the combination of sun and wind caused Jonah to become faint he again asked God to end his life, saying, 'It is better for me to die than to live' (4:8).

Asked by God whether he had the right to be angry about the plant withering, Jonah had no hesitation in replying, 'Yes, I do well to be angry, angry enough to die' (4:9). It is the last word we hear from Jonah and it shows him to be petty, self-centred and irrational, making the withering of a plant sufficient justification for wanting his life to end. The contrast between Jonah and Job could not be greater. When Job was told that in one day he had lost over 1,100 animals, seven sons and three daughters, he fell on the ground and worshipped, calling out, 'The LORD gave, and the LORD has taken away; blessed be the name of the LORD' (Job 1:21). But when God removed the sheltering plant from Jonah the prophet threw a hissy fit. In reply, God showed him how ridiculous it was for him to be concerned about a single plant yet be angry when God was having compassion on a city's people. In the book of Jonah, God has the last word—as he always does—and in this case it was to reveal his love for all, even the unlovely.

We know nothing of what happened to Jonah after this. To borrow a famous phrase from the twentieth-century American-born British poet T. S. Eliot, our last sight of Jonah sees him going out 'not with a bang but a whimper'. This helps us to see that the book bearing his name is not primarily about him, but about God. It tells us of his unqualified sovereignty in appointing and controlling the casting of the sailors' lots, the storm at sea, the great fish, the plant, the worm and the scorching east wind. It tells us of his grace in warning the Ninevites of the danger they were in. It tells us of his power in changing their thinking and way of life. In recording Jonah being thrown into the sea, swallowed by a great fish for three days, then regurgitated onto dry land, it gives us a dramatic picture of the death, burial and resurrection of the Lord Jesus Christ, one 'greater than Jonah' (Matthew 12:41). It also foreshadows what has rightly been called the church's great commission: 'Go into all the world and proclaim the gospel to the whole creation' (Mark 16:15). We can never bring the whole world to Christ, but we are under uncompromising orders to take Christ to the whole world. In the challenging words of the twentieth-century British preacher James S. Stewart, 'No church is anything more than a pathetic, pietistic backwater unless it is first and fundamentally and all the time a world missionary church.'

This comes across loud and clear as we read Jonah's remarkably honest testimony. The modern American preacher Steve Kreloff writes, 'The chief purpose of the book of Jonah is to communicate the truth that since God has a heart of compassion for the heathen, his people should reflect that same attitude by reaching out with the message of salvation to all who are alienated from God—especially those who are blatantly evil in their behaviour.' The twentieth-century American theologian and apologist Francis Schaeffer went an important step further: 'All people are our neighbours, and we are to love them as ourselves. We are to do this on the basis of creation, even if they are not redeemed, for all people have value because they are made in the image of God. Therefore, they are to be loved, even at great cost.'

The book of Jonah also confirms that God's work of salvation can never be derailed by our preferences or prejudices and that the statement he made to Moses thousands of years ago remains true: 'I will be gracious to whom I will be gracious, and will show mercy on whom I will show mercy' (Exodus 33:19). The nineteenth-century British hymn-writer Frederick William Faber put it well:

For the love of God is broader
Than the measures of man's mind
And the heart of the Eternal
Is most wonderfully kind.

MICAH

In some of the books written by the Minor Prophets we are told virtually nothing about the author. In others it is difficult to be sure when the book was written. In a few it is not easy to determine to whom they were originally addressed. In the case of Micah all three issues are solved in the first verse: 'The word of the LORD that came to Micah of Moresheth in the days of Jotham, Ahaz, and Hezekiah, kings of Judah, which he saw concerning Samaria and Jerusalem' (1:1). Samaria was the capital city of the northern kingdom of Israel and Jerusalem was the capital city of Judah. The phrase 'The word of the LORD came' occurs over 100 times in the Old Testament to indicate that in exercising their ministry the prophets' words were not 'produced by the will of man', but that they 'spoke from God as they were carried along by the Holy Spirit' (2 Peter 1:21).

By comparing the opening words of Micah with Isaiah 1:1 and Hosea 1:1 we can see that Micah was a contemporary of these two prophets, but that his ministry began a little later, after King Uzziah had died. Jotham became king in about 750 BC, followed by his son Ahaz, who, like his father, reigned for sixteen years, and his grandson Hezekiah, who reigned for twenty-nine years. This would mean that Micah flourished for about twenty years— from some time before 732 BC, when Ahaz died, and until some time after 715 BC, when Hezekiah became king.

The courageous countryman

The book of Micah is not a neat and tidy arrangement of directly related themes following a clear pattern. Perhaps Micah was one of the books Martin Luther had in mind when he wrote of the prophets, 'They have a queer way of talking, like people who, instead of proceeding in an orderly manner, ramble off from one thing to the next, so that you cannot make head or tail of them or see what they are getting at'! Despite this wry observation, scholars have not found it difficult to find an overall theme in some of the prophets' writings and to see logical links between sections. In any case, whereas some of the books have an obvious flow to them, there is no need to insist on the teaching of various subjects being tightly or obviously linked before accepting an entire book as genuine. In Micah's case it is true that he moves suddenly from one subject (and even literary form) to another, but this could easily be because his various prophecies were not all given or announced at the same time. It would be perfectly reasonable to conclude that what we read in this book reflects a number of different encounters Micah had with God, during which 'the word of the LORD' came to him and formed the basis of his written ministry.

Micah came from Moresheth (called Moresheth-gath in 1:14), a village in a fertile agricultural area about twenty-five miles south-west of Jerusalem. Whereas his contemporary prophet Isaiah lived in the city and mingled with the metropolitan movers and shakers of his day, Micah was a countryman, living a simpler life out in the fields and hills.

Micah shared with Isaiah not only the blessing of being a believer but the privilege of being a prophet and when he spoke as a prophet he was clothed with nothing less than divine authority. In those days there were false prophets who operated with self-serving motives, preaching pleasantries to people who gave them practical support, but preaching exactly the opposite to those who gave them nothing (see 3:5). Micah had no hesitation in saying, 'But as for me, I am filled with power, with the Spirit of the LORD, and with justice and might' (3:8). He may have been a simple countryman, but his message came from the very throne of God. He drew no attention to himself but emphasized that his ministry stemmed from the fact that he was filled with the Holy Spirit. Isaiah said much the same thing when he declared, 'And now the Lord GOD has sent me, and his Spirit' (Isaiah 48:16). It was this that gave the ministry of these men its dynamic impact, and it is the only thing that can give life-changing power to preaching today. As C. H. Spurgeon wrote, 'It were better to speak six words in the power of the Holy Ghost than to preach seventy years of sermons without the Spirit.'

Micah specifically said that he was filled with justice and we will see later that the cruel injustice rampant in Judah at the time was a particular burden to him. He also said he was filled with might. The original word for 'might' means 'courage', a quality the prophet certainly needed as he faced up to his commission 'to declare to Jacob his transgression and to Israel his sin' (3:8). This comes across as he directly challenged the nation's leaders: 'Hear this, you heads of the house of Jacob and rulers of the house of Israel, who detest justice and make crooked all that is straight, who build Zion with blood and Jerusalem with iniquity' (3:9–10). The nation's leadership was rotten to the core, but this unknown countryman tackled the government, the judiciary, the civic establishment and the religious leaders head-on, exposing their corruption, injustice and blatant godlessness. This kind of courage has New Testament parallels. John the Baptist, filled with the Holy Spirit, condemned the lecherous king Herod Antipas to his face and refused to back down, at the cost of his life (see Matthew 14:1–12). When the apostles were dragged before the Sanhedrin, with their lives on the line because they were preaching that Jesus had risen from the dead, they declared, 'We must obey God rather than men' (Acts 5:29). Facing the cruel Roman governor Felix, the apostle Paul refused to soften his message but declared, 'I worship the God of our fathers, believing everything laid down by the Law and written in the Prophets' (Acts 24:14).

We find the same thing as we read the lives of the great Reformers down the centuries, men like John Wycliffe, Jan Hus,

Nicholas Ridley and Hugh Latimer, who were prepared to be put to death rather than renounce their faith. Just before he was burned at the stake in 1415 the Czech Reformer Jan Hus prayed, 'O most kind Christ, draw us weaklings to yourself, for unless thou draw us we cannot follow thee. Give us a courageous spirit that it may be ready and, as the flesh is weak, may thy grace go before, for without thee we can do nothing. Give us a valiant spirit, a fearless heart, the right faith, a firm hope and perfect love, that we may offer our lives for thy sake with the greatest patience and joy.' The world has no answer to men like that. The worst it can do is to kill them, but as Augustine wrote, 'The martyrs were bound, imprisoned, scourged, racked, burnt, rent, butchered—and they multiplied.' In the deaths of martyrs godly seed is sown, which grows and bears fruit from then on, inspiring countless Christians to live and, if necessary, die for Christ in the assurance their death is 'an entrance into the eternal kingdom of our Lord and Saviour Jesus Christ' (2 Peter 1:11).

The Reformers were in the same mould as Micah, whose commitment made an indelible mark on his ministry. He was not a mechanical mouthpiece, nor was he merely a professional preacher. His ministry was deeply affected by the sin and injustice he saw: 'For this I will lament and wail; I'will go stripped and naked; I will make lamentation like the jackals, and mourning like the ostriches' (1:8). He saw his fellow countrymen rushing down a slippery slope and if they would not weep for themselves then he would do so for them. One Old Testament writer cried to God, 'My eyes shed streams of tears, because people do not keep your law' (Psalm 119:136). Jeremiah lamented, 'Oh that my head were waters, and my eyes a fountain of tears, that I might weep day and night for the slain of the daughter of my people!' (Jeremiah 9:1). Troubled that many of his fellow Jews were clinging to lifeless, formal religion and rejecting the salvation offered in Christ, the apostle Paul confessed, 'I have great sorrow and unceasing anguish in my heart' (Romans 9:2).

Is there the same kind of heartbroken concern among God's people today? How do we react when we read of the latest financial scandal, rising crime figures, an escalating divorce rate, or some other disaster in society? What do we think when a Christian leader has a moral lapse or fellow believers begin to show signs of losing their love for the things of God or make shipwreck of their faith? Do we climb up to the judge's bench or fall down at the mourner's bench? A Spirit-filled Christian will be broken-hearted for two reasons: the dishonour that sin brings to God and the disaster it brings to the sinner. A Spirit-filled Christian will yearn and pray for mercy, not judgement. Matthew Henry wrote, 'The sins of sinners are the sorrows of the saints. We must mourn for the things we cannot mend.' Do we do that, or do we draw up our robes of self-righteousness and join the Pharisee who looked down his nose at a tax collector, preened himself and prayed, 'God, I thank you that I am not like other men' (Luke 18:11)?

Micah preached and prophesied from a broken heart and God blessed him in a remarkable way. A century later, when Jeremiah's life was threatened by the authorities, some of the elders involved in dealing with him brought up Micah's case. They reminded those concerned that Micah had confronted Hezekiah, king of Judah, and warned him of impending disaster because of the nation's sin. Yet as the elders put it, 'Did he not fear the LORD and entreat the favour of the LORD, and did not the LORD relent of the disaster that he had pronounced against them?' (Jeremiah 26:19). Micah's powerful preaching brought the king to his knees, brought the country to its feet and averted the destruction of Jerusalem. This should be a constant encouragement to all faithful preachers today.

Micah's writings touch on all the great themes preached by the Old Testament prophets—the sovereignty of God, his judgement against sin, his amazing love, the need to get right with God and the coming of Messiah. As far as the last of these themes is concerned, Micah has one of the most specific prophecies in the entire Old Testament: 'But you, Bethlehem Ephrathah, who are too little to be among the clans of Judah, from you shall come forth for me one who is to be ruler in Israel, whose coming forth is from of old, from ancient days' (5:2). This points to Messiah 'coming forth' in two ways. The first refers to the humanity of Jesus, as he was born in Bethlehem, and the second to his divinity, as the phrase 'ancient days' is similar to one used by Moses, who declared that God is 'from everlasting to everlasting' (Psalm 90:2). If this is a double-barrelled prophecy, Jesus fulfilled it perfectly. He had a birth, but no beginning, and even while living here on earth 'the whole fulness of deity' (Colossians 2:9) dwelt in him. Micah goes on to say that this coming ruler would 'shepherd his flock in the strength of the LORD' (5:4) and it is impossible to miss the fulfilment of this prophecy in the life and ministry of Jesus, 'the good shepherd' (John 10:11).

God's agenda

In the course of his message Micah also gives the people specific directions as to how they should live. This will be our 'major point' and it is powerfully relevant three thousand years after the words were written.

Early in 1963, less than a year after I had entered full-time Christian service, I returned home to our tiny flat in Weston-super-Mare, Somerset, to be told by my wife that I needed to return a telephone call to a man who had left a message asking if I would speak 'at a meeting in Albert Hall'. As this was the name of a small Brethren assembly in the town, I looked forward to a convenient local engagement. However, the man I called back was the organizer of the London and Home Counties Festival of Male Voice Praise and the invitation was to speak at that year's annual united event in the Royal Albert Hall, London. I was totally nonplussed as to why I should be asked, but on 27 April 1963 I found myself standing at the famous brass-railed podium I had previously seen only on television. With hundreds of men in the choir behind me (backed by Britain's second-largest organ, with 9,999 pipes) and 5,000 people in the main body of the auditorium, it represented a unique opportunity, as I had never previously spoken to an audience of more than 400 people. Anxious to base my message on a biblical text I chose these words from Micah:

He has told you, O man, what is good; and what does

the LORD require of you but to do justice, and to love
kindness, and to walk humbly with your God?   (6:8)

These festivals were intended to be evangelistic events, as
many people who were nominal Christians or who might not
attend a preaching service came to soak up the atmosphere in
that magnificent auditorium and to hear the superb singing.
With this in mind I took Micah's words and bent them into the
shape I wanted, specifically aiming them at people who were not
Christians. Had Micah been in the audience he may have been
more than a little surprised at what I got out of them! On the
following morning I was preaching to fewer than fifty people in
a real village hall 140 miles away—and was much more at home.

Reflecting on my London experience later I learned that a text
without a context can often be a pretext. I would now add that no
text ever gains anything by being taken out of context, while
no text ever loses anything by being placed into its proper
context. Not only preachers and teachers, but all Christians
should beware of lifting a few words out of the Bible, looking
at them in isolation, and claiming to have grasped their full
meaning without paying attention to the context in which they
appear or to the sense in which the words were written. Fringe
groups and cults illustrate the danger that statements from the
Bible can be made to mean almost anything unless they are
studied sensibly, which includes studying them in their original
setting.

The Bible is not God's version of the Yellow Pages, inviting us
to pick out one statement or line and ignore everything that lies
around it. Advertisers in the Yellow Pages want us to do exactly
that and of course they hope that we will ignore all other entries
and respond only to theirs. God wants us to read the Bible very
differently. He wants us to see the big picture, which means
taking careful notice of a statement's setting and checking to
whom and in what circumstances it was written. We should
also relentlessly pursue the habit of comparing Scripture with
Scripture, as the Bible is its own best interpreter. This principle is

known as the analogy of faith and rests on the assurance that as it is the Word of God the Bible is consistent and coherent.

In his fine book *Beyond the Battle for the Bible*, J. I. Packer points us in the right direction: 'Let us, then, take our Bibles afresh and resolve by God's grace henceforth to make full use of them. Let us read them with reverence and humility, seeking the illumination of the Holy Spirit. Let us meditate on them till our sight is clear and our souls are fed. Let us live in obedience to God's will as we find it revealed to us in Scripture; and the Bible will prove itself both a lamp to our feet and a light upon our path.' Hit-and-run Bible reading can often be hit-and-miss and R. C. Sproul is right to say, 'The Word of God is deeper than a flannelgraph. It demands the closest possible scrutiny. It calls for the most excellent scholarship. It makes the finest point of technical analysis worth the effort. The yield of such effort is truth.'

That being the case, what is the context in which our 'major point' was written? The first part of Micah's message was aimed at the northern kingdom of Israel, to which God's message was, 'Therefore I will make Samaria a heap in the open country, a place for planting vineyards, and I will pour down her stones into the valley and uncover her foundations' (1:6). This prophecy was fulfilled when the northern kingdom was conquered by Assyria in 722–721 BC. The rest of his message was aimed at the southern kingdom of Judah, which was under growing threat from the aggressive Assyrian Empire. During Micah's time, Judah was ruled by a confusing mixture of kings. Jotham 'did what was right in the eyes of the LORD... But the people still followed corrupt practices' (2 Chronicles 27:2). Ahaz (Micah was a prophet throughout his sixteen-year reign) 'did not do what was right in the eyes of the LORD... He even burned his son as an offering, according to the despicable practices of the nations whom the LORD drove out before the people of Israel' (2 Kings 16:2–3). On the other hand, his successor Hezekiah 'did what was right in the eyes of the LORD' (2 Chronicles 29:2) and was a powerful reforming influence in the land. It may well be that most of Micah's ministry was exercised during the reign of

Ahaz, who followed the godly Jotham but was more interested in playing international politics than in hearing what God had to say, and as a result left his country financially bankrupt and morally ruined.

The other important context is that the nation was putting its trust in religious ritual. The first magnificent temple in Jerusalem, completed by King Solomon in 959 BC, was the official centre of the nation's worship, with its priests and other officials supervising endless rites and rituals, ceremonies and sacrifices. To all outward appearances the religious life of the country was flourishing, but the endless activity, in the temple and elsewhere, hid widespread sin. Micah summed it up in one sentence: 'Its heads give judgement for a bribe; its priests teach for a price; its prophets practise divination for money' (3:11). Yet these leaders dared to say, 'Is not the LORD in the midst of us? No disaster shall come upon us' (3:11). Under their leadership the people had become so taken up with the trappings of their religion that they imagined these were sufficient to guarantee God's presence and blessing and his protection from the disaster that had earlier wiped out the northern kingdom of Israel.

It should come as no surprise to read that Micah warned them, '... the LORD has an indictment against his people' (6:2). Through the prophet, God made his case by asking a perfectly reasonable question. He merely asked, 'O my people, what have I done to you? How have I wearied you? Answer me!' (6:3). He followed this up by reminding them how he had delivered them from slavery in Egypt, provided effective leaders for them, met all their needs during their forty-year haul through the desert, frustrated those who opposed them, and eventually led them safely into the Promised Land (see 6:4–5).

The Holy Spirit revealed to Micah that Judah's response was to try to do a deal with God and to offer him whatever sacrifice it would take to appease him. What would it take to get right with God?—'burnt offerings ... calves a year old ... thousands of rams ... ten thousands of rivers of oil ... the fruit of my body for the sin of my soul?' (6:6–7). Yet these were all external things and Micah swept aside Judah's reliance on them. In what has been called 'one of the most comprehensive and all-embracing statements in the Old Testament' Micah answered Judah's articulated question with our 'major point': 'He has told you, O man, what is good; and what does the LORD require of you but to do justice, and to love kindness, and to walk humbly with your God?' (6:8). When King David repented of his gross sin in committing adultery with Bathsheba and having her husband murdered he realized that religious ceremonies would not put things right and confessed to God, 'For you will not delight in sacrifice, or I would give it; you will not be pleased with a burnt offering' (Psalm 51:16).

Twice in the course of his approach to Judah God called them 'my people' (6:3, 5). They were not ignorant pagans who knew nothing about God and his ways. They were God's covenant people and had been born into a God-fearing culture, but they had fallen far away from the standards he had set them in his holy law. In our 'major point' Micah identified specific ways in which they were to show themselves as being set apart from the surrounding nations. He began by saying, 'He has told you...' as of course God had, not only in the Ten Commandments but in centuries of Old Testament history and teaching. The application today is obvious. How does God want his people to live in a society that is rotten to the core, dominated by materialism and greed, and in which the Christian faith is sidelined by rampant secularism or smothered by dead formalism? Micah's 'major point' to the people of his day gives three clear-cut answers to the question.

Do justice

The Old Testament concept of justice is directly related to the nature of God as revealed, for example, by Moses, who said of God, 'His work is perfect, for all his ways are justice. A God of faithfulness and without iniquity, just and upright is he' (Deuteronomy 32:4). The people of whom Micah wrote ignored this and had casually set their own convenient moral standards, which allowed confiscating other people's property, perverting the course of justice and financial chicanery. To make matters worse, they seemed to believe that this kind of behaviour was perfectly acceptable as long as they took part in a busy round of religious ceremonies.

Micah's words were a shattering reality check to these people, calling them to revolutionize their thinking and to act towards God and man in ways that reflected the divine righteousness revealed in his Word. As we should expect, Jesus did exactly the same thing and in the Sermon on the Mount taught that Christians should live such transformed lives that they would be seen to be 'sons of your Father who is in heaven' (Matthew 5:45). Paul had a similar picture in mind when he urged believers, 'Therefore be imitators of God, as beloved children' (Ephesians 5:1).

Nobody can reach perfection in this life, but God's people are called to 'press on towards the goal' (Philippians 3:14). A well-known incident will help us to get the picture. In 1924 two British mountaineers, George Mallory and Andrew Irvine, led the third British expedition to Mount Everest. On 8 June the two men set out to reach the summit via the Northeast Ridge. They never returned and in 1999 Mallory's body was finally recovered at 27,760 feet. Nobody knows whether the two men reached the summit, but Noel Odell, the expedition's oxygen officer, reported seeing them at 12.50 p.m. 'going strongly for the top'. Every Christian should strive to live in such a way as to warrant the same comment.

Tied in so closely to God's character, doing justly affects every area of life, and it will be useful to apply it a little more closely. Justice is primarily seen as a legal concept and, applied in this sense, it points to the Christian's responsibility to submit to the law of the land. Paul made this clear when he wrote, 'Let every person be subject to the governing authorities. For there is no authority except from God, and those that exist have been instituted by God' (Romans 13:1). Whether we think a particular law is good or bad is irrelevant. We are to obey the law because the authorities that exist have been established by God, who has also put the concept of law and order into our hearts to rein in our endemic lawlessness and to promote our well-being. The nineteenth-century American statesman Daniel Webster may have been over the top in saying, 'Justice is the greatest interest of man on earth', but we do have a stubborn sense that we like justice to be done and to be seen to be done. The fact that we do points to our creation by a God who 'loves righteousness and justice' (Psalm 33:5).

In disobeying the state we are disobeying God, though it is important to remember that human governments have *delegated* authority, not absolute authority, and that this delegated authority has limits. If the state demands what God forbids, the Christian's duty is to obey the greater authority. Jesus put the issue in perfect balance when he said, 'Render to Caesar the things that are Caesar's, and to God the things that are God's' (Mark 12:17). As we saw earlier in this chapter, when the authorities forbade the apostles to preach their reply was, 'We must obey God rather than men' (Acts 5:29).

In the United Kingdom today Christians very rarely face this specific challenge and unless the law demands what God forbids the law is to be obeyed. The constant challenge to believers is to be meticulous in obeying the law of the land when it does *not* clash with the law of God. The modern British preacher Stuart Olyott fine-tunes the fact that failing to obey the law of the land is more serious than it seems: 'The last time you exceeded the speed limit, or filled in your tax return late or inaccurately, or dropped litter in a public place, or kept your child from school without good reason, or crossed the road in a forbidden place, or travelled on public transport without paying the correct fare—you resisted *God!*'

As we have already seen, the biblical concept of doing justly goes beyond the legal to the ethical and the Christian is called to go much further than merely obeying the law of the land. To give some obvious examples, adultery is not illegal in our country, but it is unethical and the same is true of paying an employee less than he or she deserves. In many instances lying is not illegal, but it is unethical. Gossip, greed and covetousness are not illegal, but they are unethical, as is turning a blind eye to injustice. These are just a few examples to show that the ethical issue is a far greater test of the Christian's integrity than the legal one. The Christian is called not only to do what is legally required, but also to do what is morally right. Bible-based integrity goes far beyond keeping civic laws. It means modelling our behaviour on the higher standards revealed in the Bible and shown supremely in the life of Christ. A. W. Tozer was right to say, 'No Christian is where he ought to be spiritually until the beauty of the Lord Jesus Christ is being reproduced in daily Christian life.'

Love mercy

Secondly, it is important to notice in our 'major point' that God requires his people not merely to show mercy but to *love* it, to be gratefully glad at every opportunity of showing mercy and kindness. There is no legal element involved in mercy, which gives more than justice demands and can come only from a changed heart. The nineteenth-century American scholar Albert Barnes went so far as to say, 'Nowhere do we imitate God more than in showing mercy.' As far as giving is concerned, there is no civic law that says we should give to the poor, the homeless, the helpless, the refugee, the sick or even a needy neighbour. There is no man-made law that condemns us if we fail to respond to urgent appeals for help to people living in areas of the world ravaged by war, floods, famine or drought. Yet it is impossible to escape the Bible's teaching that showing mercy to those in need is an inflexible command to God's people and motivated firstly not by any given situation *but by the revealed nature of God*. Christians should love being merciful because God has been unimaginably merciful to them and because he 'delights in steadfast love' (7:18).

Of all the Old Testament statements that declare this truth, none is clearer than when God revealed himself to Moses as 'The LORD, the LORD, a God merciful and gracious, slow to anger, and abounding in steadfast love and faithfulness, keeping steadfast love for thousands, forgiving iniquity and transgression and sin' (Exodus 34:6–7). It is worth noting that in this first biblical revelation of the attributes of God his merciful nature is included.

Ill-informed sceptics often write off the Old Testament as showing God to be a cruel despot, but in fact it is full of references to his mercy. It says that he is 'merciful and gracious' (Psalm 86:15) and that his mercy is not expressed only to a favoured few but is 'over all that he has made' (Psalm 145:9). Thomas Brooks wrote, 'God's mercies are above all his works, and above all ours too.' Were it not for God's extravagant and indescribable mercy nobody in all of history would ever have so much as a single sin forgiven.

God's mercy can be seen throughout the entire Bible and is supremely demonstrated in the death of the Lord Jesus Christ in the place of sinners and on their behalf. Without this, all men are utterly ruined by sin and subject to God's inevitable wrath both in this world and in the world to come. Paul expressed this in one of the most glorious passages in the entire Bible. Writing to Christians in Ephesus he reminded them, 'And you were dead in the trespasses and sins in which you once walked... But God, being rich in mercy, because of the great love with which he loved us, even when we were dead in our trespasses, made us alive together with Christ—by grace you have been saved' (Ephesians 2:1–2, 4). Paul's own experience underlined the reach of God's saving mercy. He testified to having been 'a blasphemer, persecutor and insolent opponent' of God, then immediately added, 'But I received mercy' (1 Timothy 1:13). The tense of the verb he used here is such that we could literally translate it, 'I was mercied', emphasizing that he was utterly powerless to lift a finger towards his own salvation, but owed it entirely to the mercy of a loving God.

The Bible also places a heavy emphasis on God's mercy towards those with particular needs. David called God, 'Father of the fatherless and protector of widows' and said that God 'provided for the needy' (Psalm 68:5, 10) while Solomon added, 'He has pity on the weak and the needy' (Psalm 72:13). Elsewhere we read, 'He has distributed freely; he has given to the poor' (Psalm 112:9). The modern American theologian Miles Van Pelt goes so far as to say, 'There is not a section of the Old Testament that does not account, in some way, for God's care of the poor, needy, hungry or oppressed.'

There is a straight line between this and the Christian's obligation to show mercy to those in need. In the Sermon on the Mount Jesus said, '... let your light shine before others, that they may see your good works and give glory to your Father who is in heaven' (Matthew 5:16). This is not a substitute or replacement for evangelism. This kind of thinking gave rise to the modern social gospel movement, which makes the fatal mistake of marginalizing man's spiritual need. Yet this is not an either/or issue. As Matthew Henry rightly says, 'Those about us must not only *hear* our good words, but *see* our good works.' Good works are to be done not to earn praise for ourselves but so that others may see something of the powerful effect God has on our lives and be drawn to him. They contribute nothing to our salvation, but we should never neglect the fact that in being regenerated we have been 'created in Christ Jesus *for good works*, which God prepared beforehand, that we should walk in them' (Ephesians 2:10, emphasis added).

Jesus condemned scribes and Pharisees of his day as hypocrites, 'For you tithe mint and dill and cumin, and have neglected the weightier matters of the law: justice, mercy and faithfulness. These you ought to have done, without neglecting the others' (Matthew 23:23). By contrast, we find members of the early church 'selling their possessions and belongings and distributing the proceeds to all, as any had need' (Acts 2:45). Those called to preaching and other leadership roles in the church even appointed members to oversee its charitable work so that they could devote themselves 'to prayer and to the ministry of the word' (Acts 6:4). The Bible's directions to believers include: 'Do not neglect to do good and to share what you have, for such sacrifices are pleasing to God' (Hebrews 13:16); 'So then, as we have opportunity, let us do good to everyone, and especially to those who are of the household of faith' (Galatians 6:10); and 'do not grow weary in doing good' (2 Thessalonians 3:13).

The ever-practical New Testament writer James not only had something to say on the subject, but he elevated it to the highest possible level by stating, 'Religion that is pure and undefiled before God, the Father, is this: to visit orphans and widows in their affliction, and to keep oneself unspotted from the world' (James 1:27). As J. A. Motyer states, 'Caring love for the helpless is not an accidental or optional manifestation of the new nature, but part of its essence.' Showing mercy to those in need is not an option but an order. James's word 'affliction' has as its primary meaning suffering brought about by the pressure of circumstances, and this should open our eyes to the almost limitless range of human need in our twenty-first-century society. This includes the pressure of a large family or a low income, the pressure felt by the overworked or the unemployed, the pressure of chronic illness or sudden bereavement, pressures as a result of natural disasters such as earthquakes, tornadoes, hurricanes, tsunamis or floods, the pressure of a fractured relationship, a broken marriage or divorce and the particular pressures brought about by old age. There is a huge mass of human need all around us and Christians should be known as those noted for their example in providing practical help and loving support. James added the solemn warning, 'faith without works is dead' (James 2:26), then went even further and added, 'whoever knows the right thing to do and fails to do it, for him it is sin' (James 4:17).

Writing to Christians at Corinth about funds to be collected for the needs of some of their fellow believers Paul said, 'Each one must give as he has made up his mind, not reluctantly or under compulsion, for God loves a cheerful giver' (2 Corinthians 9:7). The Amplified Bible captures the meaning with the phrase 'with genuine cheerfulness and joyful eagerness'. Giving help to meet the needs of others is not a fine or a tax, nor is it to be seen as a burdensome duty. Instead, it should be recognized as a God-given privilege, enabling us to bring relief to the needy and at the same time to provide a reflection of God's mercy to us, without which we would face a disastrous destiny. The modern American scholar Simon Kistemaker says, 'When man follows God's example, he receives a divine blessing because he demonstrates that he is one of God's children.'

Walk humbly with your God

This is the third direction in our 'major point' from Micah. When Jesus was asked what was the greatest commandment in God's law he replied: 'You shall love the Lord your God with all your heart and with all your soul and with all your mind. This is the great and first commandment. And a second is like it: You shall love your neighbour as yourself' (Matthew 22:37–39). His response reflects the fact that the Ten Commandments can be divided into two sections. The first four speak of our relationship to God, while the last six speak of our relationship to our fellow men. Micah's commands to 'do justice' and to 'love mercy' obviously tie in with Jesus' summary of the last six of the Ten Commandments, while the third command—to 'walk humbly with your God'—clearly reflects what Jesus called the first four, which Jesus summarized as 'the first and great commandment'. As Jesus gave it this name, nothing is more important for anyone professing to be a Christian than seeking to obey it. The nineteenth-century American theologian W. G. T. Shedd wrote, 'It is not sufficient to commune with the truth, for truth is impersonal. We must commune with the God of truth.' There are so many things involved in walking with God that one would need to explore the entire Bible to examine the issue adequately. Instead, we will focus narrowly on the words Micah uses.

Firstly, *they imply saving faith*; they speak of walking humbly with *your* God. It has been said that Christianity is the religion of the personal pronoun. David was able to say, 'The LORD is *my* shepherd' (Psalm 23:1, emphasis added). When Thomas was told by the other disciples that they had seen the risen Jesus he was more than sceptical: 'Unless I see in his hands the mark of the nails, and place my finger into the mark of the nails, and place my hand into his side, I will never believe' (John 20:25). Thomas was present eight days later when Jesus appeared again to the disciples. Invited by Jesus to do the very things he had said would be needed to remove his doubts, Thomas simply fell at his feet and cried out, '*My* Lord and *my* God!' (John 20:28, emphasis added).

There is a world of difference between believing *about* Christ and believing *on* him, that is to say, trusting him. Saving faith goes much further than believing certain facts about Christ—or even believing all of them. Knowing the gospel is not the same as knowing the Saviour. In the course of his New Testament letter James imagines a discussion between someone who leans heavily on his doctrine and someone who leans heavily on his deeds. James has one saying to the other, 'You believe that God is one; you do well,' then immediately adding, 'Even the demons believe—and shudder!' (James 2:19). Here was a man whose doctrine was perfectly orthodox—'God is one' reflected the bedrock Old Testament statement of faith, 'The LORD our God, the LORD is one' (Deuteronomy 6:4)—but as James points out, even the demons believe this. They believe the facts, but the Christian knows Christ. Their knowledge makes them shudder, but the person with saving faith has 'peace with God through our Lord Jesus Christ' (Romans 5:1).

Secondly, *Micah's words imply an acknowledgement of God's transcendent greatness and our own smallness.* Augustine maintained, 'For those who would learn God's ways, humility is the first thing, humility is the second, and humility is the third.' Nineteen centuries later the British preacher D. Martyn Lloyd-Jones wrote, 'I sometimes think that the very essence of the whole Christian position and the secret of a successful spiritual life is just to realize two things ... I must have complete, absolute confidence in God and no confidence in myself.' It is impossible to esteem God too highly and no area of life is seen in its right perspective until we begin by humbly acknowledging his infinite majesty and sovereignty.

Finally, the words imply disciplined effort. The literal meaning of the Hebrew words translated 'walk humbly' is 'walk circumspectly', which emphasizes the care and attention needed to do this. The link with what we have just seen about the nature of God is obvious, as Jerry Bridges points out: 'Humility in every area of life, in every relationship with other people, begins with a right concept of God as the one who is infinite and eternal in his majesty and holiness.' There may be more to Micah's word 'walk' than meets the eye. Walking is something we do every day as a matter of course and there is a sense in which it lubricates everything we do between getting up in the morning and going to bed at night. In the same way, Micah saw walking with God not as a series of special moments or events but as a constant, ongoing experience of fellowship with him. A seventeenth-century French monk Brother Lawrence is best known today for his teaching about what he called 'practising the presence of God'. Writing of the determined effort this took, he said, 'As often as I could, I placed myself as a worshipper before him, fixing my mind upon his holy presence, recalling it when I found it wandering from him. This proved to be an exercise frequently painful, yet I persisted through all difficulties.'

One final word of warning needs to be given. It is good to be actively engaged in church life, but activity can be a hiding place from reality. There is a world of difference between activity and progress, and working hurriedly for God is not the same as walking humbly with him. As D. Martyn Lloyd-Jones put it, 'One of the greatest dangers in the spiritual life is to live on your own activities. In other words, the activity is not in its right place as something which you do, but has become something that keeps you going.' Ironically, having a reputation for being faithful and 'busy in the Lord's service' can feed pride, not starve it.

Walking humbly with God, the very essence of Christian discipleship, is not a press-button technique, but something that flows from a concentrated effort to place every moment of life under his lordship. It calls for daily discipline and determination and the Bible specifically warns us, 'Look carefully then how you walk' (Ephesians 5:15). One of the ways to counter self-centred pride is to reflect on Paul's question to the church at Corinth: 'What do you have that you did not receive?' (1 Corinthians 4:7). The answer is obvious. Any merit, ability or success the Christian has is entirely due to God's undeserved grace. As John Calvin put it, 'A man that extols himself is a fool and an idiot.'

The command to walk humbly with God comes with a serious warning and a sublime promise: 'God opposes the proud, but gives grace to the humble' (James 4:6). No Christian who reflects carefully on the fact that God has endless ways of frustrating the proud and limitless ways of enriching the lives of the humble should be in any doubt about the relevance of Micah's words today. The modern British hymn-writer Timothy Dudley-Smith provides a relevant prayer:

> How measureless your mercies stand,
> The hope and pledge of sins forgiven;
> Those sins, unnumbered as the sand,
> That hide the very stars of heaven:
> O God of grace, to us impart
> A penitent and contrite heart.

NAHUM

In his opening sentence Nahum tells us that he came from the town or region of Elkosh, but it is impossible to say with certainty where this might have been. There are at least two candidates. The present settlement of Elkosh, in northern Israel, was established by immigrants from Yemen and named after Nahum's birthplace, which was thought to have been somewhere in the area. Capernaum, on the north shore of the Sea of Galilee, means 'Nahum's village', but there is no solid evidence to say that this was the prophet's place of birth.

Before we go any further, this hints at a hidden lesson. The Bible's authority, integrity and value are not dependent on the background of its human authors, nor on any information about their origins. Neither do they rest on the authors' character or reputation. Instead, the Bible is to be trusted because 'All Scripture is breathed out by God' (2 Timothy 3:16). In some older English Bibles, including the Authorized (or King James) Version, the words 'breathed out by God' are rendered 'by inspiration of God', but this is open to being interpreted in a way that misses out part of the truth. It can be taken to mean merely that God 'breathed into' the Bible's human authors in such a way that they wrote what they would not otherwise have been able to write. This is certainly true, but does not go far enough. The words 'breathed out' are an accurate translation of the Greek word *theopneustos*, which tells us that God breathed out the very words that these men wrote down. The Bible will not allow us to settle for the idea the Bible's writers were merely 'inspired' in the sense that artists, musicians or sportsmen might make exceptional use of their God-given talents. Instead, it tells us that its human writers 'spoke from God as they were carried along by the Holy Spirit' (2 Peter 1:21). As we saw in the Introduction, the Holy Spirit ensured that without interfering with their individual characters, styles and language he enabled them to know and express God-breathed words in human language.

As far as the date of Nahum's book is concerned, there are two pointers. The first is his reference to the fall of the city of Thebes, in Egypt (now the site of the famous temple remains at Karnak and Luxor). In its heyday Thebes was a wealthy and powerful city, but Nahum tells us that 'she became an exile; she went into captivity; her infants were dashed in pieces at the head of every street; for her honoured men lots were cast, and all her great men were bound in chains' (3:10–11). This is a vividly accurate description of what happened when the Assyrians sacked the city in 663 BC.

The second pointer is that Nahum's book is 'An oracle concerning Nineveh' (1:1). In the prophetic writings the word 'oracle' was often used to announce a message of divine judgement. Isaiah wrote of 'The oracle concerning Babylon' (Isaiah 13:1), and the last of the Old Testament prophets is 'The oracle of the word of the LORD to Israel by Malachi' (Malachi 1:1). In Nahum's case, his message is a terrifying prophecy about the coming destruction of Nineveh—the mighty capital of the pagan Assyrian Empire—which took place in 612 BC, when it was overcome by the Chaldeans and the Medes. Taking this date together with the fall of Thebes in 663 BC, we are left with a fifty-one-year time slot, but perhaps we can get even closer. When Nahum wrote his prophecy Nineveh was still a very powerful city, but as history tells us that its disintegration began around 627 BC, this would tighten the time frame to about fifteen years and place Nahum's prophecy somewhere between 627 BC and 612 BC. This was over 100 years after Jonah's astonishing experience there and the revival of that time had long since fizzled out.

The timing may not be precise, but it is not difficult to discover Nahum's core message. In the English Standard Version of the Bible, the editors have headed the prophet's three chapters: 'God's wrath against Nineveh', 'The Destruction of Nineveh' and 'Woe to Nineveh'. In the course of his forty-seven verses Nahum uses some of the strongest language in the Bible to express God's reaction to Nineveh's sin. He writes of God's wrath being 'poured out like fire' (1:6); he says that God 'will pursue his enemies into darkness' (1:8); he records God telling the people of Nineveh, 'I will make your grave, for you are vile' (1:14); he tells of God seeing Nineveh as being 'like a pool whose waters run away' (2:8); and he has God telling its people, 'I will throw filth at you and treat you with contempt' (3:6).

The idea that Nineveh was to be destroyed would have seemed ridiculous at the time. As we saw when studying Jonah, it was a massive city that towered over all others. It owed much of its grandeur to King Sennacherib (704–681 BC)—who not only built a magnificent palace for himself (he called it 'The Palace without Rival') but transformed the city with new temples, roads, avenues, bridges, canals and parks. To meet the city's huge demand for water he also commissioned the world's first aqueduct, and to secure the city he built a massive wall surrounded by a moat.

Yet there was a dark side to Nineveh. Over a period of some 200 years it amassed massive wealth by brutally robbing other nations of their treasures. It had also become a byword for corruption—Nahum describes it as being 'full of lies and plunder' (3:1). Above all, it was passionately pagan, rejecting the one true God and worshipping the false deity Ishtar, the goddess of fertility, love, war and sex. Engravings also tell of the Ninevite leaders' sheer brutality and describes their custom of tearing off people's skin, putting their eyes out, boring through their jaws and cutting off their fingers, lips and noses. Nahum is one of only two books in the Bible (Jonah is the other) that ends with a question, which in this case is addressed to Nineveh and sums up the city's dreadful reputation: '... for who has not felt your endless cruelty?' (3:19, NIV).

This was 'the bloody city' (3:1) whose promised destruction by God takes up nearly every word of Nahum's prophecy. Yet this localized prophecy is wrapped in the timeless truth of the sovereignty of God, who controls the destiny of all nations and whose righteousness ensures that all who oppose him and oppress his people will eventually suffer a terrible fate at his hands.

Before we begin ...

Nahum has only three chapters and concentrates in terrible terms on a single subject which forms the background for our 'major point'. This background gives powerful expression to some important truths that will make the 'major point' shine with added brilliance. Spending time in examining these truths will not cut across the title of this series of studies, as we are looking at *a* major point from each prophet's writing, not *the* major point.

One of the most influential books in the history of Christian theology is *Institutes of the Christian Religion*. Written by John Calvin in 1536, it eventually became what we might call the standard systematic theology of the Protestant Reformation. Not all Christians agree with Calvin's teaching on doctrines such as election and predestination, which make him *persona non grata* as far as they are concerned. Yet Calvin's contribution went far beyond these. He was the first theologian to develop our understanding of the Lord Jesus Christ in the roles of Prophet, Priest and King. He was also the first to develop the principles of Christian ethics which are taken for granted today. What is more, no theologian in history has made a greater contribution to our understanding of the work of the Holy Spirit—so much so that Donald Grey Barnhouse has said, 'The doctrine of the Holy Spirit is a gift from John Calvin to the church of Christ.'

The opening words of the *Institutes* are these: 'Nearly all the wisdom we possess that is true and sound consists of two parts, our knowledge of God and of ourselves.' Calvin then goes on to show that these two are closely linked. The more we discover of ourselves, the more we sense our inadequacy and our need to turn elsewhere for satisfaction and fulfilment; and the more we discover about God, the more we are led to reflect on our own condition. He goes on to give a simple illustration. He imagines someone going for a walk on a bright, sunny day. As he walks along with his eyes fixed on the ground in front of him, the brilliant light from the sun enables him to see the ground beneath his feet very clearly. He might even be impressed as to how good his eyesight is, but if he were to lift his head and look directly at the sun he would be 'dazzled and confounded' by its brilliance and soon realize the limitations of his eyesight. In the same way, Calvin argues, the clearer our view of God the more we recognize our own deficiencies.

Here is another quotation, but not this time from Calvin: 'The highest science, the loftiest speculation, the mightiest philosophy which can ever engage the attention of a child of God is the name, the nature, the person, the work, the doings and the existence of the great God he calls his Father.' Those words were preached on 7 January 1855 by C. H. Spurgeon—and his text was from one of the Minor Prophets. He was putting into his own words truths that have been firmly embedded in the Bible for thousands of years, and the particular truth that binds Calvin's and Spurgeon's words together is expressed like this: 'The fear of the LORD is the beginning of wisdom, and the knowledge of the Holy One is insight' (Proverbs 9:10).

Any well-taught Christian reading those words takes three things for granted. Firstly, when the Bible speaks about knowing God it means more than knowing *about* him. Secondly, we know nothing of God unless he reveals himself to us. Thirdly, he has revealed himself to us in the pages of the Bible. When theologians try to systematize biblical truth about God they speak of God's attributes, which they then divide into his incommunicable attributes (those he alone has) and his communicable attributes (those he can in some measure give to others). His incommunicable attributes include such things as his self-existence, that is to say his utter independence of anything or anyone else in the entire universe. The same can be said about his immutability (his 'unchangeableness') and of his infinity (his complete freedom from all the restrictions that we experience as human beings). His communicable attributes include such things as his goodness, his love and his holiness. In some measure we can share in these, so that the apostle Peter, in writing about God's 'precious and very great promises' says that his people can 'become partakers of the divine nature' (2 Peter 1:4).

Tension?

So far so good, but there are times when people sense a tension when trying to put together everything the Bible says about God. For example, they ask, 'How can God be at one and the same time a God of infinite anger and infinite love?' The person with little or no understanding of Scripture balks at the idea, but the person with a thorough grasp of what the Bible has to say sees a much clearer picture.

Nobody who takes the Bible seriously can question the fact that God expresses anger. Because Aaron led the people of Israel in gross idolatry, God was 'so angry with [him] that he was ready to destroy him' (Deuteronomy 9:20). Several times in their forty years of wandering in the desert the people of Israel sinned against God in such a way that they 'provoked him to anger' and drove him to become 'full of wrath' (Psalm 78:58–59). When Solomon's heart turned away from God he was 'angry with Solomon' (1 Kings 11:9). When his people refused to listen to the word he had given the prophets to deliver, 'great anger came from the LORD of hosts' (Zechariah 7:12). The twentieth-century Bible scholar Leon Morris pointed out that in the Old Testament the subject occurs nearly 600 times, using twenty different words to express its meaning. As A. W. Pink notes, 'There are more references in Scripture to the anger, fury and wrath of God than there are to his love and tenderness'. In his superb book *Knowing God*, J. I. Packer even says that there is a sense in which the Bible could be called 'the book of God's wrath'.

In his glorious holiness, God cannot tolerate sin in any way, shape or form and the Bible leaves us in no doubt that his zero tolerance of sin finds expression in his holy anger. There can be no peaceful co-existence between God and sin, but much modern preaching stops short of revealing God's anger against it. Some try to play down God's anger by teaching that God is angry at sin but not at the sinner, but this is not the case. I have traced thirty-three places in the Bible in which God's anger is specifically expressed and in twenty-one of these the object of his anger is the sinner. If we were told of someone who was noted for his anger we would probably imagine that the person concerned was psychologically and emotionally flawed, but as God is 'perfect' in nature (Matthew 5:48) this cannot be said of him. In God's character there is not the slightest blemish, flaw, imperfection or weakness.

God's anger is the personal and passionate outworking of his perfection, something that comes powerfully across in Nahum's prophecy about God's dealings with Nineveh. He is never malicious, bad-tempered, irritable, tetchy or cruel. His anger is never irrational, impetuous, uncontrolled, unjustified or 'over the top'. The modern theologian David Baker writes, 'Any judgement by God upon sin, whether that of his own people or others, is not based on whim or uncontrollable anger, but on God's unchangingly holy character.'

Far from being a flaw, God's anger reflects his perfect holiness and justice. As R. C. Sproul puts it, 'If God is holy at all, if God has an ounce of justice in his character, indeed if God exists as God, how could he possibly be anything else but angry with us? We violate his holiness, we insult his justice, we make light of his grace. These things can hardly be pleasing to him … A God of love who has no wrath is no God. He is an idol of our own making as much as if we carved him out of stone.' Sproul is right. If God were to shrug his shoulders at sin he would be morally flawed and unworthy of our worship. His very nature makes his righteous anger at sin inevitable. God's anger at sin is one of the perfections of his character. The Bible records both 'the kindness and the severity of God' (Romans 11:22), yet while it says that 'God is love' (1 John 4:16) it never says that 'God is anger'. Instead, it teaches that God is only angry when anger is rightly called for as the proper, inevitable and personal expression of his holiness. Even then he is 'slow to anger' (1:3), tempering his response to sin in line with his moral judgements, which are 'true, and righteous altogether' (Psalm 19:9).

God's patience is even reflected in the destruction of Nineveh—the burden of Nahum's message—but so is the truth that his patience is limited. As we saw in an earlier chapter, God called the prophet Jonah in the eighth century BC to warn the people of Nineveh of impending judgement 'for their evil has come up before me' (Jonah 1:2). For a shameful reason, Jonah did his best to run away, but when he later repented God graciously re-commissioned him. Jonah then exercised an amazing ministry in the city, and saw widespread repentance among the people of Nineveh. As a result, God 'relented of the disaster that he had said he would do to them, and he did not do it' (Jonah 3:10). There was then a spiritual revival in Nineveh, though it was relatively short-lived and by the end of the century the Ninevites had not only turned their backs on God but invaded and plundered his people in Judah.

Nahum's message about Nineveh firmly underlines the principles we examined at the beginning of this chapter and it begins by asserting something that would exactly fit Nineveh's about-turn: 'The LORD is a jealous and avenging God; the LORD is avenging and wrathful; the LORD takes vengeance on his adversaries, and keeps wrath for his enemies' (1:2). Nahum then warns Nineveh that God 'will by no means clear the guilty' (1:3) and that 'His wrath is poured out like fire' (1:6). God's patience is often lasting, but it is not everlasting, as Nineveh was about to discover to its terrible cost.

There are some encouraging words for God's people in Chapter 2, as he assures them that he is 'restoring the majesty of Jacob as the majesty of Israel' (2:2) but the chapter ends with God warning Nineveh that he will come against them like an overwhelming enemy in battle: 'Behold, I am against you, declares the LORD of hosts, and I will burn your chariots in smoke and the sword shall devour your young lions. I will cut off your prey from the earth, and the voice of your messengers shall no longer be heard' (2:13). The 'young lions' may have been the nation's finest soldiers; if so, even they would be helpless against the forces God was about to unleash against them.

There is no let-up in Chapter 3, which begins with God describing himself as a terrifying warrior using foreign powers to wreak havoc on his pagan enemies: 'Horsemen charging, flashing sword and glittering spear, hosts of slain, heaps of corpses, dead bodies without end—they stumble over the bodies!' (3:3). Virtually all forty-seven verses in Nahum are taken up with a scathing denunciation of Nineveh's sin and the horrendous judgement that God is to pour out on it. When disaster eventually struck the city was so pulverized that for well over 1,000 years its exact location was uncertain. The Babylonian Chronicles, now housed in the British Museum, preserves a record of the invaders' account of its destruction and includes the phrase, 'At Nineveh a mighty assault against the city and a great slaughter was made of the people and nobles.' The museum also has reliefs from the walls of Sennacherib's 'Palace without Rival' that bear witness to the devastating fire that raged throughout the city.

Not only Nineveh

Yet God's righteous anger is not reserved only for those who descend to the same vile depths as Nineveh. The Bible's unwavering testimony is that God's face is set against all sin of every kind. This must be the case. A God of perfect holiness must *by his very nature* have zero tolerance of sin and the Bible confirms that this is so by saying that God is 'of purer eyes than to see evil and cannot look at wrong' (Habakkuk 1:13). Everyone without exception is by nature exposed to his righteous wrath. This terrifying truth applies not only to the rank pagan, the determined atheist and the serial criminal, but to the religious believer, the sophisticated pillar of society and the kind of person who 'never does anybody any harm'. Writing at the peak of his ministry the apostle Paul includes himself by saying that 'we were by nature children of wrath, like the rest of mankind' (Ephesians 2:3). Centuries earlier David went even further and confessed, 'Behold, I was brought forth in iniquity, and in sin did my mother conceive me' (Psalm 51:5). Assuming he was carried to term, David was a sinner nine months before he was born. We do not become sinners because we sin; we sin because we are sinners and every sin we commit shows what we are by nature. However respectable we may think ourselves to be, left to ourselves we are exposed to God's unrelenting anger.

Outside of Scripture, nobody may have expressed this more famously than Jonathan Edwards, the eighteenth-century American preacher and theologian. On 8 July 1741 he preached a sermon in Enfield, Connecticut, entitled 'Sinners in the hands of an angry God', perhaps the most quoted extra-biblical sermon in history. This passage captures the heart of his concern for his hearers:

> [God's] wrath towards you burns like fire; he looks upon you as worthy of nothing else, but to be cast into the fire... It is nothing but his hand that holds you from falling into the fire every moment. It is to be ascribed to nothing else, that you did not go into hell last night; that you were ever suffered to awake again in this world, after you closed your eyes in sleep. And there is no other reason to be given, why you have not dropped into hell since you arose in the morning, but that God's hand has held you up.

These truths are powerfully relevant for twenty-first-century Christians charged with the responsibility to 'Go into all the world and proclaim the gospel to the whole creation' (Mark 16:15). As the modern American theologian David Wells explains,

> It is a temptation to think that by being nice and accommodating we can make the Christian gospel seem like a great little addition to everyone's life. But the gospel is not a great little addition. It is a soul-shaking, costly, demanding reality. The church cannot hide this fact! The gospel is not about self-therapy. Despite our pressured, taut, nerve-jangling age, the Christian message is not there just to make us feel better about ourselves or more able to cope. It is about coming before our great God and Saviour, confessing our sins, entrusting ourselves to him, and surrendering our claim upon ourselves to him.

The preaching of the gospel draws its ultimate urgency from three biblical facts. The first is revealed in Paul's testimony that we are all 'children of wrath'. We are all born rebels against

God's rightful authority and with an ingrained tendency to sin. Without exception, men are exposed to God's anger not merely because of what they have done, *but because of what they are.*

Secondly, men's sinful behaviour leaves them constantly exposed to God's anger: 'For the wrath of God is revealed ... against all ungodliness and unrighteousness of men, who by their unrighteousness suppress the truth' (Romans 1:18). Left to his own devices, man lives every moment under the cloud of God's righteous anger, as 'God is a righteous judge ... who feels indignation every day' (Psalm 7:11) and 'his judgements are in all the earth' (Psalm 105:7). J. I. Packer writes, 'The subject of divine wrath has become taboo in modern society and Christians by and large have accepted the taboo and conditioned themselves never to raise the matter.' God is not an idle spectator of men's behaviour, nor is he unaffected by it. From the moment he expelled Adam and Eve from the Garden he has been expressing his holy anger against human sin. Most people blithely ignore this terrible truth. When the 'Jesus people' were hitting the headlines in the nineteen-seventies, many of them wore badges with the slogan 'Smile, God loves you!' This could have given the impression that people's lifestyles were irrelevant to him and that any behaviour out of line with what he would prefer to see would not affect his love for the people concerned. This gives a dangerously false picture. A friend of mind said at the time that the badges would have been more to the point if they had read, 'Frown, you're under judgement!'

Thirdly, God's anger will be revealed in all its fulness on the final day of judgement, then throughout eternity in hell, a truth that has been virtually eliminated from most people's thinking. Commenting that the idea of hell has been in decline for 400 years and is now on its way to extinction, Harvard University professor Gordon Kaufman says, 'I don't think there can be any future for hell.' Kaufman is not expressing his own belief but reflecting modern thinking on the subject. The Bible paints a very different picture. It will come as a double surprise to many that comparatively little about hell is found in the Old Testament and that most New Testament teaching on the subject comes from the lips of Jesus. About thirteen per cent of his recorded words are about judgement and hell and he spoke more on these two subjects than about any other. More than half of his parables relate to God's eternal judgement of sinners. I have written extensively on this in my book *Whatever Happened to Hell?* It will be sufficient here to record that in the Sermon on the Mount Jesus spoke of those who at the end of life would be 'thrown into hell' (Matthew 5:29) and elsewhere identified those who after the final day of judgement 'will go away into eternal punishment' (Matthew 25:46).

It is then that God's anger will no longer be tempered in any way, as it is at present. In one of the most terrifying statements in all of Scripture we are told that those in hell 'will drink the wine of God's wrath, poured full strength into the cup of his anger' (Revelation 14:10). Here on earth, sinners have only the merest sips of God's anger; in hell, they will 'drink it'. On earth, God's anger comes in dribbles; in hell it will be 'poured'. On earth, God's anger is diluted with his mercy and patience—'He does not deal with us according to our sins, nor repay us according to our iniquities' (Psalm 103:10)—but in hell all that will change and God's anger will be poured out 'full strength', something infinitely greater than anything that any human being has ever experienced or could possibly imagine. As the modern theologian Paul Helm rightly says, 'Hell is a place of justice, where punishment is dispensed not in accordance with the warped and partial and ignorant procedures of modern society, but immaculately, in accord with the standards of him who is supremely just.'

Bearing all of this in mind, and with the unblinking holiness of God ever before us, we can now turn to a statement that shines like a dazzlingly brilliant star against a pitch-black night sky:

> The LORD is good, a stronghold in the day of trouble; he knows those who take refuge in him.   (1:7)

This is our 'major point' from this particular Minor Prophet. It will always have a special resonance in my own heart as these words formed part of the passage set out in the daily Bible reading scheme I was following on 17 February 2010, the day my wife went to be with the Lord. In it we have three glorious truths in which God's people can rejoice.

The goodness of God

'The LORD is good' is such a stunning phrase to read immediately after Nahum's opening salvo against Nineveh that it almost seems out of place, but this is not the case. We need to bear in mind that Nahum's prophecy was given for Judah's encouragement and in the 'major point' we are now considering, God's people were given his assurance that their deadly enemy was to be wiped out while they remained secure and free to worship him without fear of invasion.

The goodness of God is a recurring theme throughout the Bible. One of the psalmists gives the simplest expression of this when he cries out to God, 'You are good and do good' (Psalm 119:68). God is essentially, infinitely, perfectly and unchangeably good and everything he does flows from this and is therefore intrinsically good. This is true even when he disciplines believers. The Bible reminds us that human fathers discipline their children 'for a short time' (Hebrews 12:10) as it seems best to them (that is, with their fallible wisdom, and sometimes with mixed motives). On the other hand, with his perfect understanding of our circumstances, God 'disciplines us for our good, that we may share in his holiness' (Hebrews 12:10). In the same passage the writer acknowledges, 'For the moment all discipline seems painful rather than pleasant, *but later* it yields the peaceful fruit of righteousness to those who have been trained by it' (Hebrews 12:11, emphasis added).

Everything that God sends or allows in a Christian's life is intended for the believer's spiritual and eternal good. In a brilliantly honest testimony Jeremiah cries out that '[God] turns his hand against me again and again' (Lamentations 3:3). Yet he also recognizes that even when he faced the most severe testing 'The steadfast love of the LORD never ceases' (Lamentations 3:22) and adds, 'The LORD is good to those who wait for him, to the soul who seeks him' (Lamentations 3:25). God sometimes turns his hand against his people (and it is amazing that he does not do so more often and more severely) *but he never turns his heart against them.*

Writing to friends on the death of an infant, the eighteenth-century British preacher John Newton told them,

> You are in the wise and merciful hands of One who prescribes for you with unerring wisdom, and has unspeakably more tenderness than can be found in all human hearts taken together! He weighs all your painful afflictions with consummate accuracy! You shall not have a single grain of trouble more, nor for a moment longer, than he will enable you to bear, and will sanctify to your good... What a blessing to be a Christian, to have a hiding place and resting place always at hand, to be assured that all things work for our good, and that our compassionate Shepherd has his eye always upon us, to support and to relieve us.

The storms of life no more indicate the absence of God than clouds indicate the absence of the sun, and the trials of life are meant to make us better, not bitter. The twentieth-century Irish preacher Herbert Carson wrote, 'Slum clearance is not an end in itself simply to satisfy the town planners. Its ultimate aim is to move people to better homes. So in all God's dealings, which may at times appear harsh, he is gently and graciously preparing us for removal.' The Puritan preacher Thomas Watson used to say that the worst God could do to his children was to whip them to heaven!

One of the clearest illustrations of what is meant by God's goodness can be seen in an Old Testament narrative. While Moses was on Mount Sinai receiving the Ten Commandments from God, his brother Aaron encouraged the Israelites to build and worship a golden calf. God was rightly angry at this blatant idolatry and 'sent a plague on the people' (Exodus 32:35). We are not told what this was, but in addition to sending it God told the people that although the remainder of their journey to the Promised Land would be safely negotiated, his own intimate presence in their midst would be replaced by that of an angel.

In the meantime God met with Moses 'face to face, as a man speaks to his friend' (Exodus 33:11). As a result of Moses' passionate intercession on behalf of the people God told him that as they moved on, 'My presence will go with you, and I will give you rest' (Exodus 33:14). Assured of this, Moses made another remarkable request: 'Please show me your glory' (Exodus 33:18). Moses wanted some indication of God's essential being—and God replied, 'I will make all my goodness pass before you and will proclaim before you my name "The LORD"' (Exodus 33:19). We dare not miss what is being said here. Asked for a statement of his nature, God expressed it in terms of his *goodness* and soon afterwards showed Moses that it lay at the heart of other attributes: 'The LORD passed before him and proclaimed, "The LORD, the LORD, a God merciful and gracious, slow to anger, and abounding in steadfast love and faithfulness, keeping steadfast love for thousands, forgiving iniquity and transgression and sin"' (Exodus 34:6–7).

A. W. Pink was right to claim, 'God's goodness is abused by the greatest part of mankind', but no Christian should ever be guilty of this. Instead, he should rejoice in being able to claim with David, 'Surely goodness and mercy shall follow me all the days of my life' (Psalm 23:6) and to share his assurance that when his earthly life ends, 'I shall look upon the goodness of the LORD in the land of the living' (Psalm 27:13). As Matthew Henry put it, 'There is nothing like the believing hope of eternal life to keep us from fainting under all the calamities of this present time.'

The stronghold

The second part of Nahum's 'major point' says that God is *'a stronghold in the day of trouble.'* 'Stronghold' is a more concrete word than 'goodness' and hardly needs any explanation. This is one of the Old Testament's favourite images of God and conveys the picture of a fortress, a position of security and safety and a place of protection from one's enemies. Looking back on a life crammed with excitement and escapes, dangers and victories, David began one of his many psalms with a series of words to make the point: 'I love you, O LORD, my strength. The LORD is my rock and my fortress and my deliverer, my God, my rock, in whom I take refuge, my shield, and the horn of my salvation, my stronghold' (Psalm 18:1–2). In what the modern author Derek Kidner has called 'this rush of metaphors' Israel's greatest king poured out his thanksgiving to God for his unfailing protection.

An anonymous psalmist struck the same note. Getting on in years, and finding the going pretty tough at times, he declared, 'In you, O LORD, do I take refuge' (Psalm 71:1). His constant prayer was, 'Be to me a rock of refuge' (Psalm 71:3). By sheer coincidence the very central one of the Bible's 31,101 verses reads, 'It is better to take refuge in the LORD than to trust in man' (Psalm 118:8). Some translations have 'princes' instead of 'man', but 'princes' may be better as it makes the point that even the most influential of men can prove fragile, limited and unreliable, whereas God is not only omnipotent but utterly trustworthy.

The opening words of Psalm 46 show where real help can be found: 'God is our refuge and strength, a very present help in trouble' (Psalm 46:1). This was Martin Luther's favourite psalm. When danger threatened he would tell his friends, 'Come, let us sing the 46th Psalm and let them do their worst.' This is exactly what he did when summoned to the Imperial Diet of Worms in 1521. Diets were powerful assemblies of the Imperial Estates of the Holy Roman Empire and Luther knew that as he could not retract his Reformation convictions his life was hanging by a thread. When his friends tried to persuade him not to face the Diet he replied, 'Even should there be as many devils in Worms as tiles on the housetops, still I would enter it.' On his long journey to Worms he wrote his famous hymn *'Ein' feste Burg ist unser Gott'* ('A mighty fortress is our God'). There have been about seventy English translations of the hymn and this version of its last verse captures the Reformer's utter assurance that whatever happened to him would be governed by the preserving providence of God:

> And though this world, with devils filled
> Should threaten to undo us;
> We will not fear, for God has willed

His truth to triumph through us.
Let goods and kindred go,
This mortal life also;
The body they may kill,
God's truth abideth still;
His kingdom is for ever.

Known by God

Finally, we are told that God *'knows those that take refuge in him'*. The metaphor of God as a refuge underlines the one that pictures God as a stronghold, but there is more to the word 'knows' than meets the eye. It clearly means more than 'he knows who they are' and when we study its use in Scripture we see that it stretches from eternity to eternity. In the first place it reaches back to the believer's eternal election. When God told Israel, 'You only have I known of all the families of the earth' (Amos 3:2) he was not saying that he knew nothing about any other nations or tribes. Instead, he was saying that out of all nations on earth he had chosen Israel to be his people in a unique way. This truth is confirmed in the New Testament, where we are told that Christians—'the Israel of God' (Galatians 6:16)—are 'a chosen race, a royal priesthood, a people for [God's] own possession' (1 Peter 2:9).

The doctrine of God's election of his people humbles everyone, because nobody deserves to be saved, nor can they make even the smallest contribution to their salvation. In the Sermon on the Mount Jesus said, 'Blessed are the poor in spirit, for theirs is the kingdom of heaven' (Matthew 5:3). There are several Greek words translated 'poor' in our English Bibles. This particular one is *ptochos,* which comes from a root meaning to crouch or cower like a beggar. Jesus used a similar word in telling the story of a man living in the lap of luxury, while just outside his gate lay 'a poor man named Lazarus, covered with sores, who desired to be fed with what fell from the rich man's table' and who was in such a wretched state that 'even the dogs came and licked his sores' (Luke 16:20–21). This man was not merely in a lower income bracket than the rich man. He was utterly destitute and completely dependent on the goodwill of others if he was not to shrivel up and die. Sinners are in the same state spiritually and nothing but God's love, expressed in his unconditional election, can rescue them and pour into their lives 'the immeasurable riches of his grace' (Ephesians 2:7).

Secondly, Nahum's use of the word 'knows' reaches forward to the believer's eternal destiny in heaven: 'The LORD knows the way of the righteous, but the way of the wicked will perish' (Psalm 1:6). The contrast with 'knows' is not 'does not know' but 'will perish'. Here is Old Testament anticipation of something Jesus made wonderfully clear in the New Testament when he promised, 'Truly, truly, I say to you, whoever hears my word and believes him who sent me has eternal life. He does not come into judgement, but has passed from death to life' (John 5:24).

Nahum's 'major point' is not only a window into God's heart. It is also a constant source of strength and assurance to his people as they make their way through a life strewn with pressure and pain, and in which there is sometimes the temptation to doubt whether they belong to God's 'chosen race'. It also looks forward to the believer's glorious home in heaven where as Richard Brooks wrote, 'We shall have everything we desire and desire everything we have.'

An enduring lesson we can take from Nahum is one endorsed by Paul, who assures us that whatever happens in this world and however the sands of time seem to be shifting under our feet, 'we have a building from God, a house not made with hands, eternal in the heavens' (2 Corinthians 5:1).

The modern British hymn-writer Christopher Idle ends his hymn 'Christ has prepared for us a place' with this prayer:

Lord, stir our hope, and give us grace
That day when all things are made new;
To find the wonder of that place,
To see and know and worship you.

HABAKKUK

Other than his name, which comes from a Hebrew root meaning 'to clasp' or 'to embrace', Habakkuk is yet another Minor Prophet who is virtually anonymous, as we know nothing about his tribe, his family, his background or his home. As he calls himself 'the prophet' (1:1) this may have been his full-time calling; it certainly seems to hint that he was recognized as a man whose message was divinely inspired. We know that he lived in Judah (possibly in Jerusalem) and that he was a contemporary of the major prophet Jeremiah, who lived during the reigns of Josiah, Jehoahaz, Jehoiakim, Jehoiachin and Zedekiah. These covered the period from 609 to 586 BC. Another clue as to the date of his prophecy is that he records God as saying, 'I am raising up the Chaldeans' (1:6). As the Chaldeans, by then the dominant military force in the Middle East, invaded Judah in 586 BC the prophecy must be dated some time before then.

What is unique about Habakkuk's writing is that it has no direct message from God to his people. Instead, it tells us what Habakkuk and God said to each other and the prophet's eventual response to their dialogue. What makes it even more remarkable is that it begins with the prophet's bewildered enquiry as to why God should apparently be sitting on his hands while his people are going through the mill. The book can be more or less divided into two complaints by Habakkuk and two answers from God, followed by a psalm of praise which ends with what has rightly been called 'one of the beautiful expressions of faith found in the Old Testament'.

Why?

Ask any group of Christians to nominate what they feel is the greatest single-verse statement in the Bible and few would be likely to choose one from the book of Habakkuk. Yet it was a New Testament quotation of something Habakkuk wrote that in the sixteenth century was used by God to change the spiritual climate of Europe. We can get a grasp of the context in which it was originally written by looking more closely at Habakkuk's overall message.

'The oracle that Habakkuk the prophet saw' (1:1) was written at a time when Judah was in a state of appalling moral and spiritual decline. Violence, strife, conflict, a paralysed legal system, the oppression of the righteous by the wicked and the perversion of justice were all rife (see 1:2–4). Anyone who thinks that the Bible is irrelevant in the twenty-first century has failed to make the obvious connection. Today's media constantly splash horrendous stories of gratuitous violence, sexual aberration, bestiality and the like that at times are difficult to believe. As I began to study this passage I read a newspaper report of a husband who had an argument with his wife, took her to the hospital at which he worked, killed her, cut her up in pieces, put her remains in an incinerator, made sure she was reduced to ashes, then casually strolled out for lunch.

News outlets are awash with reports of political skulduggery, terrorists committing suicide in order to guarantee the deaths of other people, financial corruption on an industrial scale, horrific levels of child abuse, and millions of lives ruined by chemical misuse of one kind or another. These things should make us shudder with shame, yet if we are surprised that such things happen we have failed to grasp what the Bible means when it says, 'The heart is deceitful above all things, and desperately sick' (Jeremiah 17:9). C. H. Spurgeon put his finger on the fundamental issue when he wrote, 'As the salt flavours every drop in the Atlantic, so does sin affect every atom of our nature.'

Habakkuk lived in a nation that had known a spiritual revival but was now in serious spiritual recession, yet his major difficulty was not man's actions but God's inaction. What troubled him even more than man's sin was God's silence: 'O LORD, how long shall I cry for help, and you will not hear? (1:2). His concern seems to have been shared by a minority of godly people who were praying for a revival of righteousness in the nation, yet God was apparently ignoring their prayers. The word 'hear' comes from a root meaning 'to reply by doing something'. As far as Habakkuk could see, the wicked were metaphorically (and literally) getting away with murder. Facing a similar situation, the prophet Jeremiah was equally baffled: 'Righteous are you, O LORD, when I complain to you; yet I would plead my case before you. Why does the way of the wicked prosper?' (Jeremiah 12:1). We can almost hear Jeremiah turning the issue over in his mind. He knew that God was a God of perfect justice who hated evil and had promised to bless his people; then why did he allow the faithless to 'thrive' and to 'grow and produce fruit' (Jeremiah 12:1–2)?

Another Old Testament writer reflected the same bewilderment: 'There is something else meaningless that occurs on earth: righteous men who get what the wicked deserve, and wicked men who get what the righteous deserve' (Ecclesiastes 8:14, NIV). This was precisely Habakkuk's problem. Evil was rampant and evildoers were flourishing while the righteous floundered. Even God's people were being dragged down into the general morass and there seemed to be no obvious or immediate way out. Habakkuk is completely up front with God about this and pours out his heart in genuine concern that his passionate and persistent prayers for God to intervene seem to be getting no further than the ceiling.

The 'impossible' reply

Yet Habakkuk is soon to be more baffled than ever, as we can see by taking God's response one phrase at a time.

'*I am doing a work...*' (1:5). At last, there seems to be light at the end of the tunnel. God *has* been listening and he is working to answer Habakkuk's prayers. We can almost sense the prophet's heart rate gathering pace as he realizes that he has not been praying in vain after all. It was certainly good news that God was at work, but Habakkuk would hardly be human if he did not hope that the answer would come sooner rather than later and ideally while he was still alive. Countless Christians doubtless feel the same today as they pray for a genuine, biblical revival of godliness in their own nation and in the world at large. After decades of spiritual decline in many parts of the world, how wonderful it would be if we could have just one year of our lives—a few months even—when we saw God moving in such a truly marvellous and massive way that even the secular media was forced to acknowledge it!

'*... in your days ...*' (1:5). In Habakkuk's case, God added precisely this promise: he would answer his people's petitions while Habakkuk was still alive to see it. We can imagine the prophet's pulse gathering even greater pace. God's answer to his prayer was not to come at some future date when the prophet would no longer be there to rejoice in it. Instead, it was time-sensitive, with a deadline prior to the prophet's death. Imagine how we would feel if God assured us beyond any misunderstanding that he was going to send genuine revival to our nation during our lifetime!

'*... that you would not believe if told ...*' (1:5). It was great news that God would answer his prayers during the prophet's lifetime, but what kind of answer would it be? However welcome, what if it were to be something that would affect relatively few people? If that thought had even crossed the prophet's mind it was soon swept aside by God's assurance that the answer would be so stupendous as to be beyond the normal boundaries of belief. It would not be a gentle slap on the wrist for the wicked, or a gentle boost to the fortunes of the faithful, but something so radical that had the word not come from God nobody would believe it. At this point we can imagine Habakkuk verging on tachycardia—but now comes the crunch.

'I am raising up the Chaldeans, that bitter and hasty nation, who march through the breadth of the earth, to seize dwellings not their own. They are dreaded and fearsome...' (1:6–7). Habakkuk can hardly believe his ears. The Chaldeans (also known as the Babylonians) were the very epitome of brutality and in the following verses God reminds the prophet of their track record in invading and ravaging other lands. They were 'bitter and hasty ... dreaded and fearsome ... more fierce than the evening wolves ... guilty men, whose own might is their god!' (1:6, 7, 8, 11). Yet these violent, godless hordes were to be God's instrument of his judgement on Judah and his answer to the prophet's prayer.

Human problem; divine solution

It is not difficult to see why Habakkuk was utterly confused. It was understandable that God was going to punish Judah for its abominable sin and shameless rebellion. What Habakkuk could not understand was that in order to punish his covenant people God was going to use a godless nation with which he had never even entered into a covenant. As far as Habakkuk was concerned the whole thing was inconceivable. God's punishment of his people seemed far greater than their crime and his answer to the prophet's prayer seemed to contradict his character.

To make things even more confusing to him, Habakkuk's uncertainties were fuelled by his theological certainties. We can see this in 1:12–13, a statement that begins with a rhetorical question and forms what we might call a summary of the prophet's systematic theology. It speaks of God's eternality—*'Are you not from everlasting?'*; it speaks of his holiness—*'... my God, my Holy One'*; it speaks of his faithfulness—*'We shall not die'*; it speaks of his sovereignty and justice—*'... you have ordained them as a judgement'*; it speaks of his stability—*'O Rock'*; it speaks of his purity—*'You ... are of purer eyes than to see evil'*; and it speaks of his integrity—*'... you cannot look at wrong'*. Although 'We shall not die' reflects Habakkuk's assurance that God's faithful remnant would not be wiped out when the invasion came, the prophet was still even more baffled than when he brought his original complaint to God. How could his use of the ungodly Chaldeans harmonize with his holiness?

In passing, this should alert us to the fact that getting our doctrine straight is no guarantee that everything else in life will slot seamlessly into place. We have a duty to study the Bible to the limit of our ability and to work hard at building a coherent biblical framework of doctrine, but we dare not be naïve enough to think that doing this will remove life's difficulties. Not even a solid, systematic, structured grasp of every major doctrine in the Bible is a guarantee that we will find all life's loose ends tied up and all the grey areas removed.

Habakkuk reels under the tension caused when he tries to marry God's plan for the nation with his flawless attributes. He could understand God bringing judgement on the covenant nation that had turned its back on him, but could not grasp how God could do this by means of a pagan nation with which he had never established a covenant. Surely God should be punishing the pagans, not using them to punish Judah?

Habakkuk is being transparently honest here. The Christian who never wrestles with the problem of reconciling the sovereignty of God with rampant evil has never thought seriously and honestly about the issue. J. C. Ryle, the first Bishop of Liverpool, grasped a crucial truth in assessing this kind of situation when he wrote, 'The wickedest enemies of God are only axes and saws and hammers in his hands, and are ignorantly his instruments for doing his work in the world.' Habakkuk may have begun to get a glimpse of this. He took a deep breath and determined that the right response was to trust God even when he was unable to trace him: 'I will take my stand at my watchpost and station myself on the tower and look out to see what he will say to me' (2:1). Although still reeling from the news of God's intentions he decided to wait patiently for the outworking of his promises.

God begins his second reply by asking Habakkuk to be patient and by assuring him that his intervention is certain: 'If it seems slow, wait for it; it will surely come; it will not delay' (2:3). God is never in a hurry, never caught on the hop and never fighting against a tight schedule or an unexpected deadline. While the swaggering Chaldeans were flexing their muscles and gearing themselves up for 'Operation Judah', he gives his faithful people this life-changing word:

… the righteous shall live by his faith   (2:4)

This is our 'major point' from Habakkuk and it should soon become clear why I suggest it could be one of the greatest single-verse statements in Scripture. James Montgomery Boice went so far as to say, 'To understand it is to understand the Christian gospel and the Christian life.' It is so important that it is quoted three times in the New Testament—at Romans 1:17, Galatians 3:11 and Hebrews 10:38. The Galatians reference is virtually the same as the one in Romans, so we will examine the Romans and Hebrews quotations before coming back to Habakkuk's original statement. As we do this we will see that Habakkuk's words are the key to salvation, the key to perseverance in the Christian life and the key to understanding history.

Luther's lifeline

One way of looking at how the apostle Paul uses Habakkuk's statement at Romans 1:17 is to take a historical detour. In the early part of the sixteenth century the light of the gospel had been virtually extinguished in Europe. According to *The History of Christianity*, 'Never had official religion been at a lower ebb, or the public image of Christianity more defaced.' This 'public image' was provided by the Roman Catholic Church, which dominated religious life throughout the continent and had smothered the glory of the gospel with a blanket of unbiblical traditions and practices. Among these was the granting of Indulgences, something unknown in the early church and which arose in the Middle Ages. Essentially, Indulgences were promoted as means of releasing people from sin's temporal punishment (in whole or in part) and after death of reducing or removing altogether the punishment of Purgatory (which was itself a Roman Catholic invention with no biblical basis). By the sixteenth century, the church had put Indulgences on the open market, making them available by means of a long list of rituals and other religious practices prescribed by a priest. The church taught that these Indulgences were possible not only through the sufferings of Jesus but also because the Virgin Mary and people nominated by the church as saints had by their exemplary lives achieved more than was necessary for their own salvation and had left behind a stockpile of merit that could now be tapped into. After a while the church realized that there was money to be made here and when Pope Leo X (1513–1521) needed additional funds to complete St Peter's Cathedral in Rome he offered top-of-the-range Indulgences for sale, promising forgiveness of all sins to the living and release from Purgatory for the dead. His best-known salesman was the Dominican friar Johann Tetzel, whose sales pitch was, 'As soon as the coin in the coffer rings, the soul from Purgatory springs.'

Another way of gaining indulgence was by visiting churches housing certain holy relics. At Wittenberg, a few miles south-west of Berlin, one such church claimed to have a piece of Jesus' baby blanket, thirteen pieces of the crib in which he was laid in Bethlehem, one wisp of straw from the manger, one piece of the gold brought to the infant Jesus by the wise men from the East, one hair from Jesus' beard, one of the nails used to nail him to the cross, one piece of bread left over from the Last Supper, a twig from the burning bush mentioned in Exodus 3 and nineteen holy bones. Anyone visiting this astonishing collection (and paying the going rate) was guaranteed full remission of sins.

In that very city a university student was desperately seeking to get right with God. He was so determined to solve this overwhelming problem that he joined the Hermits of St. Augustine, one of the strictest monastic orders in the Roman Catholic Church. He poured himself into a relentless round of prayer, study, meditation and rituals. In his own words, 'I was a good monk, and I kept the rule of my Order so strictly that I may say that if ever a monk got to heaven by his monkery it was I.' He sometimes went three days without a crumb of food. Even in the depths of winter he slept without a blanket, so that he almost froze to death. He claimed, 'If I had kept on any longer I would have killed myself with vigils, prayers, reading and other works.' He was overwhelmed with a sense of God's holiness and his own sin. He reasoned that if he was ever to get right with God his sins would have to be forgiven; if they were to be forgiven they would have to be confessed; if they were to be confessed they would have to be remembered; *but how could he possibly remember them all?* Needless to say, he often made his way into the confessional, sometimes spending up to six hours at a time there three times a day. It is said that at one point his confessor told him to go away and commit some sin worth confessing! He was in a torment of fear, guilt and despair and admitted, 'I was more than once driven to the very abyss of despair, so that I wished I had never been created. Love God? I hated him.'

In 1510 he went on a pilgrimage to Rome and while there he joined others in climbing on hands and knees up the twenty-eight steps leading to the church of St John's Lateran, supposedly the very steps that once stood in front of Pontius Pilate's palace in Jerusalem when Jesus was on trial. At each step the young monk kissed the stone and repeated the Lord's Prayer, yet he reached the top of the steps with no clear understanding of how to get right with God. He later commented that he had gone to Rome with onions and had returned with garlic!

The monk's name was Martin Luther and even though he was still in this confused state the church appointed him to lecture in theology at the local university! He began by lecturing on the Psalms and in April 1515 began teaching from Romans. As he worked his way through the first chapter he came across words that (in the Bible version I am using in this present book) read, 'For in [the gospel] the righteousness of God is revealed from faith for faith, as it is written, "The righteous shall live by faith"' (Romans 1:17). Far from releasing him from his spiritual torment, this statement crushed him still further. He thought the phrase 'in [the gospel] the righteousness of God is revealed' meant that the gospel emphasized how righteous God was. The law of God had already shown him that (which was why he felt so crushed), yet now he was apparently being told that the gospel underlined what the law said. The effect was predictable: 'I wished that God had not made the gospel known, because this further revelation of God seemed to make me utterly hopeless and helpless. The revelation of God blocked the way.'

Night and day he wrestled to understand the meaning of Paul's words, until one day God graciously opened his spiritual eyes to see the truth. The gospel was not underlining the law's dreadful sentence, but revealing the only righteousness that was acceptable to God. This righteousness was not a reward for self-effort or disciplined living—let alone for making financial donations. For the first time, Luther saw that the gospel was the good news that by his life and death Jesus had put an end to the law of God as a means of salvation. In his perfect life he had kept the law in every part and in his death had paid the penalty a holy God demanded from sinners. The sword of God's justice had been sheathed in the body of his Son and the fires of his wrath quenched in his blood. As a result, everyone who turned from their own self-efforts and trusted wholly in Christ received the forgiveness of sins and eternal life. When this truth broke in on Luther his assessment of Paul's words was transformed:

> Then I grasped that the justice of God is that righteousness by which through grace and sheer mercy God justifies us through faith. Thereupon I felt myself to be reborn and to have gone through open doors into paradise. The whole of Scripture took on a new meaning, and whereas before the "justice of God" had filled me with hate, now it became to me inexpressibly sweet in greater love. This passage of Paul became to me a gate to heaven.

Luther's dramatic conversion triggered off the Protestant Reformation in 1517, with justification by faith—what Thomas Watson called 'the very hinge and pillar of Christianity'—as one of its greatest principles. Paul testified that his standing before God was based not on 'a righteousness of my own that comes from the law, but that which comes through faith in Christ, the righteousness from God that depends on faith' (Philippians 3:9). This life-giving doctrine became increasingly precious to Luther and he once told his congregation, 'I have preached justification by faith so often, and I feel sometimes that you are so slow to receive it, that I could almost take the Bible and bang it about your heads'! Centuries later the British hymn-writer Edward Mote put his own testimony in these memorable words:

My hope is built on nothing less
Than Jesus' blood and righteousness;
I dare not trust the sweetest frame,
But wholly lean on Jesus' name.
On Christ, the solid Rock, I stand;
All other ground is sinking sand.

When the going gets tough ...

Paul's quotation from Habakkuk shows us that the words have a fuller meaning and can be applied more widely than the prophet would have realized at the time. The Old Testament prophets did not grasp the full meaning of their prophecies or the precise way in which they would be fulfilled. The Holy Spirit revealed to them that in exercising their ministries they were serving not only their contemporaries but future generations (see 1 Peter 1:10–12). The important thing is that the Holy Spirit by whom the prophets were 'carried along' (2 Peter 1:21) knew the full meaning of all he gave them to say, then moved New Testament authors to quote or allude to Old Testament passages over 1,000 times. Paul's quotation in Romans helps us to understand the Christian gospel and how to respond to it. We will now see another New Testament book citing Habakkuk to establish a vital principle in living the Christian life.

It is generally agreed that the book of Hebrews was written to Jews who had become Christians. We are not told where they were living at the time, but this hardly affects its background or purpose. Converting from Judaism to Christianity would have been a massive and costly leap of faith, exposing the converts to fierce opposition, especially from the Jewish religious leaders. Young, immature Christians would at times have been sorely tempted to 'lean backwards' and to hold on to at least some of the Jewish customs and rituals that had been woven into the daily fabric of their lives and had once meant so much to them.

The writer of Hebrews spends a great deal of time urging them to see that as Christians they were living under a better covenant than the old one and that in Christ they had a better sacrifice for sin, better promises, a better hope and a better destiny. The words 'better' and 'superior' are used fifteen times in the letter to drive these truths home. Yet the writer also has a pastoral concern for them and sympathizes with the fact that as soon as they were converted they 'endured a hard struggle with sufferings, sometimes being publicly exposed to reproach and affliction' (Hebrews 10:32–33). These earlier believers were openly ridiculed, mocked and exposed to contempt. Some were being tempted to run for shelter under the old umbrella of Judaism, but the writer points them in a much better direction. Reminding them that even when under the severest pressure they had 'a better possession and an abiding one', he urges them, 'Therefore do not throw away your confidence' (Hebrews 10:34–35). This was not a stark directive with no substance to it. Instead, he adds two great promises. They were to persevere 'so that when you have done the will of God you may receive what is promised. For, "Yet a little while, and the coming one will come and will not delay"' (Hebrews 10:36–37). Their problems may have been lasting, but they were not everlasting. The day was coming when they would receive what Jesus had called 'the kingdom prepared for you from the foundation of the world' (Matthew 25:34)—and this everlasting era would be ushered in by the Second Coming of Christ.

Yet these promises, however certain, were for the future. What should they do in the meantime, when they were finding the going so difficult? The writer's answer to their unspoken question was to quote Habakkuk: '... but my righteous one shall live by faith' (Hebrews 10:38). Here is a bedrock principle for Christian living, one so fundamental that Christians are said to 'walk by faith, not by sight' (2 Corinthians 5.7).

Having shown the importance of faith, the author immediately goes on to give his readers this tightly-packed explanation of what it means: 'Now faith is the assurance of things hoped for, the conviction of things not seen' (Hebrews 11:1). Unpacking the meaning of key words here will help us to understand why the writer says that believers under pressure should 'live by faith'.

Some translations have the word 'substance' instead of 'assurance', but this can give the false impression that faith brings its object into existence. The 'things not seen' (heaven and the Second Coming of Christ) are realities whether or not people believe this to be the case. *Heaven is real.* At his ascension, Jesus entered bodily 'into heaven itself' (Hebrews 9:24). For God's people, who here on earth 'have no lasting city', it is 'the city that is to come' (Hebrews 13:14). *The Second Coming of Christ is real*—as real as if it had already happened. It is mentioned some 300 times in the New Testament alone and never with even a scintilla of uncertainty about it. C. S. Lewis wrote, 'If this is not an integral part of the faith once given to the saints, I do not know what is.' Jesus could not have made it clearer when he told his disciples, 'I will come again' (John 14:3) and the author of Hebrews is so sure about this that he even uses the phrase 'the coming one' to identify Jesus.

In normal use, the word 'hope' always has uncertainty mixed into its meaning. People hope they will be able to afford something they want, or hope to get a ticket for a particular event, or hope to be in time to catch a train, or hope that they will have fine weather while they are on holiday, but in every case there is always a possibility that their hopes will be dashed. In the New Testament the word 'hope' never has this element in it. It always means *unconditional certainty,* which is its sense in the phrase 'things hoped for'. Paul assures Christians of 'the hope laid up for you in heaven' (Colossians 1:5) and when elsewhere he refers to 'the appearing of the glory of our great God and Saviour' as 'our blessed hope' (Titus 2:13) he is not writing with his fingers crossed. Writing on what he calls 'the grace of faith', Matthew Henry says, 'Faith and hope go together; and the same things that are the object of our faith are the object of our hope.'

The Greek word translated 'conviction' is used in only one other place in the New Testament, where Paul says that one of the uses of Scripture is 'reproof' (2 Timothy 3:16), that is, for enabling a person to get a clear view of the reality of his sin. In the Hebrews context faith is what we could call spiritual eyesight, convincing the believer not only beyond all reasonable doubt but beyond *all* doubt, that the thing believed in is true. Physical eyesight convinces us of a natural object's reality, so that we say, 'Seeing is believing.' Spiritual eyesight convinces Christians of supernatural realities that cannot be seen with physical eyesight, enabling them to say in effect, 'Believing is seeing.' This kind of faith goes far beyond wishful thinking. All the promises of God are fulfilled in the Lord Jesus Christ (see 2 Corinthians 1:20) and faith enables believers to lay hold of him in such a way as to give them an inner conviction that these promises are theirs. Faith is their God-given title deed of all that God has promised to his people, both in this life and in the life to come. As the modern American preacher John MacArthur puts it, 'If we follow a God whose audible voice we have never heard and believe in a Christ we have never seen, we do so because our faith has a reality, a substance, an assurance that is unshakeable.'

Neither heaven nor the return of Jesus to the earth can be seen with our physical eyes, and as Christians face up to the problems, pressures and pains of life there is a sense in which we live in blissful blindness. We have no idea how the swirling circumstances of life fit into God's perfect plan for us, *nor do we need to know.* We may not know what the future holds, but we do know who holds the future, and this should satisfy and stabilize us. This needs to be firmly grasped in these days, when there is such a craze for signs and wonders, 'words of knowledge', extra-biblical revelation, 'a special word from God', or some other exciting phenomenon. To some believers this seems to be the only way to handle the pressures they face, but this approach has a fatal flaw: *it dismantles the fundamental principle of faith.* The drive to seek for special words of wisdom and knowledge is not only eccentric, it is unbiblical. J. I. Packer is spot on when he says, 'The truth is that God in his wisdom to make and keep us humble and to teach us to walk by faith has hidden from us almost everything that we should like to know about the providential purposes which he is working out in the church and in the world.'

This applies very directly to Christians facing severe trials. The solution that naturally appeals to us is their immediate removal. When we are sick, we want instant healing; when we are in financial difficulties, we want an instant injection of cash; when we have a problem, we want a prompt and complete answer. Yet faith has another option. This is how it is expressed by Joni Eareckson Tada, who as a teenager suffered terrible injuries in a 1967 swimming accident, yet eventually came through an emotional maelstrom into a secure faith that has been an inspiration to countless others over the years: 'When we learn to lean back on God's sovereignty, fixing and settling our thoughts on that unshakeable, unmoveable reality, we can experience great inner peace. Our troubles may not change, our pain may not diminish, our loss may not be restored, our problems may not fade with the new dawn, *but the power of those things to harm us is broken as we rest in the fact that God is in control*' (emphasis added). Joni has been a paraplegic for many years, but has discovered the sublime secret that the key to perseverance is to be found in Habakkuk's statement: 'The righteous shall live by his faith'.

The Bible encourages us to bring our needs to God in prayer, but we have no right to demand instant solutions. We have no biblical basis on which to claim good health, financial riches, success in business, or any of the other things shamelessly offered by those who preach that whenever we have a need we simply imagine the instant fix, then 'name it and claim it'. What we *can* claim is the promise God gave to Paul when he declined to answer the apostle's prayer to be delivered from his 'thorn … in the flesh'. This was to assure him that, 'My grace is sufficient for you' (2 Corinthians 12:7, 9). In his book *The Sovereignty of God* A. W. Pink writes,

> Faith endures 'as seeing him who is invisible' (Hebrews 11:27). Faith endures the disappointments, the hardships and the heartaches of life by recognizing that all comes

from the hand of him who is too wise to err and too loving to be unkind. So long as we are occupied with any other object than God himself, there will be neither rest for the heart, nor peace for the mind. But when we receive all that enters our lives as from his hand, then no matter what may be our circumstances or surroundings ... we shall be enabled to say, 'The lines have fallen for me in pleasant places.' (Psalm 16:6)

His story

We can now turn back to Habakkuk and to the context in which he wrote his 'major point'. The prophet was deeply concerned for the spiritual welfare of Judah and his passionate prayer was that God would intervene to arrest its downward spiral. In response God told him that he was going to unleash the vicious Chaldeans against the nation. A modern parallel would be God responding to the prayers of Christians in the United Kingdom concerned about its spiritual decline by saying that he was going to allow the militant Islamist organization al-Qaeda to sweep into the nation and overcome it, deporting the cream of the population. It is no wonder that Habakkuk was baffled and that God's answer produced an even bigger question. It was in precisely this kind of situation that God's ultimate word to Habakkuk was, 'the righteous shall live by his faith' (2:4).

This tells us that nothing, not even the most calamitous of national or international developments, must be allowed to shake our utter confidence in the settled sovereignty of God, who 'works all things according to the counsel of his will' (Ephesians 1:11). God is not merely observing history; he is orchestrating it for his eternal glory and for his people's eternal good. *History is his story*. This is why Paul was able to write, 'And we know that for those who love God all things work together for good, for those who are called according to his purpose' (Romans 8:28). When for unbelievers things seem to be getting better and better, they are in fact getting worse and worse, as every day takes them closer to their dreadful destiny. When for even the weakest of God's people things seem to be getting worse and worse, they are in fact getting better and better as every day brings them closer to their glorious reward in heaven.

History is not going around in circles. As the modern British preacher John Benton says, 'The biblical view of history is not cyclical, it is linear. It has a definite beginning, with God's creation of the universe, and it is building to a final climax.' It is moving inexorably and at God's ordained pace towards the time when, as he revealed to Habakkuk, 'the earth will be filled with the knowledge of the glory of the LORD as the waters cover the sea' (2:14). The entire universe will eventually acknowledge that 'his kingdom rules over all' (Psalm 103:19).

Long before the days of digital technology, my father's hobby was repairing watches. When he unscrewed the back of a watch I was fascinated to see so many cogs, wheels and levers moving this way and that and seeming to make no sense at all. But when the watch was turned over and seen from the other side I realized that all the complicated and seemingly conflicting parts were combining to move the hands steadily in one secure direction. For even the best of Christians there are times when life seems so fractured and fragile that they may wonder, 'What in the world is happening?' When personal disaster strikes there is sometimes the temptation to ask, 'Why me?' Yet however severe the trial or painful the circumstances this betrays time-tied thinking. Paul pointed to a much more secure approach when he wrote, 'We are afflicted in every way, but not crushed; perplexed, but not driven to despair; persecuted, but not forsaken; struck down, but not destroyed' (2 Corinthians 4:8–9). He saw that even the worst thing that happens to God's people 'is preparing us for an eternal weight of glory beyond all comparison, as we look not to things that are seen but to the things that are unseen. For the things that are seen are transient, but the things that are unseen are eternal' (2 Corinthians 4:17–18).

When Christians 'turn the watch over' at the end of life they will see that in spite of all the pain, pressure and perplexity everything was working together for God's glory and for their good. As the nineteenth-century American theologian Tryon Edwards wrote,

'All the world's ends, arrangements, changes, disappointments, hopes and fears are without meaning if not seen and estimated by eternity.' Christians are not exempt from life's pains and pressures, conflicts and confusions, but when facing these we are to rest in the assurance that 'we are waiting for new heavens and a new earth in which righteousness dwells' (2 Peter 3:13).

PS

There is space for one last comment on Habakkuk's 'major point'. The literal translation of his words from the original Hebrew is: 'The righteous one will live by his faithfulness' and the phrase may be deliberately ambiguous. Whose faithfulness is meant? Is it the believer's or God's? The ambiguity may explain why the Septuagint rendered it, 'The righteous one will live by *my* faithfulness.' If this is what is meant, it takes away nothing of what we have seen in this chapter, as God would be saying to Habakkuk, 'Those who are truly righteous will remain faithful to me because of my faithfulness to them in giving them the grace to remain faithful to me.'

Be that as it may, by the time Habakkuk signed off he had passionately embraced the truth of what he had written. At the end of the book the prophet honestly admits that initially the thought of the Chaldean invasion was terrifying: 'I hear, and my body trembles; my lips quiver at the sound; rottenness enters into my bones; my legs tremble beneath me' (3:16). Yet he saw beyond the coming terror to the time when the Chaldeans would get their comeuppance. God had promised this by pronouncing five 'Woes' on them (see 2:6, 9, 12, 15, 19). Each one of these reflected their sins and all of them culminated in their nation's obliteration by the Persians in 539 BC. Habakkuk would not have known this timetable or precisely how God was to punish Judah's enemies for their sins, but he would 'quietly wait for the day of trouble to come upon people who invade us' (3:16).

Then comes Habakkuk's triumphant testimony that faith had overcome his fear. Even if the Chaldeans' invasion of Judah included a scorched earth policy, so that the country's crops would fail and there would be no sheep or cattle left (see 3:17, which lists the sources of the nation's staple foods) nothing would shake his confidence in God. He would still cry, 'I will rejoice in the LORD; I will take joy in the God of my salvation' (3:18). But how could he do that if everything around him was falling apart? The answer comes in his final sentence: 'GOD, the Lord, is my strength; he makes my feet like the deer's; he makes me tread on my high places' (3:19). Habakkuk's faith was not in his faith, but in the faithfulness of God, and as Anthony Sevlaggio points out, 'The Bible teaches us that our ultimate destiny is not based on our faithfulness, but rather on his'.

Habakkuk's circumstances had not changed. The nation was still a moral cesspit, the godly were still a tiny remnant—and the Chaldeans were on their way. Yet God enabled the prophet to see beyond the circumstances to the One who reigned over all of them and whose sovereign purposes for his people could never be thwarted. Habakkuk may not have understood God's ways, but he was certain that he could trust his wisdom. He had the God-given faith that was 'the assurance of things hoped for, the conviction of things not seen'. The message is hugely relevant to God's people today as we live in the period between God's biblical promises and their final fulfilment. As the modern British preacher John Legg testifies, 'The only way to honour and trust God's sovereign power and care is to exclude absolutely nothing from it.'

The eighteenth-century British poet and hymn-writer William Cowper's life was often plagued by bouts of severe depression, yet when his thinking was clear his writing reflected biblical truth in a way that has been a means of blessing to countless people over the years. In a hymn that included these words (I have quoted the last line as he originally wrote it) Cowper captured the essence of Habakkuk's 'major point':

> God moves in a mysterious way
> His wonders to perform;
> He plants his footsteps in the sea,
> And rides upon the storm.
> Judge not the Lord by feeble sense,

But trust him for his grace;
Behind a frowning providence
He hides a smiling face.
His purposes will ripen fast,
Unfolding every hour;
The bud may have a bitter taste,
But wait to smell the flower.

God's to do list
Deal, Save, Gather, Change

ZEPHANIAH

One possible reason why the Minor Prophets remain 'clean pages' in most people's Bibles is that they seem at first glance to contain little but gloom and doom, but is this a fair assessment? We would have to agree that although these twelve books contain some of the most vivid language in the entire Bible they are not to be recommended for light reading or to get a quick pick-me-up. As the twentieth-century American preacher Mario Di Gangi put it, 'If you are looking for some light-hearted scherzo or trivial minuet you won't find it here.'

Yet to write off the Minor Prophets as being nothing more than merchants of misery is to ignore some of the most exhilarating and heartening statements in Scripture. They record God saying about his people, 'I will love them freely, for my anger has turned from them' (Hosea 14:4). One Minor Prophet asks, 'Who is a God like you, pardoning iniquity and passing over transgression for the remnant of his inheritance …?' (Micah 7:18) and another looks forward to the day when 'the LORD will be king over all the earth. On that day the LORD will be one and his name one' (Zechariah 14:9).

Cue Zephaniah

This leads us directly to Zephaniah, who introduces himself

as 'the son of Cushi, son of Gedaliah, son of Amariah, son of Hezekiah' (1:1). This is the longest genealogy we have for any of the biblical prophets and tells us that as the great-great-grandson of Hezekiah, the fourteenth king of Judah, Zephaniah may have been the only one with royal blood in his veins. The prophet Isaiah was 'the son of Amoz' (Isaiah 1:1), a man Jewish tradition claims to have been a brother of Amaziah, king of Judah, but there is no written evidence of this.

Zephaniah prophesied 'in the days of Josiah the son of Amon, king of Judah' (1:1), who was also descended from Hezekiah and reigned from 640 to 609 BC. Josiah replaced his evil father Amon, whose two-year reign was riddled with immorality and corruption and who was assassinated in a palace coup. In complete contrast Josiah, who became king when he was eight years old and began to rule actively ten years later, 'did what was right in the eyes of the LORD ... and he did not turn aside to the right or to the left' (2 Kings 22:2).

Josiah may have been something of a figurehead in his pre-teen years but by the time he took over the levers of power he was truly committed to God. He destroyed centres of idolatry and vice, reformed temple worship, restored the Passover feast and worked tirelessly to clean up the polluted legacy his father had bequeathed to him. However, these reforms had yet to take place when Zephaniah was called to the prophetic ministry, at which time the nation had been in a moral and spiritual tailspin for about fifty years. Things were in such a state that he could define Jerusalem as 'rebellious and defiled' (3:1). He also pinpoints the basic reason for its ruin: 'She does not trust in the LORD; she does not draw near to her God' (3:2).

It seems very likely that he was either a native or a long-time resident of Jerusalem as he wrote of it as 'this place' (1:4) and refers to locations such as 'the Fish Gate' and 'the Second Quarter' as well as 'the hills' and 'the Mortar' (1:10–11). Be that as it may, virtually the whole of Chapter 2 is given over to pronouncing God's fearful judgement on the pagan nations that surrounded Judah. These were Philistia (including its city-states of Gaza, Ashkelon, Ashdod,

Gath and Ekron) to the west, the Philistines, Moab and Ammon to the east, Ethiopia (the Cushites) to the south and Assyria to the north. The language Zephaniah uses against these nations and people is terrifying. Gaza will become 'deserted' and Ashkelon 'a desolation'; Ashdod's population will be 'driven out'; the lands of the Cherethites will be destroyed 'until no inhabitant is left' (2:4–5); Moab and Ammon would be 'possessed by nettles and salt pits, and a waste for ever' (2:9); and Assyria would become 'a desolation, a dry waste in the desert' (2:13).

Prophecies like these prompted the Scottish preacher George Adam Smith to write, 'No hotter book lies in all the Old Testament.' Sceptics even say that passages like Zephaniah 2 show God to be totally lacking in common decency, let alone justice. Militant critics go much further. In his book *The God Delusion*, the well-known modern atheist Richard Dawkins writes, 'The God of the Old Testament is arguably the most unpleasant character in all fiction: ... a petty, unjust, unforgiving control-freak; a vindictive, bloodthirsty ethnic cleanser ... a capriciously malevolent bully.' Those familiar with his other prejudiced attempts to interpret the Bible will not be surprised to learn that this is no more than his own distorted caricature of God. As Dawkins lacks even a nodding acquaintance with biblical truth, his jaundiced opinions can be safely ignored. The distinguished American physician and geneticist Francis Collins, best-known for his leadership of the Human Genome Project, has rightly said, 'Dawkins is a master of setting up a straw man and then dismantling it with great relish.' Dawkins also overlooks the fact that the nations against which God executed such severe judgement were not perfectly respectable people who had done nothing to deserve any kind of punishment. They were pagan idolaters, sworn enemies of God and his people and steeped in violence, greed, injustice and immorality. How could a holy God of perfect justice ignore this? The Bible teaches, 'God is a righteous judge, a God who expresses his wrath every day' (Psalm 7:11, NIV). His holiness inevitably results in his anger at sin of any kind, something consistently shown throughout Scripture and no less true today.

Home truths

Zephaniah's prophecies against the heathen are terrifying, yet he has searing words to say to Judah. He begins by targeting religious leaders, singling out 'idolatrous priests' (1:4) and those who 'bow down and swear to the LORD and yet swear by Milcom' (1:5). Milcom was a pagan god described elsewhere in the Bible as 'the abomination of the Ammonites' (1 Kings 11:5) yet priests in Jerusalem were swearing by him while claiming to worship the true God. The socially elite are then condemned as those who 'array themselves in foreign attire' (1:8), which may mean that they leaned towards foreign (and pagan) trends and fashions. Next came the business community, whose members would soon 'cry' and 'wail' and be 'cut off' (1:10–11). Zephaniah does not specify their sins, but we know from his contemporary, Micah, that greed and corruption were rife in their ranks.

The general state of the nation was such that God warned, 'I will stretch out my hand against Judah and against all the inhabitants of Jerusalem' (1:4). This should have got Judah's urgent attention, but apparently it did no such thing. God had graciously sent the nation one warning after another, but as all the previous prophecies had not come to pass people believed that Zephaniah's prophecy was just another scare story. They saw no way in which God would disturb their chosen way of life: 'The LORD will not do good, nor will he do ill' (1:12). As far as they were concerned, life could go on as usual and there was no need to be concerned about divine intervention. Little did they know that Zephaniah was the last of the prophets to warn them of their impending doom.

The ungodly often take Judah's approach. One of the psalmists notes of such a person, 'He says in his heart, "God has forgotten, he has hidden his face, he will never see it"' (Psalm 10:11). Countless people with only vague ideas about the existence of God find it difficult to believe that he is aware of everything they think, say and do and rarely give any thought to the possibility that they are answerable to him for every part of their lives. They are oblivious to the fact that 'no creature is hidden from his sight; but all are naked and exposed to the eye of him to whom we must give account' (Hebrews 4:13). Zephaniah warns Judah that God would ensure that those who made that catastrophic mistake and who in their breathtaking arrogance treated him so lightly would be sought out and punished: 'I will search Jerusalem with lamps, and I will punish the men who are complacent' (1:12).

Many of the prophets wrote about 'the day of the LORD', in referring to what Gareth Crossley calls 'a complex interweaving of momentous events', each one marking God's dramatic intervention in human history. These included God's impending punishment for sin, the return of God's people to their homeland after captivity in Babylon, the first coming of Messiah and his eventual return to the earth to usher in the final day of judgement. No Minor Prophet emphasizes 'the day of the LORD' more than Zephaniah, who mentions it twenty times, including this statement which we will take as our 'major point':

The great day of the LORD is near, near and hastening fast.

(1:14)

In its immediate sense this prophecy was fulfilled shortly afterwards when the Babylonians mounted a devastating attack on the nation, ransacked Jerusalem and swept untold thousands of people off to captivity. Zephaniah also refers to 'the day of the LORD' in connection with the survivors' release from captivity and the coming of Messiah to earth. These three 'days' (the Babylonian invasion, the exiles' return to Judah and the first coming of Messiah to earth) are already past. In this chapter we will concentrate on the remaining one, which relates to the future return of Messiah and the other awesome events that this will trigger off.

It is impossible to read the Bible honestly and miss its insistence that the Second Coming of Christ will lead to a day of final judgement, when all of humanity will stand before its Maker and hear its eternal destiny declared. For Old Testament prophets this is the ultimate 'day of the LORD', the culmination of all the immediate and intermediate expressions of his holiness, justice and hatred of sin. This is what Zephaniah has in mind in the longest section of his prophecy, in which he warns of the terrible but righteous judgement that God will execute upon the world.

Sceptics try to shrug off the whole idea that they are answerable to their Maker, but one wonders whether they are ever entirely successful, as the idea of justice seems built into our moral DNA. In the opinion of the twentieth-century American philosopher, historian and theologian Rousas John Rushdoony, 'The whole of recorded history is one great longing for justice.' There is a universal instinct that people should get what they deserve; good should be rewarded and evil should be punished. This points to the world being a moral creation and at least hints at the certainty of its coming to a moral conclusion. God's interventions in time and space, both to reward and to punish—J. I. Packer says, 'Judgement does not sit twiddling its thumbs until the end of the age'—point to him being a God of *ultimate* justice. It is not difficult to work out why most people would rather not think about this, so try to suppress the whole idea, but four words about the final day of reckoning and its outcome will help to get a clear picture of what the Bible teaches.

Factual

Nothing is more clearly taught in the Bible than there will be a final and universal judgement of all mankind on what Zephaniah calls 'the great day of the LORD'. The writer of Hebrews says that 'the resurrection of the dead, and eternal judgement' (Hebrews 6:2) are not to be thought of as debatable or secondary issues, but form part of foundational biblical truth. Two-thirds of the parables Jesus told were related to the coming day of judgement. The apostle Paul told Greek philosophers in Athens, 'God ... has fixed a day on which he will judge the world in righteousness' (Acts 17:31). The word 'fixed' comes from a Greek verb meaning 'to single out'. With all of future time at his disposal God has settled on a precise moment when he will publish humankind's final accounts. Nobody on earth knows when that will be, but it is firmly fixed in God's calendar and nothing can move it.

It is important to notice that the day of final judgement will not be the day when God's final verdicts are *decided*, but when they will be *disclosed*. The apostle Paul warns evildoers, '... do you presume on the riches of (God's) kindness and forbearance and patience, not knowing that God's kindness is meant to lead you to repentance? But because of your hard and impenitent heart you are storing up wrath for yourself on the day of wrath when God's righteous judgement will be *revealed*' (Romans 2:4–5, emphasis added). This fits in perfectly with what Zephaniah tells the people of Judah. They had played fast and loose with all the warnings that earlier prophets had given them, but in doing so they were only making things worse for themselves and the day would come when their fatal behaviour would be exposed.

God's final judgement is a certainty and one of the main concerns of the Old Testament prophets is that people should see the distinction between the way God deals with the wicked not only during time but also at the end of time. Isaiah has both in mind when he writes, '... the haughtiness of man will be humbled, and the lofty pride of men shall be brought low, and the LORD alone will be exalted in that day' (Isaiah 2:17). This is a massively important issue, as the glory of God is at stake. If there is ultimately no difference between rejecting God and submitting to him, all the Christian faith has to offer is yet another brand of religious moralism—and a pretty miserable one at that for, 'If in this life only we have hoped in Christ, we are of all people most to be pitied' (1 Corinthians 15:19). If there is to be no day of reckoning, all the discipline and praying and watching, all the fighting against temptation and striving after holiness will prove to have been a waste of time. The Minor Prophets want us to realize that this is not the case, that God is a God of justice and that our eternal destiny is at stake.

When they write about the deliverance of God's people, about the yoke of the enemy being broken, about restoration and salvation the prophets are referring not only to immediate and intermediate events, but about those that will ultimately take place at the end of time, when God's elect will spend eternity in 'new heavens and a new earth, in which righteousness dwells' (2 Peter 3:13). When they write about God's enemies being captured, punished and destroyed they are again referring not only to immediate and intermediate events, but about what will ultimately take place when the ungodly will 'go away into eternal punishment' (Matthew 25:46). Malachi writes that on the day of final judgement 'you shall *see* the distinction between the righteous and the wicked, between the one who serves God and one who does not serve him' (Malachi 3:18, emphasis added). For the time being men can debate the issue with passion, some arguing that those who seek to obey God are no better off than those who deny that he even exists. On the day of final judgement endless debate will be replaced by an eternal distinction.

Throughout history there have always been those who rejected the whole idea of a day of reckoning. In the long term, to say, 'The LORD will not do good, nor will he do ill' (1:12) is to rule God out altogether and therefore to say that 'the day of the LORD' is merely religious fiction. Foremost among the 'day deniers' are *annihilationists*, who say with the Roman philosopher Seneca, a contemporary of Jesus, 'There is nothing after death and death itself is nothing.' The twentieth-century British thinker Bertrand Russell put it more bluntly: 'When I die I shall rot'. Annihilationism is the logical position of four major philosophies followed by countless millions of people today.

The first is atheism. As this denies the existence of God, the idea that God stands at the end of time as the universal judge of humankind is treated as pure fiction. The second is materialism, which says that as matter is the only reality we can discount any thought of moral and spiritual accountability. The third is existentialism, which says that the only real meaning life has is that which the individual concerned gives to it during his or her lifetime, and that when that life comes to an end, nothing of value remains. The fourth is secular humanism, which rejects the supernatural in any way, shape or form. All four philosophies are not only crude but cruel, as they imply that good and evil are of no eternal consequence and that there will never be a righting of the present life's myriad wrongs. They also contradict the Bible's clear teaching that the day is coming when 'God will judge the righteous and the wicked' (Ecclesiastes 3:17).

Other 'judgement day deniers' are universalists. Some of them believe in God, while others have vague ideas left over from their religious upbringing, or cling to scraps of information about God picked up as they have gone through life. What they share is the belief that at the end of life God will receive everybody into heaven regardless of what they believed and how they behaved and without any need to show a moral 'passport'. The Kray Twins, Reggie and Ronnie, were notorious London gangsters during the nineteen-fifties and the nineteen-sixties and were involved in murders, violent assaults, armed robberies, arson and protection rackets. Ronnie died in prison in 1995 and five years later Reggie was released on compassionate grounds shortly before his death. Writing the day after Reggie's funeral, a reporter told *Daily Mail* readers, 'His sins, which were many, were forgiven and forgotten the moment he met God.' This kind of universalism, with no concrete evidence to back it up, is no more than wishful thinking. It implies that meeting with God after death is a glorified prize-giving, with everybody a winner. The Bible says otherwise and declares, '[God] will judge the world with righteousness, and the peoples with equity' (Psalm 98:9). There is no way in which this declaration can be spun to mean that good and evil will be treated in exactly the same way. Nobody who reads Zephaniah seriously can ever come to the conclusion that 'the great day of the LORD' can be confidently brushed aside. Six times in the first four verses of his book he records God emphasizing the certainty of his judgement with the words 'I will' and these four verses alone are sufficient to put an end to the hopes of the annihilationist and the dreams of the universalist.

Fearful

The modern American film producer Woody Allen famously said, 'I'm not afraid of dying. I just don't want to be there when it happens.' Countless people with no faith in God claim to have no fear of death, but they ignore the fact that although death is certain it does not mean the end of personal existence. As the Bible makes clear, '... it is appointed for man to die once, *and after that comes judgement*' (Hebrews 9:27, emphasis added). Death marks the end of temporal existence here on earth, but the beginning of eternal existence beyond the grave. To have no fear of death is an irrelevance, as it is only the first of two appointments we all face, the second being final judgement at God's hands. The British racing driver Stirling Moss, winner of sixteen Formula One Grand Prix races, reflected this when at the height of his career in the nineteen-fifties he confessed, 'I am frightened of death. I know it means going to meet one's Maker, and one shouldn't be afraid of that. But I am.'

For the rest of this chapter we will concentrate on what death will bring to the ungodly, whose destiny will be revealed on 'the day of the LORD' by a righteous and holy God who is 'the Judge of all the earth' (Genesis 18:25) and who has already declared that as far as heaven is concerned, 'nothing unclean will ever enter it' (Revelation 21:27). When we consider the holiness of God, his perfect and complete knowledge of every thought, word and action of every human being who has ever lived, his righteous anger against sin of every kind and his perfect justice, it is easy to see why the Bible says that as far as unforgiven sinners are concerned, 'It is a fearful thing to fall into the hands of the living God' (Hebrews 10:31). Wrongdoers and lawbreakers can go through life cleverly evading many of the consequences they deserve, but death puts an end to dodging and they will ultimately be brought to account. As John Calvin bluntly put it, 'We often escape from men; we cannot escape the judgement of God.'

Some people give occasional thought to the final day of judgement, but think of it as rather like going through Customs at an airport, hoping that they will not be stopped and questioned too closely. I returned home from the United States on one occasion when my wife was with me (usually a guarantee that we would return with heavier suitcases and lighter wallets!). I did some quick calculations on the homeward flight and estimated that we might have to pay £150.00 in duty. When the Customs officer asked if we had anything to declare, we showed him a list of items and a sheaf of receipts. He looked briefly at these and then to our amazement said, 'Go on through. I won't charge you anything.' I nearly asked for his name and details of when he was normally on duty! On the final day of judgement the picture will be very different, as the verdict will not depend on the judge's mood or whim. For those who did not get right with God while living on earth it will be 'a day of distress and anguish, a day of ruin and devastation, a day of darkness and gloom, a day of clouds and thick darkness' (1:15). In Matthew Henry's words, 'Those who will not deliver themselves into the hand of God's mercy cannot be delivered out of the hand of his justice.'

For such people, this judgement is truly fearful, as they will hear the dreadful words, 'Depart from me, you cursed, into the eternal fire prepared for the devil and his angels' (Matthew 25:41). The Bible's most common word for this is 'hell'. Over the centuries poets and other authors have come up with many lurid descriptions of hell. One wrote of the ungodly 'hanging by their tongues, while the flaming fire torments them from beneath'. Another described a vision in which he saw a man suffering such torments in hell that 'The flames of fire gushed out from his ears and eyes and nostrils and at every pore.' In his famous fourteenth-century work *La Divina Commedia (The Divine Comedy)* the Italian poet Dante Alighiere wrote of souls being battered by an 'infernal hurricane', which describes hell's victims 'tearing each other apart with their teeth'. Yet these descriptions, and others like them are nothing more than speculation and we need to look elsewhere for solid truth on the subject.

To believe in heaven but not in hell is to claim that there were times when Jesus was telling truth and times when he was lying. It has been calculated that of 1,870 verses recording words spoken by Jesus, thirteen per cent are about judgement and hell. Then what is hell like? A few years ago a report circulated saying that scientists in Siberia had drilled a hole nine miles deep and that a sensitive listening device had picked up the sound of millions of humans screaming in agony from a massive subterranean cavern calculated by the scientists to be over 1,000 degrees

Celsius. This led to speculation that they had eavesdropped on hell, but the report eventually proved to be a hoax, and in any case its findings have no basis in the Bible. The modern theologian Reinhold Niebuhr writes, 'It is unwise for Christians to claim any knowledge of either the furniture of heaven or of the temperature of hell', but this disguises the fact that the Bible gives us a number of telling images that are sufficient for us to know that it is what someone has called 'the ultimate horror of God's universe'.

It is a rubbish dump. When Jesus warned hypocrites that they would be 'sentenced to hell' (Matthew 23:33) the word he used for 'hell' was *Gehenna*. This was based on *Ge Hinnom*, a place just outside of Jerusalem into which all the city's filth was dumped, along with the bodies of dead animals and the corpses of criminals. All of this was then left to rot or to be destroyed by the fire that was always burning there. I often think of hell when I visit my local rubbish dump, as everything taken there is considered by its owner to be of no further value. There are mountains of refuse from people's gardens and rubbish from their homes, all of it considered worthless. There is not a single attractive feature about the site and I always get away from it as soon as I can. Jesus used the word *Gehenna* a further ten times, as if to underline the gruesome truth that all who go to hell are utterly worthless. C. S. Lewis captured some of what this means when he wrote, 'To enter hell is to be banished from humanity.'

It is a prison. Jesus urged people to get right with God while they had opportunity to do so. He said that doing this would be like settling a lawsuit out of court rather than letting the accuser 'drag you to the judge, and the judge hand you over to the officer, and the officer put you in prison' (Luke 12:58). Many years ago I was Secretary to the States of Guernsey Prison Board and my duties often took me into the island's prison. My emotions were always stirred when I saw prisoners locked away from society in that miserable place, yet they were never abused or ill-treated. They had regular meals, opportunities for recreation and access to other amenities. Prisons in civilized countries sometimes have comfortable beds, libraries, colour television and reasonable exercise facilities as well as opportunities to develop friendships, learn a trade, study for examinations or even earn a university degree. Hell is very different. There will be no comforts, pleasures or friendships, nor will there be any facilities for rest or recreation. Its inmates are in 'the pit of destruction' (Psalm 55:23) and are utterly without instinct or opportunity to achieve anything. In earthly prisons only the body is confined, while the spirit is free to create, imagine, anticipate, hope—and even worship—but in hell both 'soul and body' (Matthew 10:28) are imprisoned.

It is a place of utter darkness. Jesus said that on the day of final judgement the ungodly will be 'thrown into the outer darkness' (Matthew 8:12) and the apostle Peter calls it 'gloomy darkness' (2 Peter 2:4). In both cases the emphasis points to hell being infinitely worse than any physical, mental or spiritual darkness ever experienced on earth. Zephaniah prophesies that 'the great day of the LORD' will be 'a day of darkness and gloom, a day of clouds and thick darkness' (1:15) for God's enemies. It may be impossible for us to imagine a place with no dawns, no morning sunlight, no clear blue sky and no soft evening light, but Matthew Henry reflected the Bible's teaching when he wrote of hell as a place of darkness 'without any remainder, or mixture, or hope, of light; not the least gleam or glimpse of it'.

It is a place of fire. The Bible uses fire as a picture of hell over twenty times. One of the Minor Prophets wrote of God's anger at sin being 'poured out like fire' (Nahum 1:6) and in the Sermon on the Mount (which many people who would not accept the Bible as the Word of God claim to be the basis of their moral code) Jesus warned that the ungodly were 'liable to the hell of fire' (Matthew 5:22).

The image of hell as a place of fire is terrifying and when we grasp what it means it becomes even worse. It is common for people to think of hell in terms of being separated from God for ever, but the Bible does not say this. Instead, it teaches that the ungodly will spend eternity *in the presence of God*, who is described in the Bible as 'a consuming fire' (Hebrews 12:29). People resolutely opposed to God would gladly settle for being separated from him for ever. The twentieth-century French philosopher (and passionate atheist) Jean-Paul Sartre, wrote, 'The last thing I want is to be subject to the unremitting gaze of a holy God.' Yet the Bible makes it clear that in eternity those who reject God will be 'be tormented ... in the presence of the holy angels *and in the presence of the Lamb*' (Revelation 14:10, emphasis added), enduring un-ending, conscious punishment. As 'the Lamb' is a biblical title for the Lord Jesus Christ, into whose hands the judgement of all mankind has been committed, this tells us that the ungodly will be inescapably faced with the glory, majesty and holiness of the one they rejected while on earth. They will know nothing of his grace, love, mercy, kindness, forgiveness or patience, but will be relentlessly exposed to the awesome fire of his righteous and unrestricted anger. After a careful study of what the Bible taught on the subject the Puritan preacher John Flavel concluded, 'The worst terrors of the prisoners in hell come from the presence of the Lamb.' Small wonder that for those who reject God there remains nothing but 'a fearful expectation of judgement' (Hebrews 10:27).

Fair

Time and again I have been asked, 'How can a God of love send anybody to hell?' but the question misses two criticially important points. The first is that God is not only a God of love but a God of utter holiness whose very nature ensures his unchanging anger at sin—and as 'all have sinned and fall short of the glory of God' (Romans 3:23) all men are by nature exposed to it. The Bible says more about God's anger than it does about his love and we dare not ignore one and concentrate on the other; as an article in *Punch* put it, 'You can't just have the bits of God you like and leave out the stuff you're not so happy with.' God does not send *people* to hell, he sends *sinners* to hell and as Zechariah declares that 'The LORD ... is righteous' and 'does no injustice' (3:5), God condemning unrepentant sinners to hell leaves no stain on his character. He is 'the righteous judge' (2 Timothy 4:8) and takes no vindictive pleasure in doing so. A human judge is not taking revenge on a criminal when sentencing him a life imprisonment and when the divine Judge sentences sinners to eternal punishment he is not acting out of spite or in retaliation. As it is impossible for God to do anything that would violate who he is, the question to ask is, 'How can a God of holiness allow anyone into heaven?'

The second point is that those who despise God's authority and reject God's patience and love are designing their own appalling destiny. J. I. Packer says, 'Nobody stands under the wrath of God save those who have chosen to do so. The essence of God's action in wrath is to give men what they choose, in all its implications; nothing more, and equally nothing less.' Jesus described himself as 'the light of the world' (John 8:12) and warned, '... the light has come into the world, and people loved the darkness rather than the light because their deeds were evil' (John 3:19). Even in countries ruled by authorities opposed to biblical teaching there are no man-made laws that make it impossible for people to acknowledge God's existence, thank him for his goodness, seek his forgiveness and grace, pray for his help or try to live in a way that would be acceptable to him. Although doing all of these things falls short of what is needed to experience a living relationship with God, millions of people choose to ignore them all and 'do their own thing'. C. S. Lewis is right when he says, 'There are only two kinds of people in the end: those who say to God, "Thy will be done" and those to whom God says, in the end, "Thy will be done". All that are in hell choose it.'

Final

Most judicial systems have a carefully designed structure that allows convicted criminals to appeal to a higher court. In England, serious crime is tried in the Crown Court. A person convicted there could appeal on a point of law to the Criminal Division of the Court of Appeal. If this appeal failed, he could then appeal to the Supreme Court. This is the final court of appeal in England, but the appellant could then take his case one step further, to the European Court of Human Rights. That would be the end of the road, as England recognizes no higher court. By contrast, God's verdicts on 'the day of the LORD' are irreversible as there is no higher authority to which anyone could possibly appeal. God's word is absolutely final.

The other sense in which God's verdict on the ungodly is final is that those condemned to hell will never be released from their sentence. Zephaniah suggests this when he prophesies that Moab will be 'a waste for ever' (2:9). In June 1964 Nelson Mandela, an anti-apartheid campaigner in South Africa convicted of trying to overthrow the government, was sentenced to life imprisonment. For the first fifteen years this included hard labour, breaking boulders in a limestone quarry on Robben Island, a penal colony offshore from Cape Town. He was later moved to Pollsmoor Prison, then Victor Verster Prison Farm near Cape Town and on 11 February 1990 was released from captivity in a massive media event seen on television by millions all around the world. Including time spent awaiting his trial, Mandela had spent nearly 10,000 days in prison. He was in his late forties when jailed and in his late seventies when released. Writing in *TIME* magazine he told of 'long, lonely, wasted years' yet said that he never gave up hope because he knew of the constant pressure being brought to bear for his release. He spent twenty-seven years in prison, but the rest of his life in freedom.

For those imprisoned in hell the story is very different. The Bible never mentions Purgatory or parole, but says, 'When the wicked dies, his hope will perish' (Proverbs 11:7). It clearly teaches that nobody in hell will ever be released. The twentieth-century British evangelist Leonard Ravenhill used to preach, 'There are a million roads into hell, but not one road out of it.' Nowhere does this terrible truth come across more clearly than when Jesus told people what would happen when he judged the world. After warning his hearers that he would tell the ungodly, 'Depart from me, you cursed, into the *eternal* fire prepared for the devil and his angels', he added, 'And these will go away into *eternal* punishment, but the righteous into *eternal* life' (Matthew 25:41, 46, emphasis added). The words I have emphasized translate the identical Greek word *aionios* and it is important to realize that Jesus was not teaching philosophers, theologians or professors of linguistics. He was speaking to ordinary men and women and he made it crystal clear to them that both destinies are endless. The thought of countless people enduring appalling agony for ever pounds at our emotions like a relentless sledgehammer, yet we must submit to all that Scripture says and not merely to whatever sits comfortably with our instincts or feelings. When we stand under Scripture we will be forced to agree with the Puritan preacher Thomas Brooks, who wrote, 'The damned shall live as long in hell as God himself shall live in heaven.'

Near and getting nearer

Zephaniah's prophecy about 'the day of the LORD' had a note of urgency about it. He warned his hearers that it was not only 'near' (1:7) but 'near and hastening fast' (1:14). As far as the first stage of its fulfilment was concerned, Judah's devastation was only a few years away, but what of its ultimate future fulfilment?

The end of time will be ushered in by the personal return of the Lord Jesus Christ to the earth, something prophesied some 300 times in the New Testament alone. Is this 'near and hastening fast'? Preaching on the Day of Pentecost, seven weeks after Jesus had risen from the dead, Peter said that the world was then in 'the last days' before 'the day of the Lord comes' (Acts 2:17, 20), while some time later one of Jesus' brothers wrote, '... the coming of the Lord is at hand ... the Judge is standing at the door' (James 5:8–9). Countless books have been written on the subject of eschatology (doctrines broadly covering the end of time and specifically about death, judgement, heaven and hell) and the subject has often generated more heat than light.

Much of the output centres on the mention in the last book in the Bible of a period of 'a thousand years' (Revelation 20:4, 7). Will this 'golden age' come before or after Jesus returns to the earth, or is this 'thousand years' to be taken symbolically, not literally, and as meaning the present Christian age? All three views have passionately dogmatic supporters, and this is not the place to join the debate. Instead, we can concentrate on biblical statements that are beyond dispute.

Firstly, however we interpret what Jesus called 'the signs of the times' (Matthew 16:3) his return to the earth is now over 2,700 years nearer than when Zephaniah prophesied and 2,000 years nearer than when Peter preached. In one sense 'the day of the LORD' dawned when Jesus was born, and it will come in its fulness when he returns to the earth. The whole concept of his return is ridiculed by most people, but the Bible anticipates this and warns that 'scoffers will come in the last days ... [and] will say, "Where is the promise of his coming?"' (2 Peter 3:3–4).

Secondly, 'the day of the Lord will come like a thief in the night' (1 Thessalonians 5:2). None of those who burgled my home three times over the years gave notice of their intentions. All three break-ins took my wife and me completely by surprise. If on the day of any one of these burglaries we had reason to believe that our house would be broken into before morning we would have made sure we were prepared. Yet Jesus warned his hearers that he would return 'at an hour you do not expect' (Matthew 24:44). Everybody will be surprised—but nobody will be in any doubt that he has come.

Thirdly, the Lord's return will be a dreadful day for all who reject God, as he will come 'to execute judgement on all and to convict all the ungodly of all their deeds of ungodliness that they have committed in such an ungodly way' (Jude 15). It is impossible to miss the emphasis here. As John Benton writes, 'When the Lord comes, all the truth will be exposed. Everything will be open; every deception will be unravelled and seen for what it is. And not only every deception, but every self-deception, will be unravelled.' Every godless thought, word and action will join in condemning the ungodly.

Fourthly, the Lord's return will be a glorious day for God's people, as he will come 'to save those who are eagerly waiting for him' (Hebrews 9:28). The nineteenth-century Scottish preacher and theologian John Brown expressed what this salvation will mean: '[It will be] for their complete and eternal deliverance from evil in all its forms and degrees, and for their being made happy, according to all their various susceptibilities of happiness, up to their largest capacity of enjoyment, and during the entire eternity of their being.' Zephaniah goes even further and in an amazing statement says that when all of his elect are securely

gathered in heaven God 'will rejoice over you with gladness ...
he will exult over you with loud singing' (3:17). Not only will
all the redeemed sing 'a new song' (Revelation 5:9) but God
himself will sing, rejoicing in the glorious fulfilment of the plan
of salvation he put in place when in Christ he chose a people
for himself 'before the foundation of the world' (Ephesians 1:4).
No wonder J. A. Motyer calls the book of Zephaniah 'a carefully
constructed and polished literary work' that 'reads like an
elegant study of the Lord's triumphant plans for world history.'

With all of this in mind, Zephaniah's command comes across
loud and clear: 'Be silent before the LORD' (1:7). Other prophets
use the same kind of language, which in essence means, 'Set
aside your own ideas and instincts, preferences and prejudices
and listen to what God is saying.' If the ungodly do this they will
hear him saying, 'Seek the LORD while he may be found; call
upon him while he is near' (Isaiah 55:6). Christians waiting for
'new heavens and a new earth' should take careful note of Peter's
next words: 'Therefore, beloved, since you are waiting for these,
be diligent to be found by him without spot or blemish, and at
peace' (2 Peter 3:13–14). Elsewhere, the apostle John urges us
to live in such a way that 'when [Jesus] appears we may have
confidence and not shrink from him in shame at his coming'
(1 John 2:28). It is always a bad sign when people settle for
discussing eschatology rather than preparing for the coming of
Christ by their daily determination to live in a way worthy of the
gospel. Augustine wrote, 'He who loves the coming of the Lord
is not he who affirms it is far off, nor is it he who says it is near.
It is he who, whether it be far or near, awaits it with sincere faith,
steadfast hope and fervent love.' An anonymous hymn-writer
tells us how we should respond to the Bible's teaching about the
Lord's coming:

> Great God, what do I see and hear!
> The end of things created:
> The Judge of mankind doth appear
> On clouds of glory seated;
> The trumpet sounds, the graves restore

The dead which they contained before:
Prepare, my soul, to meet him!

HAGGAI

As with many of the Minor Prophets we know nothing about Haggai, who merely identifies himself as 'the prophet' (1:1). He was probably born during Judah's exile in Babylon, and as his name means 'my feast' or 'my festival' he may have been born at the time of one of the great Jewish festivals. If so, his parents may have been putting down a marker as to the reality of their faith even though they had been wrenched from their homeland and were being forced to live in an alien country.

Uniquely among the Minor Prophets, Haggai's message was directed almost exclusively to two people: 'Zerubbabel the son of Shealtiel, governor of Judah' and 'Joshua the son of Jehozadak, the high priest' (1:1). This alone helps us to date his prophecy, but we have no need for guesswork as Haggai tells us precisely when God's prophetic word came to him. The book consists of five messages, the first of which came to Haggai 'in the second year of Darius the king, in the sixth month, on the first day of the month' (1:1). The second message was given three weeks later, 'on the twenty-fourth day of the month, in the sixth month, in the second year of Darius the king' (1:15). Nearly four weeks later the third message was given, 'in the seventh month, on the twenty-first day of the month' (2:1). Almost exactly two months later came the fourth message, 'on the twenty-fourth day of the ninth month, in the second year of Darius' (2:10); and on the same day, 'the twenty-fourth day of the month' (2:20) God delivered his final message to this prophet. Using our modern dating system, this would indicate that the first of Haggai's messages was in August 520 BC and the last in December of the same year, meaning that his entire written ministry covered slightly less than four months.

The background to Haggai's prophecy is fairly straightforward. In the last of three attacks the Babylonians, under their founder and ruler Nebuchadrezzar overran the Middle East, besieged and captured Jerusalem in 586 BC, destroyed the temple and carried off most of the city's inhabitants to Babylon (roughly speaking, modern-day Iraq). As we saw in earlier chapters, seventy years later the exile ended in a remarkable way. By then Babylon had been declining in power and had been overthrown by Cyrus, the founder of the Persian Empire. Finding that he had to control countless foreigners who had been uprooted from their homelands and held in exile in Babylon, he issued a decree allowing them to return home and reinstate their national gods. Yet Cyrus' surprising decision was not merely politically useful, it was the fulfilment of an astonishing prophecy made by Isaiah two hundred years earlier, when God told him that Cyrus would come to power 'and he shall fulfil all my purpose … saying of Jerusalem, "She shall be built", and of the temple, "Your foundation shall be laid"' (Isaiah 44:28). The Jews' deliverance was in God's plan long before Cyrus arrived on the scene. As J. A. Motyer rightly says, '[Cyrus] stepped onto the world stage without any idea of the only God whose tool he was to be.'

Not all the Jews wanted to accept Cyrus' offer. Babylon had become their home and almost all had been born there. What is more, some years earlier the prophet Jeremiah had managed to get a message from God through to them, encouraging them to settle down in Babylon, build houses, marry (among fellow exiles only) and raise families. Jeremiah's message contained another important instruction: 'But seek the welfare of the city where I have sent you into exile, and pray to the LORD on its behalf, for in its welfare you will find your welfare' (Jeremiah

29:7). Two things stand out here. The first is the clear indication that the exile had been planned by God and was not merely another incident in the constant clash of nations. The second is the command to pray for those who now ruled over them, even though they did not share their faith. This finds an echo in the New Testament, where the apostle Paul urges Christians to pray 'for kings and all who are in high positions, that we may lead a peaceful and quiet life, godly and dignified in every way' (1 Timothy 2:2).

These instructions to the exiles in no way conflicted with God's sovereign intervention through Cyrus. In spite of the fact that by now their homeland would have been in a pretty sorry state, some 50,000 jumped at the offer to return and in 538 BC Zerubbabel, who had been governor of Jerusalem at the time of the exile, was joined by the high priest Jeshua in leading them back home. Soon after they had settled back in Jerusalem they began the mammoth task of rebuilding the temple, which had stood for nearly 400 years before being destroyed by the Babylonians. At first, everything went well. In about two years the foundations were laid, the altar was built and worship services were reinstated, but trouble was looming. Neighbouring Samaritans offered to help them, but the Jews' leaders turned them away, saying, '... we alone will build to the LORD, the God of Israel, as King Cyrus the king of Persia has commanded us' (Ezra 4:3). Stung by this, the Samaritans changed their tactics and 'discouraged the people of Judah and made them afraid to build and bribed counsellors against them to frustrate their purpose' (Ezra 4:4–5). Their schemes worked so well that the Jews gradually lost interest in the project and it ground to a halt for about sixteen years.

In the meantime, King Cyrus had died and Darius, the great reorganizer of the Persian Empire, had taken over as ruler of Babylon. When he discovered from the official records that the Jews had Cyrus' authority to rebuild the temple he added his endorsement. In no uncertain fashion he directed Tattenai, the governor of Trans-Euphrates, and others to stop their opposition to the work: 'Leave the work on this house of God alone. Let the governor of the Jews and the elders of the Jews rebuild this house of God on its site... May the God who has caused his name to dwell there overthrow any king or people who shall put out a hand to alter this, or to destroy this house of God that is in Jerusalem' (Ezra 6:7, 12).

It was during this time that God raised up the prophets Haggai and Zechariah to join with Zerubbabel in reigniting the people's enthusiasm and driving the work on. Four years later it was completed and the temple was dedicated on what by our present dating system would have been 12 March 516 BC

Priorities

Haggai is the second smallest book in the Old Testament but the prophet's message was urgent, clear and uncompromising. It also came with ultimate authority. The name 'The LORD of hosts' is used as a title for God well over 200 times in the Old Testament and Haggai uses the phrases 'Thus says the LORD of hosts', 'The word of the LORD came' and similar terms over twenty times in thirty-eight verses. There can be only a few passages in the Bible in which the divine authority of the human writer's words is more constantly emphasized. Haggai is a clear reminder to us that the authority of the Bible comes not from the calibre of its human authors but from the character of its divine Author. Donald Grey Barnhouse is right to say, 'The shortest road to an understanding of the Bible is the acceptance of the fact that God is speaking in every line.'

God's first message through Haggai was delivered when the people had stopped working on the rebuilding of the temple and were concentrating on self-serving agendas that included developing their own properties or building new ones. Suddenly, as the twentieth-century Irish scholar J. McIlmoyle put it, Haggai broke into their lives 'like a dispatch-rider from the headquarters of the supreme commander'. He began with a rhetorical rebuke: 'Is it a time for you yourselves to dwell in your panelled houses, while this house lies in ruins?' (1:4). These people may have agreed that rebuilding the temple was a worthy project, but the nation's finances were in a mess after its years in exile, money was tight, and they had decided that work on the temple would have to be put on hold, at least for the time being. At first glance this might sound perfectly reasonable but it was far from it, because while work on the temple had ground to a halt, the people had spent time, money and energy on their own homes and many of them were now living in the relative comfort (and, for some, perhaps even luxury) of 'panelled houses'.

God's question was aimed at pricking their consciences: 'Consider your ways. You have sown much, and harvested little. You eat, but you never have enough; you drink, but you never have your fill. You clothe yourselves, but no one is warm. And he who earns wages does so to put them into a bag with holes' (1:5–6). These people were misusing resources that should have gone towards the rebuilding of the temple, but God urged them to open their eyes and see where their approach had got them. If they did, they would have to admit that their self-centred policy had backfired. Using a different metaphor, the modern scholar Joyce Baldwin says, 'Their money disappeared like flour through a sieve.'

The Bible has a great deal to say about the stewardship of a Christian's resources and we will take a close look at this when we reach the book of Malachi. A believer's giving to God's work should be 'in keeping with his income' (1 Corinthians 16:2, NIV) and should be done 'not reluctantly or under compulsion, for God loves a cheerful giver' (2 Corinthians 9:7). The people to whom Haggai was writing were not cheerful givers, but cheerful keepers. They had got their priorities wrong and were more intent on spending money on their own comfort and pleasure than on supporting God's work.

The effect of Haggai's message was dramatic. Leaders and people alike 'obeyed the voice of the LORD their God, and the words of Haggai the prophet, as the LORD their God had sent him' (1:12). We are even told the exact day in which they reported for work—'on the twenty-fourth day of the month, in the sixth month, in the second year of Darius the king' (1:15). Using our modern Western calendar this would have been on

21 September 520 BC. Another Old Testament writer confirms that God blessed their obedience: 'The elders of the Jews built and prospered through the prophesying of Haggai the prophet and Zechariah the son of Iddo' (Ezra 6:14). This made them two of very few prophets who saw obvious and outstanding results from their ministries. A small cloud arose when some older people, who had seen the glorious original temple built by King Solomon, doubted whether the replacement could match it. In reply, God urged them to keep working on the project, 'for I am with you... My Spirit remains in your midst' (2:4–5).

Beyond Judah

This was what we might call the immediate and local outworking of the prophecy, but God also declared, 'I will shake all nations, so that the treasures of all nations shall come in' (2:7). At least two major meanings are packed into this amazing statement. As well as referring to the rebuilt temple it looks forward to the coming into being of the church of Christ, a 'house' much greater than any temple built in Jerusalem. For all its rebuilt glory this temple was also destroyed during the Roman siege of Jerusalem in AD 70, but by then the Messiah, someone infinitely greater than Solomon, had come. From then on his living presence in the Christian church has given it a glory far exceeding that of even the most elaborate temple built by man. With Christ as 'the cornerstone' (Ephesians 2:20), the Christian church is 'a kingdom that cannot be shaken' (Hebrews 12:28), steadily growing into 'a holy temple in the Lord' in which believers are 'being built together into a dwelling place for God by the Spirit' (Ephesians 2:21–22). This building will one day be seen to include people of 'every tribe and language and people and nation' (Revelation 5:9), redeemed by the precious blood of Christ and by his grace belonging to a spiritual building so secure that 'the gates of hell shall not prevail against it' (Matthew 16:18). This seems to be the main meaning of God's additional promise, 'The latter glory of this house shall be greater than the former' (2:9). The twentieth-century Dutch theologian R. B. Kuiper wrote, 'The glory of the greatest, wealthiest, most powerful and most resplendent empire of all history was as nothing, yes less than nothing, in comparison with the glory of the church of Christ.'

There is yet another strand to the prophecy, one reflected in the New Testament, where God promises, 'Yet once more I will shake not only the earth but also the heavens' and explains that 'things that have been made' will be shaken 'in order that the things that cannot be shaken may remain' (Hebrews 12:26–27). As these words were being written, the old covenant was already 'becoming obsolete and growing old' and was 'ready to vanish away' (Hebrews 8:13), but a final shaking will bring the present physical world order to an end, to be replaced by 'new heavens and a new earth' (2 Peter 3:13). As the writer of Hebrews points out, Christians should hold fast to this promise, be grateful that they are receiving 'a kingdom that cannot be shaken' and 'offer to God acceptable worship, with reverence and awe' (Hebrews 12:28).

In his next message, given in the course of a question and answer session with the priests, God warns the people of Judah that neither returning to their homeland nor being involved in rebuilding the house of God would automatically render the people holy in his sight, or guarantee that they would be rewarded with his blessing. More than a decade of poor harvests had been a sign of this and they should have woken up to the fact. They were now urged to give this serious consideration and it seems that they did so, because a genuine change of heart was now met with this gracious and glorious promise: 'But from this day on I will bless you' (2:19). Throughout the history of Christianity formalism has always been a deadly obstacle to the progress of both churches and individuals, leading the twentieth-century American preacher Vance Havner to say, 'Many a Christian, many a church, has everything in the showcase and nothing on the shelves.'

Finally, on 'the twenty-fourth day of the ninth month, in the second year of Darius' (2:10, 20), which by our current reckoning would be 18 December 520 BC, God sent a message to Zerubbabel, the governor of Judah. We will concentrate on this for the rest of this chapter as it includes our 'major point'. Simply put, it was a word of great encouragement. Someone has said, 'Encouragement is oxygen to the soul'; in which case God's message to Zerubbabel was like a massive injection! In the first place it was an assurance that all the enemies of God's people would be defeated: 'I am about to shake the heavens and the earth, and to overthrow the throne of kingdoms. I am about to destroy the strength of the kingdoms of the nations, and overthrow the chariots and their riders. And the horses and their riders shall go down, every one by the sword of his brother' (2:21–22). Judah was a relatively small nation, always in danger of being overcome by more powerful enemies, but God promised Zerubbabel that he would never allow it to be eliminated, whereas its enemies were heading for disaster. Governments would collapse, alliances would disintegrate and armies would be defeated, but Judah would remain. In the years to come, the Persian, Syrian, Egyptian and Roman empires all fell in fulfilment of this prophecy. This brings us to our 'major point':

> On that day, declares the LORD of hosts, I will take you, O Zerubbabel my servant, the son of Shealtiel, declares the LORD, and make you like a signet ring, for I have chosen you, declares the LORD of hosts.   (2:23)

One helpful way of reading any passage of Scripture is to ask two questions: 'What did it mean at that time?' and 'When read in the light of all of Scripture, what is its intended meaning for all time?' Asking the first question makes the reader examine both the text and the context, to discover, for example, whether the passage is recording history, prophecy, an allegory, a parable or using some other literary form. Asking the second question means looking for an unchanging principle in the passage.

A New Testament example will illustrate how this works. Paul tells the Christians at Corinth that 'a thorn was given me in the flesh' and that three times he 'pleaded with the Lord about this, that it should leave me' (2 Corinthians 12:7–8). In response, God determined that the 'thorn' should remain, but assured Paul, 'My grace is sufficient for you, for my power is made perfect in weakness' (2 Corinthians 12:9). What did it mean to Paul at that time? All kinds of theories have been suggested as to what this 'thorn' was. The word translates the Greek *skolops*, a sharply pointed stake or pole, which suggests something that brought the apostle acute pain in either his body or spirit. It was natural for him to ask God for its removal, and God could certainly have done this, but instead he assured Paul of something even better—supernatural grace to go on serving God faithfully in spite of the 'thorn'. What is more, Paul was enabled to see that God allowed the thorn 'to keep me from being conceited because of the surpassing greatness of the revelations' (2 Corinthians 12:7). It would have been natural for others to have been awestruck at Paul because of the 'visions and revelations' (2 Corinthians 12:1) he had received and equally natural for him to boast of these. In an answer that went far beyond the apostle's prayer, God showed him that it was better for the 'thorn' to remain so that the apostle would constantly see that all his privileges, gifts and effectiveness were due entirely to the grace of God.

Getting the message

The clear principle we need to learn from Paul's testimony about this 'thorn' is that God's grace is always sufficient to meet the needs of his people, whatever those needs might be. It may not mean that the situation will dramatically change, or that the pain will immediately be eased. What it does mean is that if their particular 'thorn' remains they will be given God's grace to endure it and to accept it as part of God's providential ordering of their situation. In a delightful analogy, Vance Havner said, 'The ocean will hold a boat or a battleship, and God's grace will stand any weight you put on it'.

All over the world God's people are being put under severe pressure because of their faith. I have before me a monthly Christian newspaper that on one page alone reports the following current events. In Algeria, 'absurd' criminal charges were being levied against church leaders. In China, police and security officials broke up a church house group and smashed furniture before taking twenty Christians to the local police station and demanding money for their release. In Ethiopia, the homes of eighty Christians were burned down and a convert from Islam was stabbed. In India, a Christian pastor was beaten up during a church service. In Morocco, a Christian jailed for his faith was five years into a prison sentence and other Christians were expelled from the country. In Nepal, church leaders were threatened with violence if they did not give in to extortion demands. In Pakistan, Christians were attacked with rifles, axes and clubs. In Saudi Arabia, where conversion from Islam carries the death penalty, Christians were arrested for 'proselytizing'. These cases are only a glimpse of the countless ways in which Christians are being persecuted today.

The vast majority of believers may never face such pressure, yet even in these dire situations God's grace is sufficient. I have met countless Christians who have been able to confirm my experience that at a time of pain, sorrow, grief, doubt, disappointment, fear, uncertainty, loss or some other 'thorn' God has made 'the immeasurable riches of his grace' (Ephesians 2:7) powerfully real. For some, the experience has been so vivid that they would call 2 Corinthians 12:9 their 'life verse', Bible words that have meant more to them than any others.

That said, in searching for the principle behind this it is important to understand that God's all-sufficient grace is constant, whether or not an individual senses it to be a living reality to them at any given moment. Each one of us is utterly dependent on God's grace for every breath we take and sensing it at special moments does not affect its permanent reality. As the twentieth-century British preacher George Duncan wrote, 'A Christian never lacks what he needs when he possesses in Christ the unsearchable riches of God's grace.' Viewing any of God's attributes merely through the lens of our own current experience or emotions will always lead to restricted or distorted vision.

Having looked at some of the principles we need to bear in mind whenever we read the Bible, we can now turn back to our 'major point', which begins with God saying, 'I will take you, O Zerubbabel my servant, the son of Shealtiel' (2:23). The prophecy and the promise go far beyond anything that Zerubbabel could have imagined, as they placed him in Messiah's family tree. This is confirmed in a New Testament genealogy of Jesus, which includes 'Shealtiel the father of Zerubbabel, and Zerubbabel the father of Abiud' (Matthew 1:12–13).

This takes us a little further in understanding the meaning of the message, but there is much more to come, as Zerubbabel was not only a human ancestor of Jesus but also an Old Testament 'type', or picture, of the Saviour. We can see this by noticing two words used of him at the beginning of our 'major point' and a further statement at the end. In the first place God calls him 'my servant' (2:23), a phrase frequently used of Jesus by the prophet Isaiah, especially in Chapters 40–55. Secondly, God tells Zerubbabel, 'I have chosen you' (2:23) and Isaiah records God as referring to the coming Messiah as 'my chosen, in whom my soul delights' (Isaiah 42:1). The New Testament picks up this same truth and says of Jesus, 'He was chosen before the creation of the world' (1 Peter 1:20, NIV).

As we saw in the Introduction, all the Old Testament prophets were signposts pointing to the coming Messiah. Only if we keep this in mind can we fully understand their message. In our present 'major point' this means seeing far beyond Zerubbabel. Just as the promises of deliverance for God's people in Haggai's day were 'personalized' in Zerubbabel, so the great promises of the gospel are secured in Jesus Christ. Paul confirms that 'all the promises of God find their Yes in him' (2 Corinthians 1:20). All the great biblical promises of grace in this world and glory in the world to come find their meaning in Jesus the Messiah. In Paul's words, Jesus is the One 'whom God made our wisdom and our righteousness and sanctification and redemption' (1 Corinthians 1:30). These are all found in Jesus and only in him are they settled and secure. Outside of him there is no shelter from the wrath of God; in him there is salvation, security and satisfaction.

Dignity

In the first verse of his book Haggai calls Zerubbabel 'governor of Judah' (1:1) and in the last verse God calls him 'my servant' (2:23). There is a certain dignity about the title of 'governor', even though Judah was only a tiny nation and at that time was under the supervision of a foreign power. Zerubbabel's real dignity was based on the fact that God told him, 'I have chosen you.' No greater dignity or honour than that could ever be conferred on a human being. Writing to New Testament Christians, Peter called them 'elect exiles of the dispersion in Pontus, Galatia, Cappadocia, Asia and Bithynia, according to the foreknowledge of God the Father' (1 Peter 1:1–2). Calling them 'elect exiles' points to the very different ways in which they were seen by men and by God. As far as the world was concerned they were 'exiles', persecuted by their enemies, driven from their homeland and scattered throughout much of Asia Minor. Yet to God they were 'elect' and, as Peter assured them, '... you are a chosen race, a royal priesthood, a holy nation, a people for his own possession' (1 Peter 2:9). Isaiah uses the same kind of phrase when he records God calling believers 'the people whom I formed for myself' (Isaiah 43:21). Yet this corporate truth is also personal and individual, leading the twentieth-century Greek scholar Kenneth Wuest to comment, 'Each saint is God's unique possession just as if that saint were the only human being in existence.'

This is a staggering truth, leading John to write, 'See what kind of love the Father has given to us, that we should be called children of God' (1 John 3:1). Reflecting on the word 'us' drives the meaning home. Knowing as we do at least something of the depravity of our sinful natures (to say nothing of our erratic track record) it is surely amazing that God should choose us to be his children and welcome us into his family. John's wording almost has the feeling of a question—as if he is asking, 'What kind of love is this...?' My ministry means that I spend a great deal of time in airports. While there I sometimes enjoy looking at the logos on the tail fins of aircraft, then trying to work out the airline concerned. By now I am very familiar with many and quite good at recognizing others, but occasionally I am stumped and need to look on the fuselage of the aircraft concerned. John's statement has this kind of feel to it. We all know examples of human love, some of them deeply moving, but what kind of love is this that God has poured out on those he calls his children? Why, for instance, would God choose to lavish this special love on those who have nothing in their background, social standing, education, influence, wealth, ability or moral status to commend them?

Human choices are never made in this way. Being chosen for a job, a sports team, or some other position depends on skill or ability, or at the very least on perceived potential. In complete contrast, God never uses these criteria. As one New Testament writer asks, '... has not God chosen those who are poor in the world to be rich in faith and heirs of the kingdom, which he has promised to those who love him?' (James 2:5). Paul invites the Christians at Corinth to check that this is the case: 'For consider your calling, brothers: not many of you were wise according to worldly standards, not many were powerful, not many were of noble birth. But God chose what is foolish in the world to shame the wise; God chose what is weak in the world to shame the strong; God chose what is low and despised in the world, even things that are not, to bring to nothing things that are, so that no human being might boast in the presence of God' (1 Corinthians 1:26–29). Paul was not saying that anybody who was wise, powerful or of noble birth was rejected, but that no human qualification affected God's choice. God chose the foolish to become faithful, the weak to be his witnesses, the lowly to become loyal, the despised to become disciples and the world's nobodies to become his nobility. As we will see when we reach Malachi, God's choosing of his people is not only unconventional but unconditional, in the sense that they contribute nothing to it.

When Paul affirmed that 'Christ Jesus came into the world to save sinners' he had no hesitation in adding, 'of whom I am the foremost' (1 Timothy 1:15) and at the very height of his ministry he confessed, 'For I know that nothing good dwells in me, that is, in my flesh' (Romans 7:18). Even in his position as an apostle, being greatly used by God, his own nature remained hostile to the very gospel by which God in his loving grace had saved him. John Newton underlined the same sobering truth and confessed, 'I find not one corruption of my vile heart is dead, though some seem now and then asleep.' How amazing that God should stoop to such depths to bring sinners to himself! In the Bible's own words, 'He raises up the poor from the dust; he lifts the needy from the ash heap to make them sit with princes and inherit a seat of honour' (1 Samuel 2:8). Christians should never lose sight of this.

The signet ring

We can now concentrate on the other important statement that God makes to Zerubbabel in our 'major point': 'I will … make you like a signet ring'. Three great truths spring out of the text.

Firstly, the signet ring speaks of security. A signet was a stone set into a ring and engraved with the owner's personal symbol. It was used to endorse official documents by being pressed into soft wax or clay, so guaranteeing that the documents were authentic. In an Old Testament incident, the Persian King Xerxes declared, '… no document written in the king's name and sealed with his ring can be revoked' (Esther 8:8, NIV).

The picture is one of certainty and security and is used by God to assure Zerubbabel that whatever storms broke over the land neither he nor the nation would ever be forsaken. There is a parallel picture elsewhere in the Old Testament. When at some point during the exile there were those who began to despair and to cry out, 'The LORD has forsaken me; my Lord has forgotten me', God replied, 'Can a woman forget her nursing child that she should have no compassion on the son of her womb? Even these may forget, yet I will not forget you. Behold, I have engraved you on the palms of my hands' (Isaiah 49:14–16). There was a custom in those days of tying an emblem on the hand or wearing a ring on the finger as a token that the person represented would never be forgotten or forsaken. A somewhat similar thing is done today in the United States when yellow ribbons are placed in prominent places as a token that those in military service overseas are not forgotten.

The picture in Isaiah is even more vivid, with the names of God's people being engraved on his hand, the ultimate guarantee of security. Augustus Montague Toplady expressed it beautifully in his hymn 'A debtor to mercy alone':

> My name from the palm of his hands
> Eternity will not erase;
> Inscribed on his heart it remains,
> In marks of indelible grace.
> Yes, I to the end shall endure,
> As sure as the earnest is given;
> More happy, but not more secure,
> The glorified spirits in heaven.

The last two lines of Toplady's hymn should make every Christian sing with bewildered joy. The glorified spirits in heaven are obviously happier than even the most contented Christian on earth. They have no aches or pains, no sorrows or sins, no doubts or disappointments, no fears or failings, no trials or tribulations—yet even in God's immediate presence *they are not more secure*.

The feeblest Christian, the one racked with doubt over some issue or another, the one wrestling with some chronic temptation, the one whose faith is being severely tested, the one whose assurance of salvation is not as strong as it used to be, the one who feels useless or ineffective in God's service—none is less secure than the glorified spirits in heaven. God calls believers his 'treasured possession' (Malachi 3:17), leading Thomas Brooks to comment, 'Earthly jewels sometimes get separated from their owner, Christ's jewels never... Earthly jewels are sometimes lost, Christ's jewels never... Earthly jewels are sometimes stolen, Christ's jewels never.'

Secondly, the signet ring speaks of beauty. As Christmas 1979 approached, my wife Joyce and I discussed whether all the necessary presents had been bought. Lists were carefully checked and the children's presents had been hidden safely away. On Christmas Eve I was quietly confident that everything had been taken care of when Joyce broke the news that she had not yet bought a present for me. She had seen something she wanted to give me, but was not sure that I would like it. When she told me that it was a ring, my face fell. I had never worn a ring in my life, not even a wedding ring and, as she sensed, the thought of wearing one held no appeal for me. I tried to tell her gently, but the words were hardly out of my mouth before I realized that I had hurt her badly. We had gone through some difficult times together and Joyce had suffered a period of severe depression from which God had wonderfully delivered her. Through all of this there had been such a deepening of our relationship with each other that she obviously intended the ring to be something very special from her to me.

Realizing this and knowing that the shops would close within the hour, I suggested we go and take a look at it right away. As we got to the jeweller's I churlishly almost hoped that the ring had been sold, but when we looked in the window it was still there. Although its price was probably close to the limit Joyce could sensibly afford it was not expensive and was almost the only ring in the case, presumably because people had gone for higher-priced items. We went into the shop and I tried it on. As I had never worn a ring before it felt strangely heavy and uncomfortable. Then I looked at Joyce's face and saw the glow of pleasure she had at seeing the ring on my finger. A few minutes later, with a beaming smile, she took my arm and we walked out of the shop with the gift-wrapped ring firmly in her possession.

It is still on my finger as I write these words. It never attracts attention from other people, but to me it is the most precious ring in the world and as I look at it now it speaks to me of something that takes my breath away. As God sweeps his eye over the unspeakable glories of heaven, the vast array of galactic space, the intricate beauty of planet Earth and the marvellous intricacies of sub-microscopic creation he can find nothing more precious in his sight than a redeemed sinner. What God told his people in Old Testament times, and what he told Zerubbabel, he tells every individual believer today: '… you are precious in my eyes, and honoured, and I love you' (Isaiah 43:4). How precious are believers to God? The answer is that he was prepared to pay for their redemption 'not with perishable things such as silver or gold, but with the precious blood of Christ' (1 Peter 1:19).

Thirdly, it speaks of authority. The seal on a king's signet ring represented the king, so that any document sealed with the ring had regal authority and power. Zerubbabel was a descendant of David and a member of the nation's royal family, but being God's 'signet ring' gave him much greater status and authority as he directed the people in the temple rebuilding programme.

Serving God in obedience to Christ's command to 'proclaim the gospel to the whole creation' (Mark 16:15) is a great privilege, but Christians need to face the fact that the message we preach is not one the world wants to hear. God warned the prophet Jeremiah that his message would be treated as 'an object of scorn' (Jeremiah 6:10) and Paul told his readers that the gospel was 'folly to those who are perishing' (1 Corinthians 1:18). Nothing has changed. The primary challenge Christian churches face today is not numerical but spiritual. We are not surrounded by billions of people who are spiritually neutral and open to persuasion that the gospel is true. Instead, 'the whole world lies in the power of the evil one' (1 John 5:19) and is diametrically opposed to biblical truth.

Yet it is the Christian's God-given responsibility to share the gospel with other people seriously, passionately and urgently 'whether they hear or refuse to hear' (Ezekiel 2:5). As Vance Havner put it, 'The gospel is not a secret to be hoarded but a story to be heralded.' This should never be done with a sense of superiority, but neither should Christian witness be hesitant or defeatist. Instead, we should be confident that because the gospel originates with God it has divine authority. Paul's statement '... we are ambassadors for Christ' (2 Corinthians 5:20) points to an electrifying truth. In salvation, Christ took the place of sinners; in evangelism the redeemed sinner takes the place of Christ. In John Newton's deeply challenging words, 'Christ went away into heaven with our nature to represent us there, and has left us on earth with his nature to represent him here.'

The dignity of serving God is second only to the dignity of belonging to his family, but if the Christian's message is to have real authority, with Christ central to the message, there is a price to be paid—the price of dying to self. The modern British preacher Michael Green is not overstating the case when he says, 'What is needed is not only the message of crucifixion but the crucifixion of the messenger.' We must die to our appetite for men's approval and to our nervous concern about their criticism. Everyone who shares the gospel with others should bear in mind that their message is not something the church has put together. It is nothing less than 'the gospel of God' (Romans 1:1) and those who hear it are called to respond not to the messenger but to the divine Author of the message.

The English missionary Bishop Frank Houghton, who died in 1972, put into words the spirit in which Christians should seek to take the gospel to the world:

Facing a task unfinished,
That drives us to our knees,
A need that, undiminished,
Rebukes our slothful ease,
We, who rejoice to know you,
Renew before your throne
The solemn pledge we owe you
To go and make you known.

ZECHARIAH

I n the Introduction we highlighted the five major themes to be found in the Minor Prophets. As we come towards the end of our studies it would be good to remind ourselves what they are.

The first is *the sovereignty of God*. The prophets often emphasize this in their teaching by the simple means of calling him 'the Lord GOD' (Amos 7:1). The New International Version has 'the Sovereign LORD', a title underlining the fact that God is in active control of all reality outside of himself, with every element in creation at his disposal. As we saw earlier, history is his story.

The second is *God's inflexible and righteous judgement of sin*. Not a single sin in all of history will be unaccounted for or unpunished, but dealt with either in the death of Jesus or in hell. Perhaps the most succinct statement of this truth in the Minor Prophets is: '… the LORD will by no means clear the guilty' (Nahum 1:3).

The third is *God's amazing love*, beautifully expressed in the statement: 'The LORD your God … is gracious and merciful, slow to anger, and abounding in steadfast love' (Joel 2:13). Nothing the Minor Prophets say about God's anger affects this great truth.

The fourth is *the need to get right with God*. The Minor Prophets were not executioners but exhorters. Their concern was not to see people ruined but redeemed and their earnest cry was: 'Come, let us return to the LORD' (Hosea 6:1).

The fifth is *the coming of Messiah*. This runs like a rich seam of truth through the entire prophetic canon, reflected in the statement, 'But you, O Bethlehem Ephrathah, who are too little to be among the clans of Judah, from you shall come forth for me one who is to be ruler in Israel, whose coming forth is from of old, from ancient days' (Micah 5:2).

When we come to Zechariah we find all five of these major themes. On *the sovereignty of God*, Zechariah uses the term 'the LORD of hosts' (1:3) about fifty times and moves towards the climax of his book by declaring, 'And the LORD will be king over all the earth. On that day the LORD will be one and his name one' (14:9). On *God's inflexible and righteous judgement of sin*, Zechariah prophesies of God's enemies that as they face the consequences of their sins 'a great panic from the LORD shall fall on them' (14:13). On *God's amazing love*, Zechariah records God saying of Judah, 'I will bring them back because I have compassion on them' (10:6). On *the need to get right with God*, Zechariah writes, 'Return from your evil ways and from your evil deeds' (1:4). As to *the coming of Messiah*, Zechariah writes not only of his first coming but of his triumphant return to earth at the end of time, and closes his prophecy by referring again and again to what will happen 'On that day' (14:9).

The fact that Zechariah deals with all five of these major themes is significant. He is the penultimate Old Testament prophet—with only Malachi to come—and God moves him to address the five main themes that have dominated the ministries of his predecessors. God had been declaring these same truths for centuries, yet chose to repeat them through Zechariah. The important message here for twenty-first-century man is that we do not need a new message. 'New' is one of the most enticing words in our vocabulary, which is why it is so frequently used in the advertising world. When something is promoted as coming in a new colour, a new flavour, a new shape or a new size, or with a new formula, a new ingredient or a new additive, we rush to get it, blithely assuming that if it is new it must be better (and often discovering that it is not). Yet the passion for something new also reaches into religion. The apostle Paul was fully aware of this when he warned Timothy, 'For the time is coming when people will not endure sound teaching, but having itching ears they will accumulate for themselves teachers to suit their own passions, and will turn away from listening to the truth and wander off into myths' (2 Timothy 4:2–4).

In some ways Zechariah is a particularly significant prophet; we could call him a major among the minors. He is quoted more often in the New Testament than any other Old Testament book except Isaiah, with portions of his book cited in over seventy different places, one-third of these in the Gospels. The book of Revelation has more references to Zechariah than to any Old Testament prophet except Ezekiel. Martin Luther called him 'the quintessence of the prophets', and in effect wrote two commentaries on Zechariah, one in Latin (prepared by others from Luther's lecture notes) and one in German. Zechariah is the longest book among the Minor Prophets and thought by many to be the most difficult to interpret, as so much of it is in symbolic language.

Meet the man

There are about thirty people called Zechariah in the Old Testament and the author of this particular book identifies himself as 'the son of Berechiah, son of Iddo' (1:1). References in Ezra and elsewhere suggest that he was born into one of the Jewish priestly families that returned from the Babylonian exile and there are clues that Zechariah may have been a priest before God chose him be to a prophet. We cannot be certain of this, but we can be precise about when he began to prophesy. His first prophetic declaration was 'In the eighth month, in the second year of Darius' (1:1). This month began on the equivalent date of 27 October 520 BC. This was just a few weeks after Haggai's ministry had persuaded people to abandon their self-serving plans and resume rebuilding the temple.

If we compare the dates of Zechariah's prophecies (which were delivered over a period of three years) with the precise dates given for Haggai's ministry (which was condensed into less than four months—the sixth, seventh and ninth months of the second year of Darius), we can see that their prophecies overlapped and were all given about eighteen years after the Jews had returned from captivity in Babylon. A start had been made on the rebuilding of the Jerusalem temple, but the work had been stopped by opposition from neighbouring tribes, mainly Samaritans. It was restarted after a few years, but the work had nothing like the drive it deserved and many Jews had lost interest in the project. It was then that God raised up Haggai and Zechariah to challenge, motivate and energize his people. In modern terms the two men had what we would call a team ministry, though they were very different in style. Joyce Baldwin puts it very neatly: 'If Haggai was the builder, responsible for the solid structure of the new temple, Zechariah was more like the artist, adding colourful windows and their symbolism, gaiety and light.'

The message Zechariah was charged with bringing seems to be aimed particularly at those who were not yet committed to the project. It begins on a note sounded throughout the ministries of the Minor Prophets: 'Return to me, says the LORD of hosts, and I will return to you' (1:3). As a powerful motive to obedience, the people were told to reflect on the fate of their forefathers, who had heard the same message, but 'did not hear or pay attention' (1:4). This had made God 'very angry with your fathers' (1:2) and as a horrific outcome the nation had been overrun, Jerusalem had been ransacked, the temple had been destroyed and the people deported to Babylon. What more evidence could they need of the folly of turning their backs on God and the wisdom of obeying him? As with Haggai, the prophet's message produced remarkable results as the people responded and drove the work of rebuilding forward, so that Ezra recorded, 'And the elders of the Jews built and prospered through the prophesying of Haggai the prophet and Zechariah the son of Iddo' (Ezra 6:14).

Some critics have suggested that the same man may not have written the entire book of Zechariah, as there is a different feel from Chapter 9 onwards. This is not the place to discuss the issue, but there seems to be sufficient evidence to accept that Zechariah wrote it all. In the early part, before the rebuilding of the temple was complete, Zechariah was a 'young man' (2:4). By the time we reach Chapter 9 the temple is complete and the prophet turns his attention from purely national matters to the world at large and to issues that are not merely immediate but ultimate. It is not difficult to see this as the wider approach of a mature minister of God's Word.

This moves us towards our 'major point' in Zechariah. I have chosen it because it underlines why some consider this to be the most Messianic of the Old Testament books. In the course of his prophecy Zechariah wrote extensively not only about the first coming to earth of Jesus the Messiah but of his return to earth at the end of time. Our 'major point' sums up what we could properly call Zechariah's magnificent obsession:

> It is he who shall build the temple of the LORD and shall bear royal honour, and shall sit and rule on his throne. And there shall be a priest on his throne, and the counsel of peace shall be between them both.   (6:13)

The immediate reference here is to Joshua (a.k.a. Jeshua), the high priest who returned to Jerusalem in the first batch of expatriates to take up the offer to come home from Babylon. Joshua helped Zerubbabel to lead God's people after their return, and Zechariah's words speak of a signal honour paid to him, but 'Joshua' is the same name as 'Jesus' and the prophecy is bursting with Messianic meaning. The 'temple of the LORD' obviously refers to the rebuilt temple in Jerusalem; and the New Testament calls the Christian church 'a holy temple in the Lord' (Ephesians 2:21). Joshua had a temporary role of honour, but Jesus is the one who is to receive 'honour and glory for ever and ever' (1 Timothy 1:17).

A few verses earlier we are told that Joshua was to have 'a crown' (6:11) placed on his head, while here he is said to 'rule on his throne'. No other Old Testament priests wore crowns, nor did priests act as kings, as this was forbidden by God, whereas Jesus is 'King of kings' (Revelation 17:14) and 'a high priest for ever' (Hebrews 6:20). Lastly, the 'counsel of peace' (6:13) foreshadows Jesus 'making peace by the blood of his cross' (Colossians 1:20). It is difficult to think of many other verses in the entire Old Testament more tightly packed with truth about the coming Messiah than this one. After his resurrection Jesus told two of his disciples, '… everything written about me in the Law of Moses and the Prophets and the Psalms must be fulfilled' (Luke 24:44). In this study we will see how the 'major point' we have identified in Zechariah, together with five related prophecies, all direct our attention to him.

Lowly and insignificant

The first comes in the course of a vision about Joshua and shows him standing before 'the angel of the LORD' (representing God himself) with Satan 'standing at his right hand to accuse him' (3:1). Joshua represents not only the entire priesthood but the whole nation and his 'filthy garments' (3:3) are symbolic of sin, a picture used by Isaiah when he says that even our righteous deeds 'are like a polluted garment' (Isaiah 64:6).

Satan seems to have a good case, but before he can develop it he is told, 'The LORD rebuke you, O Satan! The LORD who has chosen Jerusalem rebuke you! Is this not a brand plucked from the fire?' (3:2). In the eighteenth century this metaphor made a profound impression on the Methodist leader John Wesley. As a five-year-old he had been rescued from a devastating fire at his home in Epworth, Lincolnshire, seconds before the roof caved in. From then on he called himself 'a brand plucked from the burning' and after his conversion many years later he invested the phrase with another, more profound, meaning. Left to themselves all men are polluted with sin, but in his sovereign grace God has chosen a people as his 'Jerusalem'.

Not only is Satan ruled out of court, but at God's direction

Joshua's filthy garments are removed and he is told, 'Behold, I have taken your iniquity away from you, and I will clothe you with pure vestments' (3:4). The imagery in Zechariah is powerful and wonderfully applicable to God's people today. Satan's otherwise justifiable case against them no longer stands because their sin has been dealt with by the Lord Jesus Christ, who in his death on the cross took their sin upon him and in his own body and spirit paid in full the penalty it deserved. In Isaiah's words, 'But he was wounded for our transgressions; he was crushed for our iniquities' (Isaiah 53:5). In the most breathtaking New Testament statement on this we are told, 'For our sake [God] made him to be sin who knew no sin' (2 Corinthians 5:21). As the nineteenth-century biblical scholar Samuel P. Tregelles pointed out, 'Christ assumed every consequence of sin which was not itself sinful.' Paul makes it clear that 'Christ is the end of the law for righteousness to everyone who believes' (Romans 10:4), so that all who put their trust in Christ are declared righteous in God's sight. In the language of Zechariah's vision, they are clothed with 'pure vestments'. Paul testified that his own standing before God was based on 'not having a righteousness of my own that comes from the law, but that which comes through faith in Christ' (Philippians 3:9).

Zechariah's vision goes on to record God saying, 'I will bring forth my servant the Branch' (3:8), two titles the Bible gives to Christ. At one point Isaiah writes of God announcing, 'Behold my servant, whom I uphold, my chosen, in whom my soul delights. I have put my Spirit upon him; he will bring forth justice to the nations' (Isaiah 42:1). In the New Testament, Jesus is said to be the exact fulfilment of this prophecy (see Matthew 12:15–21).

We will concentrate here on the other title—'the Branch'— which Zechariah develops later in the book. God tells him to tell Joshua: 'Thus says the LORD of hosts, "Behold the man whose name is the Branch: for he shall branch out from his place, and he shall build the temple of the LORD. It is he who shall build the temple of the LORD and shall bear royal honour, and shall sit and rule on his throne"' (6:12–13).

This clearly points to Jesus, the greater Joshua. A branch can sometimes be massive, as in the case of the giant sequoias I recall seeing in Yosemite Park, California, some of which reach to a height of 300 feet. One called the Grizzly Giant has a branch ninety feet above the ground and six feet in diameter. Yet the Hebrew word translated 'Branch' in Zechariah could be translated 'sprout' or 'shoot', something quite unimpressive but with the potential to grow and spread. Isaiah reflects this when prophesying, 'There shall come forth a shoot from the stump of Jesse, and a branch from his roots shall bear fruit' (Isaiah 11:1).

My wife was once given a tiny cutting from a lovely flowering plant in a friend's house and she carefully tended it when we returned home. To her delighted surprise it not only survived but grew so strongly that she was able to take her own cuttings from it and plant them elsewhere in the house. Before long these tiny cuttings led to beautiful red flowering houseplants in several rooms. In Zechariah's prophecy Jesus is referred to as a tiny sprout or shoot, something that seemed initially insignificant. His family tribe of Judah had been ravaged and wrecked by its enemies. He was born into a working-class family and brought up in Nazareth, something of a backwater and with an unenviable reputation. When Philip, one of his early disciples, told his friend Nathaniel that Jesus was the promised Messiah, Nathaniel replied, 'Can anything good come out of Nazareth? (John 1:46). Whenever he was not preaching in his role as Bishop of Liverpool, J. C. Ryle and his family worshipped at St Nathaniel's Church in the Windsor area of Liverpool. There was a time when an advertisement for labourers added the rider, 'No Windsor man need apply.' In Jesus' day, the same kind of thing might have been said of Nazareth. It is almost impossible to imagine a scenario further removed from what might have been expected of the promised Messiah, but Zechariah got it exactly right. This apparently insignificant Branch, brought up on the wrong side of the tracks, would 'bear royal honour' and 'sit and rule on his throne'.

There is no greater miracle in the Bible than that of God assuming a human nature in the person of Jesus in order to rescue sinners. It is infinitely beyond our grasp and even Paul calls it 'the mystery of godliness' (1 Timothy 3:16). Martin Luther was right to say, 'The mystery of the humanity of Christ that he sunk himself into our flesh, is beyond all human understanding.' As the eighteenth-century British hymn-writer Charles Wesley wrote in his well-known hymn 'Let earth and heaven combine', in the incarnation we have 'Our God contracted to a span, incomprehensibly made man'. It is even impossible for us to come up with anything like an analogy, though C. S. Lewis tried to give us a glimpse of one aspect of what was involved. He wrote,

> Lying at your feet is your dog. Imagine, for the moment, that your dog and every dog is in deep distress. Some of us love dogs very much. If it would help all the dogs in the world to become like men, would you be willing to become a dog? Would you put down your human nature, leave your loved ones, your job, hobbies, your art and literature and music, and choose instead of the intimate communion with your beloved, the poor substitute of looking into the beloved's face and wagging your tail, unable to smile or speak? Christ by becoming man limited the thing which to him was the most precious thing in the world; his unhampered, unhindered communion with the Father.

Zechariah's vision teems with truth about the promised Messiah, not least in emphasizing that '*he* shall build the temple of the Lord'. This is no mere earthly building, but the Christian church, 'God's temple' (1 Corinthians 3:16), with Christ himself as the 'foundation' (1 Corinthians 3:11) and the 'cornerstone' (Ephesians 2:20) and with believers 'being built up ... to be a spiritual house' (1 Peter 2:5). As the seventeenth-century British preacher William Gurnall beautifully put it, 'The church is nothing but Christ displayed.'

Glorious yet submissive

In the second of his five prophecies Zechariah says of the pledged Messiah, 'Rejoice greatly, O daughter of Zion! Shout aloud, O daughter of Jerusalem! Behold, your king is coming to you; righteous and having salvation is he, humble and mounted on a donkey, on a colt, the foal of a donkey' (9:9). This is one of the best-known of Zechariah's prophecies, largely because of its striking fulfilment recorded in Matthew 21:1–11, which describes the occasion when Jesus rode into Jerusalem shortly before his crucifixion. The words 'glorious' and 'submissive' certainly describe the Messiah prophesied by Zechariah and each of these is expressed in two ways.

The first glorious thing about the coming king is that he would be 'righteous'. This refers not only to the king's character but also to the just way in which he would rule. This would shine as a beacon of hope to the prophet's first hearers, as their nation had suffered under a succession of kings whose obituaries could have been headed '... did what was evil in the sight of the LORD' (2 Kings 21:2). They had been arrogant, ruthless and corrupt and had often made a mockery of justice, but one prophet after another announced that the coming Messiah would be utterly different. As Joyce Baldwin comments, 'When rogues continually succeed in getting away with their crimes, while innocent people suffer and find no redress, to be promised that right will triumph, that the righteous will be vindicated, is a cause for deep joy.' Isaiah calls the coming Messiah 'the righteous one' (Isaiah 53:11), while Jeremiah elaborates and describes him as one who will 'reign as king and deal wisely, and shall execute justice and righteousness' (Jeremiah 23:5). Centuries later, having spent several years in Jesus' company, the apostle Peter called him 'the Holy and Righteous One' (Acts 3:14). It is impossible to miss the ultimate meaning of Zechariah's prophecy.

The second glorious thing about the coming king is that he would be the one 'having salvation'. Not even the finest of the nation's kings had been able to bestow salvation on his people. Some had helped to turn the economy around, won great military battles, or rekindled national pride or spiritual enthusiasm, but even the best of their achievements had been temporary. What is more, none had been able to give their people salvation in its full biblical sense, which essentially means deliverance from sin. Only the Messiah of whom the prophets spoke could do this; as Peter said at Pentecost, '... there is salvation in no one else, for there is no other name under heaven given among men by which we must be saved' (Acts 4:12).

Another striking thing about Zechariah's prophecy is that the coming king is not merely said to bring salvation but is described as 'having salvation'. In other words salvation is *Messiah himself*. Jesus does not offer salvation as one might hand over a gift to someone else; *he offers himself*. Salvation does not come from listening to him, agreeing with his teaching, trying to follow him, or even admiring him. As the apostle John put it, 'And this is the testimony, that God gave us eternal life, and *this life is in his Son*. Whoever has the Son has life; whoever does not have the Son does not have life' (1 John 5:11–12, emphasis added). Nothing could be clearer; Jesus is not only the Saviour, he is salvation.

This comes across beautifully in a New Testament incident. When, in accordance with the Law of Moses, Joseph and Mary took the baby Jesus up to Jerusalem to present him in the temple forty days after his birth, the priest on duty was an old man called Simeon, who had been fervently looking for the coming of Messiah. When he took Jesus in his arms he began a paean of praise by saying, 'Lord, now you are letting your servant depart in peace, according to your word; for *my eyes have seen your salvation*' (Luke 2:29–30, emphasis added). In words clearly given to him by the Holy Spirit, Simeon confirmed that Jesus is not merely the one who brings salvation; he *is* salvation. In a striking phrase, the nineteenth-century Scottish evangelist Henry Drummond pointed out, 'The death-struck sinner, like the wan, anaemic, dying invalid, is saved by having poured into his veins the healthier blood of Christ.' Yet for all his saving power it was also prophesied about this coming Messiah that he would be submissive. This is also expressed in two ways.

He would be submissive by being humble. Zechariah uses this very word, one that combines the ideas of gentleness and humility, qualities totally out of line with those of typical Middle Eastern kings of Old Testament times. Many of them were surrounded with extravagant trimmings of pomp and circumstance, lived in luxurious palaces with hordes of servants at their disposal, and had lifestyles that demonstrated their exalted status. The contrast with the coming Messiah could not be greater. Rather than surrounding himself with fawning flunkeys, Jesus said, '… the Son of Man came not to be served but to serve' (Mark 10:45). On another occasion he urged his followers, 'Take my yoke upon you, and learn from me, for I am gentle and lowly in heart' (Matthew 11:29). This is the only time in the Bible where the heart of Jesus is mentioned and the word translated 'gentle' has the sense of a quiet acceptance of God's sovereign and perfect will. This ties in perfectly with Paul's reference to 'the meekness and gentleness of Christ' (2 Corinthians 10:1). No other man in history has ever humbled himself so greatly, and no other man has ever been so exalted as a result.

He would be submissive by riding on a donkey. In earlier times Middle Eastern rulers often rode on donkeys, but from King Solomon's time onwards the picture changed and they rode on magnificent horses chosen to reflect their royal owners' status. Horses stood for power—armies would often be ranked by the number of horses they could field—while donkeys stood for the daily grind of agricultural work and were often a sign of poverty. This makes Zechariah's prophecy all the more stunning. This glorious, triumphant Messiah would ride into Jerusalem ('Zion') not on a magnificent warhorse but on a lowly farm animal—and centuries later that is exactly what happened. Making his way into Jerusalem at the beginning of the last week of his earthly life, Jesus sent two disciples on ahead to find 'a donkey tied, and a colt with her' (Matthew 21:2). They did as they were told, then 'brought the colt to Jesus and threw their cloaks on it, and he sat on it' (Mark 11:7), fulfilling Zechariah's prophecy in meticulous detail.

The incident is also one of several that show the way in which Jesus submitted to his Father's will while on earth by accepting the limitations of his lowly upbringing. Just as he had to borrow a donkey on which to ride, so he had to borrow a boat in which to sail across the Sea of Galilee (see Matthew 9:1) and a coin with which to give an illustration (see Luke 20:19–26). The one who created water as a liquid compound with its molecule made up of one oxygen atom and two hydrogen atoms (H_2O) had to ask someone to give him a drink when he became thirsty (see John 4:1–7). Throughout his ministry he could even be said to be of 'no fixed abode'; he said that while even birds and animals had their homes, 'the Son of Man has nowhere to lay his head' (Matthew 8:20).

Rejected and betrayed

The third prophecy comes from the latter part of Zechariah, which is packed with visions and imagery. Because of the remarkable detail in the prophecies it contains, Chapter 11 alone has been described as 'one of the greatest of all demonstrations of the divine inspiration of Holy Scripture'. In this chapter the prophecy is given in a very unusual way, in that Zechariah is told to act out the part of two shepherds, one good and one bad. With the coming Messiah as our focal point, only the first of these shepherds is immediately relevant here and the text reveals six things about him.

The first tells us what the shepherd did. 'Thus says the LORD my God: "Become shepherd of the flock doomed to slaughter"' (11:4). In its immediate context the shepherd was to care for God's people, who were being inhumanely treated by their oppressors, but it is also a picture of Jesus the Messiah, who called himself 'the good shepherd' (John 10:11). Yet in spite of his amazing ministry, most of his own people, the Jews, rejected him. 'He came to his own, and his own people did not receive him' (John 1:11), and as a result were 'doomed to slaughter', a picture of eternal punishment.

The second tells of two staffs (commonly used by shepherds), given the names Favour and Union. Zechariah writes, 'I took my staff Favour, and I broke it, annulling the covenant that I had made with all the peoples' (11:10). This seems to follow on from what was said earlier and points to God withdrawing his favour from those who rejected him, so leaving them exposed to their enemies. Less than forty years after Jesus died the Roman Emperor Titus led an invasion that besieged and conquered Jerusalem, slaughtering 1.5 million Jews in the process.

Zechariah goes on, 'Then I broke my second staff Union, annulling the brotherhood between Judah and Israel' (11:14). Judah and Israel had separated much earlier, but this vision refers to a chronic civil war that began to rage within Judea. Commenting on the breaking of these two staffs, Thomas Moore wrote, 'The staff of protection from evil abroad and the staff of continued union at home were both broken, and the double horrors of foreign and domestic war paid the fearful penalty of rejecting the Lord of life.'

The third has Zechariah writing, 'In one month I destroyed the three shepherds' (11:8). Bible students have come up with over forty different explanations of this enigmatic passage, but there is at least one direct line to the coming Messiah. Under the Old Covenant, the three principal offices instituted by God were those of Prophet, Priest and King. Over the centuries not one measured up to his God-given role and when Jesus, the divine Shepherd came, he instituted the New Covenant and abolished all three old covenant offices. John the Baptist, the contemporary and immediate forerunner of Jesus was in effect the last Old Testament prophet; no priest was ever appointed after the Jerusalem temple was destroyed; and no king has ever ruled over the Jewish state from that day to this. In the fulfilment of Messianic prophecy Jesus came into the world as Prophet, Priest and King. In the common prophetic use of time periods Zechariah's 'one month' simply means what John Calvin calls 'a short space of time' and its Messianic meaning here would cover the earthly lifetime of Jesus.

The fourth has the shepherd declaring of the people, 'They also detested me'. The Messianic message is clear. In spite of the Good Shepherd's love and kindness, most people rejected both him and his message. As Isaiah prophesied, 'He was despised and rejected by men; a man of sorrows and acquainted with grief' (Isaiah 53:3). Shortly before his arrest and crucifixion Jesus cried, 'O Jerusalem, Jerusalem, the city that kills the prophets and stones those who are sent to it! How often would I have gathered your children together as a hen gathers her brood under her wings, and you would not!' (Matthew 23:37).

The fifth follows on: 'So I said, "I will not be your shepherd. What is to die, let it die. What is to be destroyed, let it be destroyed"' (11:9). Jesus the Good Shepherd did everything he possibly could to turn people from sin and its dreadful penalty, but when they adamantly refused he allowed things to run their inevitable course. The symbolism here clearly speaks firstly of the destruction of Jerusalem a few years later, but also of the ultimate horror of hell for those who reject the one and only Saviour.

The sixth speaks of the shepherd's work being ridiculed. Zechariah, acting the part of the good shepherd, asks the people to value his work and pay him as they see fit. In response, 'they weighed out as my wages thirty pieces of silver' (11:12). This was no more than a man would pay someone if his ox had gored his neighbour's slave (see Exodus 21:32). Considering all that the shepherd had done for them, it was an insult; Zechariah wryly refers to it as 'the lordly price at which I was priced by them' (11:13). When God then told Zechariah, 'Throw it to the potter' he 'took the thirty pieces of silver and threw them into the house of the LORD, to the potter' (11:13).

This is a notoriously difficult allegory to interpret, but it can certainly be seen as foreshadowing something that happened some 500 years later. Jesus was betrayed by Judas Iscariot to the chief priests for exactly 'thirty pieces of silver' (Matthew 26:15). Later, when Judas saw that Jesus had been condemned he tried to give the money back. When the priests refused to accept it Judas threw the money into the temple and committed suicide. Seeing this, the priests considered it blood money, took the thirty pieces of silver 'and bought with them the potter's field as a burial place for strangers' (Matthew 27:7).

Matthew goes on to say that this 'fulfilled what had been spoken by the prophet Jeremiah' (Matthew 27:9), not Zechariah. This may be because there are similarities between Zechariah's prophecy and one recorded at Jeremiah 18:1–4; 19:1 and 32:6–15 and that Matthew chooses to name the major prophet and not the minor one. John Calvin admitted, 'How the name of Jeremiah crept in I do not know, nor do I give myself much trouble to enquire.' Whatever the true explanation, the links between the prophecy and the incidents involving Judas Iscariot are striking. Jesus, the Good Shepherd, is valued at thirty pieces of silver and this derisory amount is thrown into the house of the Lord and then, in effect, to the potter.

Violent and vicarious death

The fourth prophecy comes in the course of another vision: "'Awake, O sword, against my shepherd, against the man who stands next to me,' declares the LORD of hosts. "Strike the shepherd, and the sheep will be scattered'" (13:7). In the Messianic fulfilment of this prophecy, the first amazing thing to notice is that it is *God* who orders the sword to strike the shepherd. There can be no question as to the identity of the shepherd, as God calls him 'the man who stands next to me', a phrase meaning 'the man who has fellowship with me on equal terms'. This can only mean Jesus, the Good Shepherd, of whom John was to write, 'In the beginning was the Word, and the Word was with God, and the Word was God' (John 1:1). The victim was not only human but also divine and therefore sinless.

If we asked who was responsible for the death of Jesus, several answers could be given. It could be said that Satan was, as he put it into Judas Iscariot's heart to betray Jesus. It could for obvious reasons be said that Judas was. It could be said that the Jews were, as they planted false witnesses to testify against Jesus. It could be said that Pontius Pilate was, as he pronounced the death sentence. It could even be said that Jesus was, as he said, 'I am the good shepherd. The good shepherd lays down his life for the sheep' (John 10:11) and added, 'No one takes [my life] from me, but I lay it down of my own accord' (John 10:18). Yet there is another answer to the question: *God was responsible for Jesus' death*. Peter made this clear when on the Day of Pentecost he told the crowd that Jesus had been 'delivered up according to the definite plan and foreknowledge of God' (Acts 2:23). This did nothing to absolve those who carried out his crucifixion—Jesus was still 'killed by the hands of lawless men' (Acts 2:23)—but God had already planned that this would happen. The death of Jesus was not an afterthought or a last-minute idea, but a pivotal part of God's amazing plan to rescue sinners from eternal disaster. As J. A. Motyer writes, 'Out of the wealth of his resources God has paid debts that were no concern of his.'

That the divine Father should put the divine Son to death in order to bear the punishment rightly due to rebellious sinners should leave us utterly amazed. Thomas Moore calls it, 'The most awful illustration of the repulsive and separating power of sin that the history of the world affords.' One other detail can be mentioned. On the night before his crucifixion Jesus underlined the fulfilment of Zechariah's prophecy that 'the sheep will be scattered' by quoting it to his disciples alongside his prediction (soon to be fulfilled), 'You will all fall away because of me this night' (Matthew 26:31).

Coming in glory

Zechariah begins his final chapter by declaring, 'Behold, a day is coming for the LORD' (14:1). Whatever the immediate fulfilment of this prophecy, it is the ultimate fulfilment that shines through most clearly. The wording in the translation we are using is especially helpful. When a girl is to get married, we often say of the wedding day, 'This is *her* day.' Everything is subservient to her wishes and the other members of her family do everything they can to make sure that she is the centre of attention and attraction. In the New Testament the church of Christ is described as 'a bride adorned for her husband' (Revelation 21:2) and Zechariah uses wedding-day language to emphasize that over and above everything else the day of which he is speaking is the heavenly Bridegroom's day. He is obviously referring to the Second Coming of Christ, the day when the entire universe will acknowledge his eternal sovereignty, majesty, glory and power.

From this final vision we have space to note only a few details. Zechariah says that this day is 'a unique day, which is known to the LORD' (14:7), the clear meaning being that it is known *only* to him. This is reflected in the New Testament. When teaching his disciples about his return to the earth, Jesus told them, 'But concerning that day and hour no one knows, not even the angels of heaven, nor the Son, but the Father only' (Matthew 24:36). In his human nature, not even Jesus knew the day of his return, yet only someone whose nature was also divine could know of the angels' ignorance. This shows how futile it is for man to say when it might be. The twentieth-century scholar William Hendriksen makes the wry comment, 'Curiosity is wonderful. For nosiness, intrusiveness, impertinence there is no excuse.'

The prophet then tells us that the Lord will return 'and all the holy ones with him' (14:5), a prophecy precisely endorsed by Jesus who said that the Son of Man would come 'and all the angels with him' (Matthew 25:31). He also tells us that this day will be 'neither day nor night, but at evening time there shall be light' (14:7). In speaking of the day of his return Jesus said, '... the sun will be darkened and the moon will not give its light, and the stars will be falling from heaven, and the powers in the heavens shall be shaken' (Mark 13:24–25). The two prophecies are closely linked and William Hendriksen is wise to say that as the second is deeply rooted in the first, which is in visionary language, we will probably not know how much must be taken literally and how much figuratively 'until this prophetic picture becomes history'.

On the other hand we can be quite clear as to the meaning of one of Zechariah's final statements: 'And the LORD will be king over all the earth' (14:9). The same glorious reign is anticipated throughout the Old Testament. Solomon longed for a coming king who would 'have dominion from sea to sea' (Psalm 72:8) and Zechariah turns this prayer into prophecy by quoting Solomon and declaring of the coming king that 'his rule will be from sea to sea' (9:10). In the New Testament this same truth is at the heart of Paul's statement that 'at the name of Jesus every knee should bow, in heaven and on earth and under the earth, and every tongue confess that Jesus Christ is Lord, to the glory of God the Father' (Philippians 2:10–11).

In Old Testament times countless people dismissed the idea of a coming Messiah. In Jesus' lifetime most people rejected him and today billions deliberately disown him—but the day is coming when every being in existence, without exception, will acknowledge him to be Lord. Those already in heaven, those living on earth at his return and those condemned to spend eternity in hell will cry out in unison, *though not in harmony*. Not everyone will be in the kingdom, but everyone will acknowledge the King. Some will do so with everlasting joy and others with everlasting horror, but nobody will be in any doubt as to the truth. There will be no atheists, agnostics or sceptics on that day, nor will there be any opportunity for those who rejected Christ to repent and be saved from their appalling destiny. Instead, they will all be forced to realize that his words were true, his promises genuine and his warnings real. As Tryon Edwards so precisely put it, 'Hell is truth seen too late.'

Three things stand out as we close Zechariah's prophecy. The first is the perfection of Scripture, clearly seen in the way in which his prophecies were fulfilled. Zechariah gives us good reason for believing that the Bible is 'the living and abiding word of God' (1 Peter 1:23). The second is the perfection of the Lord Jesus Christ; whether we see him as a Branch, a Shepherd or a King he always fulfils these roles to perfection. The third is the perfection of salvation Jesus provides, which is not something tentative or temporary but secure and eternal and which will be universally demonstrated when Jesus returns in glory. A modern version of words by the nineteenth-century British hymn-writer Frances Ridley Havergal expresses what Christians' emotions should be as they anticipate this:

> O the joy to see you reigning,
> You, my own beloved Lord;
> Every tongue your name confessing—
> Worship, honour, glory, blessing,
> Brought to you with one accord:
> You my master and my friend,
> vindicated and enthroned;
> To the earth's remotest end
> Glorified, adored and crowned!

MALACHI

It is possible to read Malachi in less than ten minutes—but impossible to read it comfortably, as its message is as powerfully disturbing now as it was when first written. 'Malachi' means 'my messenger' and may refer to the writer's ministry, but we will assume here that Malachi was the writer's name. We can come fairly close to dating the book, even though it has no information about which king of Israel or Judah was reigning at the time it was written. This might be a good point at which to remind ourselves of where the Minor Prophets fit into Old Testament history.

- We are not sure when Joel, Obadiah and Jonah were written.
- Hosea and Amos prophesied to the northern kingdom of Israel prior to its exile to Assyria in 722 BC.
- Micah, Habakkuk, Zephaniah (and possibly Nahum) prophesied to the southern kingdom of Judah prior to its exile to Babylon in 586 BC.
- Haggai, Zechariah and Malachi prophesied to Judah after its return from captivity, which took place in three stages between 538 BC and 444 BC.

There are some clues as to the precise period when Malachi was written. Firstly, he mentions Judah as having a 'governor' (1:8). This was an office established by the Persians, who had overthrown Babylon during Judah's exile (though we are not told who held that office when Malachi prophesied). Secondly, Malachi indicates many of the problems mentioned by two of the Major Prophets, Ezra and Nehemiah, who also wrote after Judah's return from exile. Thirdly, while Haggai and Zechariah wrote about the rebuilding of the temple in Jerusalem, Malachi makes no mention of it. As it was completed in 515 BC, Malachi clearly wrote after that date. It may have been considerably later, as by Malachi's time the temple services had degenerated into mere religious formality.

Malachi's message is said to be 'to Israel' (1:1) though in fact he was speaking to the southern kingdom of Judah. The explanation is that 'Israel' was originally the name given to the entire Jewish nation, then after the nation was divided it was used to mean the ten tribes of the northern kingdom, later taken captive in Assyria. The two tribes of the southern kingdom of Judah were later deported to Babylon. As Israel had by then been wiped out, the name 'Israel' was used of the people who returned to Judah after being released from their captivity. This is the nation Malachi has in mind. More immediately relevant to twenty-first-century believers is that Israel in the Old Testament is a picture of the Christian church. We must therefore read Malachi as a word to 'the Israel of God' (Galatians 6:16), that is, all God's people, whether or not they are Jewish by birth. This makes Malachi required reading for all Christians today.

The dialogues

When Malachi came on the scene Haggai and Zechariah had already died—and so had the religious renewal their ministries had sparked off. The temple and the walls of Jerusalem had been rebuilt, but the spiritual and social life of the nation had been reduced to rubble. Both Haggai and Zechariah had promised glorious things for the nation, but there seemed no sign of these and people were becoming disillusioned and disheartened. There was a growing scepticism about God's covenant love for his people, their religion had degenerated into meaningless ritual and they had lost any concern for godly living. To make matters worse, the nation was in the throes of severe economic recession. It had slipped from the best of times to the worst of times.

This is the background to Malachi's message, which is called 'The oracle of the word of the LORD' (1:1). The word 'oracle' comes from a Hebrew verb meaning 'to carry a burden' and reflects the weight of responsibility Malachi felt when delivering his message. He was not offering his opinion on the current state of the nation's affairs. He was bringing God's word to the people and was impelled to do so. In his book *The Beacon Lights of Prophecy*, the twentieth-century American theologian Albert Knudson wrote, 'There are two classes of preachers—the good preachers who have something to say and the poor preachers who have to say something. But there is yet another and higher class. It consists of those who both have something to say and who have to say it. Such are the prophets.' Malachi qualified.

Malachi's message is given mainly in the form of a series of dialogues between God and his people. These often see God charging them with sin, the people questioning the charge, then God vindicating it. Of the fifty-five verses in Malachi, forty-seven are spoken directly by God, a higher proportion than in any other book in the Bible. As we will see, the issues raised range from public worship to personal morality and as Malachi is the last of the prophets his book gives us a vivid picture of the closing period of Old Testament history. We will also see that the issues he dealt with were not confined to his day but are relevant to the twenty-first century believers.

The covenant

God begins the first dialogue with the sublimely simple statement, 'I have loved you' (1:2). We will dig into this at the end of this chapter, but concentrate here on the people's puzzled (and outrageously insolent) response: 'How have you loved us?' God had made wonderful promises to them through Haggai and Zechariah. If he had meant what he said surely the nation would be in much better shape. In thinking like this they were making the classic mistake of judging God by their present circumstances and not by what he had revealed of his nature and purposes. In the absence of a 'quick fix' to their predicaments they felt justified in casting aspersions on God's character.

God's response is to give them a refresher course on part of their nation's history. We looked at this when studying Obadiah, but it will be useful to summarize it here. The great patriarch Abraham, with whom God made the covenant that undergirded Israel's very existence, was the father of twin sons, Jacob and Esau. Although Esau was born a few moments before Jacob, God had already told their mother, Rebekah, that he would serve his younger brother, the exact opposite of the custom embedded in their culture. As they grew up, the two brothers often confronted each other and eventually went their separate ways, becoming the heads of two nations, Edom (the name Esau took) and Israel (the name God gave to Jacob). Edom became a byword for arrogance and for bitter opposition against the people of God in Israel, and as we saw in Obadiah its antagonism reached a vicious climax in 586 BC.

It is important to grasp that God had sovereignly chosen to bestow his blessing on Jacob and his descendants and to execute terrible judgement on Esau and his ungodly descendants *before the brothers were born*. Now, in his message through Malachi, God headlines the nation's history: "'Is not Esau Jacob's brother?" declares the LORD. "Yet I have loved Jacob but Esau have I hated. I have laid waste his hill country and left his heritage to jackals of the desert'" (1:2–3). When Malachi wrote these words, God's people had been settled back in Judea for over half a century, while Edom had been ransacked by the Nabateans and swept into the desert. The Edomites' arrogant response was to swear that they would one day recapture their land, but they reckoned without God's irresistible judgement on them: 'If Edom says, "We are shattered but we will rebuild the ruins," the LORD of hosts says, "They may build, but I will tear down, and they will be called 'the wicked country', and 'the people with whom the LORD is angry for ever''" (1:4). This terrible warning was fulfilled to the letter some 500 years later when the entire nation of Edom was wiped out.

God had therefore revealed his special love for his people, not merely by frustrating the plans of their enemies and eventually eliminating them altogether, but also by declaring his unchangeable love for those who put their trust in him. Their spiritual vision had become so clouded that they were unable to see this and had reached the stage where they had no assurance of God's presence. In one of his psalms David had cried out, 'Bless the LORD, O my soul, and forget not all his benefits' (Psalm 103:2), but the people Malachi addresses failed on both counts. Matthew Henry explains why believers should not repeat their mistake: 'In thanking God, we fasten upon his favours to us; in praising and adoring God, we fasten upon his perfections in himself.'

A perverted priesthood

Respect

The second (and longest) dialogue is between God and Israel's spiritual leaders. God begins by reminding them of a proverbial statement of social morality: 'A son honours his father, and a servant his master' (1:6). He then points out that although he was their Father (see Deuteronomy 32:6) and their Master they did the opposite: 'If then I am a father, where is my honour? And if I am a master, where is my fear?' (1:6). Respect for parents and masters was part of Mosaic law, but the priests failed to honour their divine Father and Master, the One to whom they owed their very existence as a nation.

The priests were so out of touch with reality they did not even realize their sin and wondered, 'How have we despised your name?' (1:6). When God answered, 'By offering polluted food upon my altar', they asked, 'How have we polluted you?' (1:7). God's reply was very specific. Old Testament law required that animals offered in sacrifice had to be perfect, without a blemish of any kind. Those that were 'blind or disabled or mutilated or having a discharge or an itch or scabs' (Leviticus 22:22) must never be offered. Yet these priests were ignoring what the law said and offering animals that were 'blind', 'lame' and 'sick'

(1:8), presumably those the owners were glad to get rid of. John Benton comments, 'Sacrifice is the giving up of something we genuinely value in order to express our devotion to God. But the "sacrificing" of diseased animals was like offering someone as a birthday present the contents of our dustbin!' Their behaviour was an insult to God, as he pointed out by ironically asking, 'Present that to your governor; will he accept you or show you favour?' (1:8).

In addition, the priests' hearts were not in what they were doing. They moaned, 'What a weariness this is' (1:13). They acted as if they were in a boring job, not a privileged ministry. The phrase 'you snort at it' (1:13) should probably read, 'you snort at *me*'; in today's vernacular they were turning their noses up at God. They had lost sight of God's majesty and glory and had no vibrant fellowship with him. Their religious ceremonies were a drudge rather than a delight. At no point do any of the prophets condemn the people's time-honoured religious rituals, as they were God-ordained means of leading the people to repentance and faith, but God was never going to be hoodwinked by priests merely going through the motions. R. C. Sproul outlines the prophets' ministry in this area: 'They called the people to return to orthodoxy, not to abandon their history. They called for a return to the terms of the original covenants that God had made with them, to obedience to the law that God had revealed through Moses, and, most importantly, to the practice of true worship as distinguished from all forms of idolatry and hypocrisy.'

A second indictment against the priests centred on their preaching: 'For the lips of a priest should guard knowledge, and people should seek instruction from his mouth, for he is the messenger of the LORD of hosts. But you have turned aside from the way. You have caused many to stumble by your instruction. You have corrupted the covenant of Levi' (2:7–8). The priests were not only prostituting the sacrifices by offering second-rate animals, they were failing to teach the truth of God's holy law and as a result 'caused many to stumble' (2:8).

The Christian ministry is an awesome calling and D. Martyn Lloyd-Jones was perfectly right when he wrote, 'Preaching is the most amazing, the most thrilling activity that one can ever be engaged in, because of all that it holds out for us in the present, and because of the glorious endless possibilities in an eternal future.' This is undeniably true, yet the advice I always give to any young man who says he is considering whether to be a preacher or something else is to choose the alternative. To stand before a congregation week after week and claim to be teaching what the Bible says and means is a serious responsibility. It ought not to be undertaken without a deep and tested conviction that one has been called by God to be his mouthpiece and that one has no alternative but to respond to that call. What is more, a Christian preacher is to be passionately committed to the relentless study of Scripture and to preaching only what it says, not basing his teaching on the latest theological fad or trying to come up with his own doctrinal inventions. Speculation is no substitute for revelation and there is some merit in the statement: 'He who thinks by the inch and talks by the yard deserves to be kicked by the foot.' John Stott put the issue well: 'The Christian preacher is to be neither a speculator who invents new doctrines which please him, nor an editor who excises old doctrines which displease him, but a steward, God's steward, dispensing faithfully to God's household the truths committed to him in the Scriptures, nothing more, nothing less and nothing else.'

This is light years away from what one often sees on so-called 'Christian' television programmes. Shamelessly tearing Scripture out of context, 'televangelists' prepare viewers for the punchline by passionately assuring them that if they will 'sow a seed' to support the preacher's ministry ('All major credit cards accepted') the donors will be guaranteed a breakthrough in their lives, delivering them from all their physical, financial and relational difficulties. Diseases will be healed, malignant tumours will vanish, debts will disappear and fractured relationships will be healed.

Claims like these are aired twenty-four hours a day, yet it is amazing that anybody could believe such unbiblical nonsense for a single minute. Jesus did not shed his blood to guarantee that his followers get the best jobs, or to boost their bank balances, or to keep them in perfect physical condition. He died to deliver people from the penalty and power of sin, and eventually from its very presence. Leonard Ravenhill may have had 'health and wealth' preachers in mind when he wrote, 'I would sooner expect a frog to sit down and play Beethoven's *Moonlight Sonata* than expect to see some of the slick preachers of this hour preaching with an anointing that would cause godly fear among the people.'

The apostle Paul pointed the way to truly biblical preaching when telling his young friend Timothy, '... preach the word; be ready in season and out of season; reprove, rebuke, and exhort, with complete patience and teaching' (2 Timothy 4:2) and every Christian preacher and teacher should have these words written on his heart. A preacher's mandate is not to find some new 'truth' but to preach and teach the old truths with conviction and passion.

Wrecking the covenant

Malachi himself takes part in the next dialogue, which he begins by asking two rhetorical questions: 'Have we not all one Father? Has not one God created us?' (2:10). Malachi is not referring to the universal fatherhood of God and brotherhood of man, but rather to God as the Father of his covenant people. Malachi's question harks back to the fact that in establishing his covenant at Sinai God had forged a unique spiritual relationship with them, setting them apart from the rest of mankind and calling them 'my sons' and 'my daughters' (Isaiah 43:6).

Malachi leaned on this covenant family theme in asking, 'Why then are we faithless to one another, profaning the covenant of our fathers?' (2:10) and in mentioning two ways in which people had broken faith. The first was that they had 'married the daughter of a foreign god' (2:11), something expressly forbidden in the Law of Moses (see Deuteronomy 7:3–4). This blatant disobedience was 'abomination' (2:10) in God's sight, not on racial grounds but because the brides concerned were pagans, worshipping 'a foreign god'.

The same principle is underlined in the New Testament. God's clear word to Christians is: 'Do not be unequally yoked with unbelievers. For what partnership has righteousness with lawlessness. Or what fellowship has light with darkness. What accord has Christ with Belial?' (2 Corinthians 6:14–15). This principle is repeated in the advice that a Christian widow 'is free to be married to whom she wishes, *only in the Lord*' (1 Corinthians 7:39, emphasis added). There are no loopholes here. The Christian who chooses to marry a non-Christian in the hope that their spouse will be converted is committing not one sin but many. They are gambling with God, denying the authority of the Bible as his Word, creating an unnecessary division in the unity of the church (Malachi calls it being 'faithless to one another') and guaranteeing that the marriage will start off on the wrong foot, with man and wife divided where they should be most firmly united. God *may* graciously save the unconverted spouse, but many more mixed marriages end in separation or divorce. Christians are called to avoid the risk by marrying only within the faith, then to live together until death parts them, and to do so in a loving and supportive relationship that reflects the beautiful bond between Christ and his bride, the church.

The second sin pinpointed by Malachi was that of a person divorcing 'the wife of your youth ... though she is your companion and your wife by covenant' (2:14). Malachi asks, 'Did [God] not make them one, with a portion of the Spirit in their union?' (2:15). Marriage was not just a legal contract but a covenant to which 'the LORD was witness' (2:14). Breaking that covenant was a serious sin and no amount of emotion (see 2:13), trying to sweet-talk God into letting them do what they wanted, would solve the problem. God said that the person divorcing his wife 'covers his garment with violence' (2:16), a phrase suggesting that he smothers himself in sin. He could hardly have used stronger language. Addressing the same subject, Jesus pointed out that Old Testament teaching (in Deuteronomy 24:1–4) did not justify divorce, but was given because of 'your hardness of heart' (Matthew 19:8) and to protect a divorced wife. He then added, '... whoever divorces his wife, except for sexual adultery, and marries another, commits adultery' (Matthew 19:9). As in Malachi's time, divorce in many countries today is seen as a perfectly acceptable option; in the United Kingdom between forty and fifty per cent of marriages end that way. Every divorce involves sin of some kind and God hates sin of every kind. This is why in his command through Malachi to every married person he puts his finger on the spot: 'Guard yourselves in your spirit, and do not be faithless' (2:16).

With Ephesians 5:22–23 in mind, the modern American scholar Iain Duguid adds an important point in a combined comment on both sins identified by Malachi: 'Confining marriage to the limits of the community of faith and remaining faithful within marriage are crucial in the Bible *because marriage is the principal metaphor for the relationship of Christ and his church*' (emphasis added).

Questioning God's providence

The next dialogue is very brief, but says a great deal. God opens it with the accusation 'You have wearied the LORD with your words'. When the people protest, 'How have we wearied him?' they are told, 'By saying, "Everyone who does evil is good in the sight of the LORD, and he delights in them." Or by asking, "Where is the God of justice?"' (2:17). They were making the monstrous suggestion that as evil men seemed to be enjoying God's favour he could no longer claim to be just. Joyce Baldwin goes so far as to say that the question 'Where is the God of justice?' was tantamount to denying God's existence. Scepticism as to whether God exists, means all that he says, or does all that he claims or promises has a long history. The very first question in the Bible was one Satan asked Eve, the first woman in human history: 'Did God actually say, "You shall not eat of any tree in the garden"?' (Genesis 3:1). From the moment she and Adam took the bait and fell into sin, questioning God's providence has been embedded into mankind's corrupted DNA.

Even the prophet Jeremiah was affected and complained, 'Why does the way of the wicked prosper? Why do all who are treacherous thrive?', pointing out to God, 'You plant them and they take root; they grow and produce fruit' (Jeremiah 12:1–2).

One of the psalmists had gone even further and admitted that at one point, 'I was envious of the arrogant when I saw the prosperity of the wicked' (Psalm 73:3). He complained that although they 'set their mouths against the heavens' they were 'not in trouble as others are' or 'stricken like the rest of mankind', but were 'always at ease' (see Psalm 73:1–12). He was 'over the top' in saying this, as were the people of Malachi's day who complained that 'everyone who does evil' was thriving. It was not until the psalmist 'entered the sanctuary of God' that he 'discerned their end' (Psalm 73:17) and only when our relationship with God is living and thriving that we can get our circumstances into the right perspective.

There is a sense in which the dialogue ends with God's explanation of how the people's complaint had wearied him, but he adds a dramatic announcement to the effect that he is not indifferent to the sins of either believers or unbelievers but is going to intervene in a way that will make it clear he will judge sin wherever he finds it. A king visiting his people would often send messengers to prepare the way for his coming and God's promise to Malachi was: 'Behold, I send my messenger, and he will prepare the way before me' (3:1).

Although Malachi's name means 'my messenger', he is not the one God has in mind here, as later he is more specific: 'Behold, I will send you Elijah the prophet before the great and awesome day of the LORD comes' (4:5). This 'Elijah' was to be John the Baptist, the immediate forerunner of Jesus who came on the scene 400 years later. We know this because at one point in his ministry Jesus quoted Malachi, then said of John, '… he is Elijah who is to come' (Matthew 11:14). This confirmed words spoken before John the Baptist was born, when an angel told his father, Zechariah, that when the child grew up he would 'turn many of the children of Israel to the Lord their God' and 'go before him in the spirit and power of Elijah' (Luke 1:16, 17).

There was to be a further, greater messenger. God had predicted the arrival of John the Baptist by announcing, 'A voice cries: "In the wilderness prepare the way of the LORD; make straight in the desert a highway for our God"' (Isaiah 40:3 and see Mark 1:1–3).

Now, God tells the people of Malachi's day, 'And *the Lord whom you seek* will suddenly come to his temple; and the messenger of the covenant in whom you delight, behold, he is coming' (3:1, emphasis added). This is clearly the Lord Jesus Christ, the Messiah. God's covenant with his people is a prominent theme in Malachi (see 2:8, 10, 14; 3:1) and 400 years later Jesus came as Mediator of the 'new covenant' (Hebrews 12:24) that was promised in Jeremiah 31:31–34. Jesus was more than a messenger; *he was the message.* His birth, sinless life, substitutionary death and resurrection from the dead are the only way through which sinners can get right with God and be freed from sin's curse.

Messiah's arrival would not be to announce a universal prize-giving. Instead, God warned, 'I will draw near to you for judgement. I will be a swift witness against the sorcerers, against the adulterers … against those who oppress the hired worker in his wages, the widow and the fatherless, against those who thrust aside the sojourner, and do not fear me, says the LORD of hosts' (3:5). There would be no hiding place for those who were routinely trampling the covenant underfoot: '… who can endure the day of his coming, and who can stand when he appears?' (3:2). Those who brazenly asked, 'Where is the God of justice?' would have a devastating answer to their question.

Yet there was a hopeful strand to Malachi's message. Messiah would come not only to condemn but also to cleanse. He would come 'as a refiner and purifier of silver' and would 'purify the sons of Levi and refine them like gold and silver' (3:3). Beginning with the priests, he would purge from sin those who truly repented, transforming their lives so that they would 'bring offerings in righteousness to the LORD' (3:3). The result would radically change things: 'Then the offering of Judah and Jerusalem will be pleasing to the LORD as in the days of old and as in former years' (3:4). All of this prophecy was played out as Jesus transformed lives during his ministry and its promises continue to be true today to all who truly turn to him.

The God robbers

In the next dialogue God reminds the Israelites that they owed their very survival to his unchanging faithfulness: 'For I the LORD do not change; therefore you, O children of Jacob, are not consumed' (3:6). The people are described as 'children of Jacob', their unreliable forefather, but the Lord never changes. Even if God's people behave like Jacobs, he remains Jehovah, utterly true to his eternal covenant. The Israelites' chronic disobedience had lasted from 'the days of your fathers' (3:7), the time when God had miraculously delivered them from captivity in Egypt. In spite of this, God now promised, 'Return to me, and I will return to you' (3:7). Some 400 years earlier Joel wrote, 'Return to the LORD your God, for he is gracious and merciful' (Joel 2:13); 300 years earlier Hosea wrote, 'Return, O Israel, to the LORD your God' who promised, 'I will love them freely' (Hosea 14:1, 4); 100 years earlier God's message through Zechariah was, 'Return to me … and I will return to you' (Zechariah 1:3). God had not changed, nor had his promise, but these people were so arrogantly satisfied simply to go through the religious routines that they asked, 'How shall we return?' (3:7). God bluntly replied, 'Will man rob God? Yet you are robbing me' (3:8). When they asked, 'How have we robbed you?' God's answer was crystal clear: 'In your tithes and contributions' (3:8).

We will spend some time on the subject of tithing (the giving of one-tenth) because it raises a controversial question in today's church: *are Christians under a biblical direction to give one-tenth of their income to Christian causes?* The biblical picture will become clear as we trace what Scripture says about tithing before the Old Covenant was instituted, during its lifetime and after it was replaced by the New Covenant.

There are only two references to tithing before the law was established under Moses. One is in Genesis 14:17–20 when Abraham (then called Abram) won a military battle and chose to give one-tenth of the spoils of war (not of his own possessions or regular income) to a king called Melchizedek, who as 'priest of God Most High' had pronounced God's blessing on the patriarch. The second is in Genesis 28:20–22, when after an amazing experience of God's presence Jacob vowed to give 'a full tenth' of all that God would provide for him in the future. Like Abraham, Jacob was under no obligation to do this. His gift was a voluntary and spontaneous thank offering in response to God's goodness.

Under the Mosaic law tithing was part of an elaborate system spelled out in Leviticus, Numbers and Deuteronomy. In an agricultural setting, tithing involved livestock, grain, wine, oil and other products. Probably on a yearly basis, the tithe was to be shared with the Levites, the only tribe that had no inheritance in the land of Canaan, and they in turn were to give one-tenth of what they received to the priests (see Numbers 18:20–28). In addition, another tithe of people's produce was to provide for an annual religious festival in Jerusalem. Those living far away from the city could sell their produce, bring the money to Jerusalem, and there spend it on food and drink for the festival, which was a time of celebrating God's goodness to them (see Deuteronomy 14:22–27).

Every third year yet another tithe was to be used for the benefit of 'the Levite ... the sojourner, the fatherless, and the widow, who are within your towns' (Deuteronomy 14:29). Israel was both a spiritual community and a theocratic nation under God's direct rule, with priests as the nation's leaders. These three tithes (the Levite tithe, the festival tithe and what we could call the social welfare tithe) were in effect taxes levied to support both church and state. It has been calculated that when other stipulated offerings and taxes are added—Malachi calls them 'contributions' (3:8)—the average Israelite might give over thirty per cent of his income.

Tithing in the New Testament has to be seen in two different periods, because during Jesus' lifetime all the Mosaic Law was still in place. This explains why he was circumcised (Luke 2:21), dedicated in the temple at Jerusalem (see Luke 2:22–32), attended the major religious festivals there (see, for example, John 2:13; 5:1), paid the half-shekel temple tax (see Matthew 17:24–27) and did not stop Pharisees from tithing (see Matthew 23:23).

The situation changed radically after Jesus' death, resurrection and ascension, because he was 'the mediator of a new covenant' (Hebrews 9:15), also referred to as 'a better covenant' (Hebrews 7:22). The Old Covenant sacrificial system had served its purpose and had been replaced by Jesus, who in his death 'put away sin by the sacrifice of himself' (Hebrews 9:26). As the Jerusalem temple was destroyed in AD 70 it is obviously no longer the designated place for corporate worship, and Christians no longer need priests to act as intercessors, because they form 'a royal priesthood' (1 Peter 2:9). The word 'tithe' does not appear in the New Testament after Jesus' ascension, and the giving of one-tenth is mentioned only in Hebrews 7:1–9 when the writer refers back to Melchizedek and to the priests receiving tithes from the Levites.

Present believers are directed to be baptized, to join a church, to pray, to study God's Word, to witness, and to live in a way 'worthy of the gospel of Christ' (Philippians 1:27) *but nowhere are they commanded to give at least ten per cent of their financial income or resources to Christian causes.* Those who insist that this remains a legal requirement should logically also insist on obedience to Old Covenant inheritance laws and those mandating animal sacrifices and circumcision. They should also comply with laws that forbid eating pork or shellfish and others that give specific instructions about slavery, money-lending, the payment of employees, the valuation of property, sheep-shearing and eating fruit—to say nothing of burnt offerings, drink offerings, grain offerings, heave offerings, peace offerings, sin offerings, trespass offerings, and wave offerings. They should also insist on visiting Jerusalem three times a year—and never travel more than five-eighths of a mile on the Sabbath. Yet this kind of response would deny the glorious truth that in terms of getting right with God believers are 'not under law but under grace' (Romans 6:14).

When the people of Malachi's day failed to keep their covenant obligations they were 'cursed with a curse' (3:9). Believers are under no such threat today because 'Christ redeemed us from the curse of the law by becoming a curse for us' (Galatians 3:13). The command, 'Bring the full tithe into the storehouse, that there may be food in my house'; the invitation, '... put me to the test'; and the promise to 'open the windows of heaven for you and pour down for you a blessing until there is no more need' (3:10) fit Israel's situation perfectly. If they repented and tithed as required, God would send sufficient rain to guarantee abundant harvests and also prevent the 'devourer' (the locust) from destroying 'the fruits of your soil, and your vine in the field' (3:11).

Malachi's teaching on tithing says nothing about money, but many television preachers and other 'peddlers of God's word' (2 Corinthians 2:17) today use what he has to say as a bargaining chip and tell their hearers that if they sow 'seed faith' (by sending money to the preacher's ministry) God will reward them with riches that will clear their debts, repay their mortgages and meet all their other financial needs. This slanderous nonsense has no biblical basis. Believers should be motivated not by the potential for personal gain but by 'the grace of our Lord Jesus Christ', who 'though he was rich, yet for your sake ... became poor, so that you by his poverty might become rich' (2 Corinthians 8:9). The New Testament gives two particular guidelines for Christian giving:

It is to be done freely and willingly: 'Each one must give as he has decided in his heart, not reluctantly or under compulsion, for God loves a cheerful giver' (2 Corinthians 9:7). Although Christian giving is not an option but an obligation; there is no compulsion here as to the amount to be given. As Christians are free to give whatever they choose this cannot be a legal percentage, as was the Old Testament tithe. The Greek word translated 'cheerful' is *hilaros*, the root of our English word 'hilarious'. This reflects the Old Testament proverb 'Whoever has a bountiful eye will be blessed' (Proverbs 22:9), where the word 'bountiful' means 'good'. The picture suggests someone with a gleam in his eye as he gives because it is something he loves doing. The nineteenth-century American theologian Charles Hodge went so far as to say, 'Unless we feel it is an honour and a joy to give, God does not honour the offering.'

It is to be done regularly and proportionately. In raising funds for hard-pressed believers in Jerusalem Paul told church members at Corinth, 'On the first day of every week, each of you is to put something aside and store it up, as he may prosper, so that there will be no collecting when I come' (1 Corinthians 16:2). As this passage is about an emergency relief fund, it is not a perfectly detailed template for the practice of taking up weekly offerings in church (and many churches make other arrangements) but it does point to some important principles. Truly Christian giving is a response to God's gift of salvation, and as churches meet 'on the first day of the week' their services present an obvious and appropriate opportunity to make financial gifts as part of a corporate act of worship. In addition, the givers—'each of you'—can join with other worshippers in thanking God for his gracious provision of their own needs and in praying for his blessing on their gifts.

Although the New Testament nowhere directs believers to give a tithe of their income to God's work no right-thinking Christian will use this as an escape clause and as an excuse to be tight-fisted. James Montgomery Boice points out that New Testament obligations are generally greater, not less, than those under Old Testament legislation and goes so far as to say, 'So while we are not required to give a specific tenth of our income, it is hard to think of a normal Christian, blessed with the fulness of the gospel of Jesus Christ, doing less. Under reasonable circumstances any true believer should give more than the tenth, for all we have is the Lord's.'

Key words in what Boice says are 'under reasonable circum-stances'. Some Christians are so hard-pressed financially that they may be able to afford only a tiny proportion of their income for God's work; others could comfortably give one-tenth of what they earn; and there are others who could give even more without feeling the pinch. The guideline in 1 Corinthians 16:2 is 'as he may prosper'. This takes into account any changes in a person's financial situation, including unemployment, redundancy and retirement on the one hand and promotion or some other increase in income on the other. The Bible is totally realistic about this: 'If the readiness is there, it is acceptable according to what a person has, not according to what he does not have' (2 Corinthians 8:12). Nothing could be clearer.

Regular giving in a church will be used in part to maintain that church's ministry, and in particular will include the honourable support of those 'who labour in preaching and teaching' (1 Timothy 5:17). Beyond that, both for individuals and for churches, there is open-ended scope for giving to support missionaries and biblically sound para-church ministries as well as to help the poor and those suffering as the result of war, natural disasters and man's inhumanity to man. It is a matter of individual conscience, not law, as to how believers' total giving should be divided, though this does not give us warrant to ignore the abiding value of the Law of Moses as a guide to godly living. Writing in the September 2011 issue of *Evangelical Times,* my close friend and fellow preacher Peter Anderson asks a highly relevant question: 'Surely genuine love for the Lord should find expression in faithful stewardship. You cannot serve God and money, but you can serve God with money. How you respond is a significant indication of your Christian discipleship.'

In practice, today's believers can give to Christian causes in many ways, including by the Internet, by bank standing order and by making use of government concessions (such as Gift Aid in the United Kingdom). The all-important principle is that a Christian's giving should be regular and proportionate, not spasmodic and unrelated to their own means.

Quite apart from regular giving, there are times when an emergency or a special project calls for additional funds. For one particular Old Testament project, people gave so generously that Moses had to stop them giving any more! (see Exodus 36:1–7). Paul wrote of believers who at a time of special need gave 'according to their means, as I can testify, and beyond their means, of their own free will' (2 Corinthians 8:3). Nobody is called upon to deny their family members basic necessities or to run into debt, but there are times when special needs call for special action and Christians should seek God's guidance in how to respond.

Before we leave the subject, my own testimony may be an encouragement to some. When an earnest Christian friend in Guernsey pressed my then fiancée Joyce and me on the subject of tithing, we each began to give one-tenth of our gross income to Christian causes. When we got married we tithed our joint income; the accounts for our first month as a married couple include these two entries: 'Two salaries £73.12.3d ... tithe £7.6.0d.' Even when raising five sons on what would be considered by many to be a shoestring, we were enabled to keep giving at least the same proportion, treating it as a floor, not as a ceiling. When we grew in our knowledge of Scripture and discovered that we were not legally bound to do this we saw no reason for cutting back and throughout even the most difficult of years we found that God unfailingly supplied all our needs 'according to his riches in glory in Christ Jesus' (Philippians 4:19).

The murmurers

The final dialogue can be looked at much more briefly as it underlines what we read in 2:17 about questioning God's providence. The fact that God returns to the subject shows that this was not something that could be glossed over. It also shows that the people concerned were oblivious to the fact that, as Thomas Watson put it, 'Our murmuring is the devil's music.'

When God tells the people, 'Your words have been hard against me' and (true to form) they reply, 'How have we spoken against you?' (3:13), God quotes them word for word: 'It is vain to serve God. What is the profit of our keeping his charge or of walking as in mourning before the LORD of hosts? And now we call the arrogant blessed. Evildoers not only prosper but they put God to the test and they escape' (3:14–15). The murmurers had not left the worshipping community and turned their backs on God, but they complained that their worship and service seemed to be getting them nowhere. This may not have been an organized protest movement, but many individuals had come to this conclusion and vented their frustration to one another. One can imagine friends meeting socially and sharing their complaints. John Benton even suggests, 'Perhaps they were words said under the breath. Perhaps they might have been simply thoughts which were nurtured in the mind but never spoken audibly.' Either way, their thoughts and words were not hidden from God, but were 'naked and exposed to the eyes of him to whom we must give account' (Hebrews 4:13).

They even complained that the ungodly were not only 'arrogant' but daring to put God to the test—and getting away with it. They were not the first to think like this. As we saw earlier, the psalmist Asaph was at one point 'envious of the arrogant' when he 'saw the prosperity of the wicked' (Psalm 73:3). God's response through Malachi was to draw their attention to the fuller picture. There was a faithful remnant that 'feared the LORD and esteemed his name' (3:16). God heard them, too, and when he finally settled people's destinies they would be seen to be his 'treasured possession' (3:17). On that day those who had doubted and slandered God would 'see the distinction between the righteous and the wicked, between one who serves God and one who does not serve him' (3:18).

Writing to the church at Corinth, Paul reminded his hearers of God's severe judgement on the Israelites when at one point in their forty-year desert odyssey they grumbled against his dealings with them (see Numbers 14:1–23). He then told them that Christians should not 'grumble, as some of them did' (1 Corinthians 10:10). Although God's ways are always perfect, they are sometimes perplexing, yet we are called to trust him even when we cannot trace him, assured that his eternal purposes for us will never fail. The American missionary Jim Elliot, who was murdered by Auca Indians in Ecuador in 1956, wrote, 'Eternity shall be at one and the same time a great eye-opener and a great mouth-shutter.' Christians can afford to wait.

Famous last words

People's final words often have special meaning. In the Bible, Joseph's prophetic words to his brothers in Genesis 50:24–25 come into this category. So do David's last words in 2 Samuel 23:1–7, Stephen's last words as he was being stoned to death (see Acts 7:59–60) and Paul's last words to the Ephesian elders in

Acts 20:32–35. Then there were Jesus' last words on the cross, when he cried, 'Father, into your hands I commit my spirit' (Luke 23:46) and after his resurrection his final words to his disciples at Matthew 28:18–20 when he gave them the church's great commission before he ascended into heaven.

The book of Malachi records God's last words in the Old Testament (it was to be 400 years before he 'spoke' again, this time by sending the promised Messiah) and they begin with the statement that will be our 'major point':

'I have loved you,' says the LORD. (1:2)

It has been said that 'God is love' (1 John 4:8, 16) is the greatest statement about him in the entire Bible. Commenting on these three amazing words, the nineteenth-century Scottish preacher Robert Candlish wrote, 'He is, he has ever been, love. From all eternity, from before all worlds, God is love. Love never is or can be, never was or could be, absent from his being. He never is or can be God—he never was or could be God—without also being love; without loving. I say without loving; actually loving.'

The Bible teems with declarations of the love of God and with illustrations of ways in which he has demonstrated it. Psalm 136 begins with the exhortation: 'Give thanks to the LORD' and every one of its twenty-six verses ends with the overriding reason why we should do so—'for his steadfast love endures for ever'. The psalmist reveals God as 'the God of gods', 'the Lord of lords' (vv. 2–3) and 'the God of heaven (v.26), whose 'great wonders' include creating the heavens and the earth (vv. 4–9). It then moves on to show that the Israelites' entire history resonated with examples of God's love in action. He had rescued them from captivity in Egypt, dividing the Red Sea, overthrowing Pharaoh and his army (vv. 10–15) and leading them through their years of wandering in the desert (v.16). He had overcome all their powerful enemies (vv. 17–20) and paved the way for them to settle in the Promised Land (vv. 21–25). No wonder they were called to give thanks!

Love is the mainspring of everything God does and while

Malachi's message contains only one direct reference to it (in the dialogue at 1:1–2) this comes at the very beginning of God's last prophetic word for 400 years, as if to show that his 'last words' were framed in the context of his unchanging commitment to his people. In spite of the fact that their history was a roller-coaster ride stained with compromise, lethargy and downright disobedience, they could always be assured of the 'steadfast love' of which other prophets had spoken. As Iain Duguid rightly says, God's love for his people 'is not an emotional feeling, but rather a covenantal term that expresses the behaviour that flows out of a committed relationship'. But why should God commit himself to his people in this way? Moses seemed on the brink of answering the question after he had received and announced the Ten Commandments. He told the people, 'It was not because you were more in number than any other people that the LORD set his love on you, for you were the fewest of all peoples, but …'

The next words are obviously the answer to the question every believer longs to hear—and here they are: '… it is because the LORD loves you and is keeping the oath that he swore to your fathers' (Deuteronomy 7:7–8). *No further explanation is given anywhere in the Bible.* God used to speak to him 'face to face, as a man speaks to his friend' (Exodus 33:11), but not even to Moses did he go any further than this. God's love was the ground of his people's election and the driving force of the covenant of grace he had established with them. Even after their forty years of wandering in the desert between Egypt and Canaan, when their lives were hanging by a thread and they frequently grieved him, God assured his people, 'I have loved you with an everlasting love; therefore I have continued my faithfulness to you' (Jeremiah 31:3). Addressing modern believers, John MacArthur said, 'When God saved you and granted you an eternal inheritance, it wasn't because you were special or more deserving of his love and grace than others. It was because he sovereignly chose to love you and to extend his great mercy to you.' As the Old Testament closes, God tells Malachi to remind Israel of this glorious truth.

As we saw when studying Amos, all those who put their trust in Christ form 'the Israel of God' (Galatians 6:16), which means that God's assurance of his everlasting love applies as fully to each one of them as it did to those to whom Jeremiah and Malachi originally wrote. Paul reflected this when he wrote about 'the breadth and length and depth' of God's love for his people, shown supremely in Christ, even though the apostle confessed that it 'surpasses knowledge' (Ephesians 3:18–19). There is no way known to man by which the everlasting love of God can be measured. It is without parallel and beyond explanation or analogy. The clearest demonstration of it is that 'while we were still sinners, Christ died for us' (Romans 5:8). Earlier in the same chapter Paul says that we were 'weak' (the literal meaning of the word is 'utterly powerless') and 'ungodly' (Romans 5:6) and later says we were God's 'enemies' (Romans 5:10). Yet for powerless, godless rebels, God 'did not spare his own Son but gave him up for us all' (Romans 8:32). As the nineteenth-century British preacher Alexander MacLaren said, 'God's love is not drawn out by our lovableness, but wells up, like an artesian spring, from the depths of his nature.'

It is surely no coincidence that in the last book in the New Testament (since when there has now been a similar prophetic silence for nearly 2,000 years) God ensures that we hear the same uncomplicated message. John's remarkable prophetic visions in Revelation include separate messages to each of seven churches from the glorified Jesus Christ, who described himself as 'the holy one' (Revelation 3:7), the exact title God gives himself at Isaiah 40:25. One message was to the church at Philadelphia, a city in the Roman province of Asia Minor. The church was relatively small, with 'little power' and constantly persecuted by 'the synagogue of Satan' (Revelation 3:8–9), God's fearful name for fundamentalist Jews who rejected the need for conversion to Christ and claimed that they alone were God's people. In response, God promised not only to sustain the Christians in their present difficulties, but added, 'I will keep you from the hour of trial that is coming on the whole world' (Revelation 3:10), an even greater wave of persecution during which the pagan worship of the Roman Emperor was to be enforced.

What is more, they were promised that the day was coming

when all their enemies 'will learn that *I have loved you*' (Revelation 3:9, emphasis added). God's abiding love for his chosen people would ensure that in the world to come they would be seen to be 'a pillar' (Revelation 3:12) in God's glorious and eternal temple. This particular message would have special meaning for the Philadelphians as their city was in an area prone to earthquakes, which frequently destroyed man-made pillars. Heaven's temple is 'the Lord God the Almighty and the Lamb' (Revelation 21:22), leading the modern British preacher Richard Brooks to comment that 'to be made a pillar in the temple of God is to enter for ever into the closest, richest, loveliest, sweetest, brightest, most blissful relationship imaginable with God in heaven.'

There is no earthly or heavenly limit to God's love for those who trust in Christ, which is infinite and unconditional, constant and irresistible. There is nothing they can do to make God love them more and nothing they can do to make him love them less. The Bible makes this crystal clear in the staggering statement that 'neither death nor life, nor angels nor rulers, nor things present nor things to come, nor powers, nor height nor depth, nor anything else in all creation, will be able to separate us from the love of God in Christ Jesus our Lord' (Romans 8:38–39). The nineteenth-century Scottish preacher Horatius Bonar put it well when he wrote, 'Nothing in us, nothing in the world, nothing in heaven or earth, nothing in man or angel produced the love of God. It was uncreated, unbought, undeserved, and unfathomable. God loved the sinner because he was God, and because the sinner was a sinner. That is the end of the matter.'

The 1980 film *The Elephant Man* was based on the true life story of Joseph Merrick (called John Merrick in the film), a nineteenth-century Englishman who was horribly disfigured by the worst recorded case of Proteus syndrome, an abnormal and incurable growth of bones, skin and other systems. After spending years as a side-show freak he was rescued by a Victorian surgeon who found a permanent home for him in what is now the Royal London Hospital, where he was eventually revealed to be a person of intelligence and sensitivity. At one point during his rehabilitation Merrick cried out, 'My life is full because I know

I am loved.' Christians can use the same words to testify that they are loved in an infinitely greater way by an infinitely greater Saviour who has delivered them from an infinitely greater disease.

The eighteenth-century British preacher and hymn-writer Augustus Montague Toplady put it beautifully:

> The work which his goodness began,
> The arm of his strength will complete;
> His promise is Yea and Amen
> And never was forfeited yet;
> Things future, nor things that are now,
> Nor all things below nor above,
> Can make him his promise forego,
> Or sever my soul from his love.

We could have no more glorious note on which to end these studies in the Bible's 'clean pages'.